CONTESTED SITES

Contested Sites

Commemoration, Memorial and Popular
Politics in Nineteenth-Century Britain

PAUL A. PICKERING and ALEX TYRRELL

with Michael T. Davies, Nicholas Mansfield and James Walvin
Preface by Iain McCalman

ASHGATE

Published by
Ashgate Publishing Limited
Gower House, Croft Road
Aldershot, Hants
GU11 3HR
England

Ashgate Publishing Company
Suite 420
101 Cherry Street
Burlingon, VT 05401–4405
USA

Ashgate website: http://www.ashgate.com

British Library Cataloguing in Publication Data
Contested sites : commemoration, memorial and popular
  Politics in nineteenth-century Britain. – (Studies in
  labour history)
  1. Memorials–Political aspects–Great Britain–History–
  19th century 2. Monuments–Great Britain–History–19th
  century 3. Memory–Political aspects–Great Britain–
  History–19th century 4. Politics, Practical–Great
  Britain–History–19th century 5. Political psychology
  6. Great Britain–Politics and government–19th century
  I. Pickering, Paul A. II. Tyrrell, Alex
  320.9'41'09034

US Library of Congress Cataloging-in-Publication Data
Contested sites : Commemoration, memorial and popular politics in nineteenth century
  Britain / Paul A. Pickering, Alex Tyrrell.
    p. cm. – (Studies in labour history)
  Includes bibliographical references and index.
  ISBN 0–7546–3229–6 (hardback : alk. Paper)
  1. Historic sites–Conservation and restoration–Government policy–Great
  Britain–History–19th century. 2. Cultural property–Protection–Great
  Britain–History–19th century. 3. Historical markers–Great Britain–History–19th
  Century. 4. Popular culture–Great Britain–History–19th century. 5. Labor
  Movement–Great Britain–History–19th century. 6. Historic sites–Great
  Britain–History–19th century. 7. Great Britain–Politics and government–19th century.
  8. Monuments–Great Britain–History–19th century. 9. Memorials–Great
  Britain–History–19th century. 10. Statues–Great Britain–History–19th century.
  I. Pickering, Paul A. II. Tyrrell, Alex. III. Studies in labour history (Ashgate(Firm))

  DA655.C565 2004
  363.6'9'094109034–dc22   2003056933

ISBN 0 7546 3229 6

This book is printed on acid-free paper

Typeset in Times Roman by Express Typesetters Ltd, Farnham, Surrey

Printed and bound in Great Britain by MPG Books Ltd, Bodmin, Cornwall

Contents

Studies in Labour History
General Editor's Preface

Labour history has often been a fertile area of history. Since the Second World War its best practitioners – such as E.P. Thompson and E.J. Hobsbawm, both Presidents of the British Society for the Study of Labour History – have written works which have provoked fruitful and wide-ranging debates and further research, and which have influenced not only social history but history generally. These historians, and many others, have helped to widen labour history beyond the study of organized labour to labour generally, sometimes to industrial relations in particular, and most frequently to society and culture in national and comparative dimensions.

The assumptions and ideologies underpinning much of the older labour history have been challenged by feminist and later postmodernist and anti-Marxist thinking. These challenges have often led to thoughtful reappraisals, perhaps intellectual equivalents of coming to terms with a new post-Cold War political landscape.

By the end of the twentieth century, labour history had emerged reinvigorated and positive from much introspection and external criticism. Very few would wish to confine its scope to the study of organized labour. Yet, equally few would wish now to write the existence and influence of organized labour out of nations' histories, any more than they would wish to ignore working-class lives and focus only on the upper echelons.

This series of books provides reassessments of broad themes of labour history as well as some more detailed studies arising from recent research. Most books are single-authored but there are also volumes of essays centred on important themes or periods, arising from major conferences organized by the Society for the Study of Labour History. The series also includes studies of labour organizations, including international ones, as many of these are much in need of a modern reassessment.

Chris Wrigley
British Society for the Study of Labour History
University of Nottingham

List of Figures

Foreword

History has been written with quipo-threads, with feather-pictures, with-wampum-belts; still oftener with earth-mounds and monumental stone heaps, whether as pyramids or cairns ...

Thomas Carlyle, 'On History' (1830)

This book began several years ago as an idea for a very short-term project in the form of a joint article. It has subsequently grown, if not like Topsy, then certainly in ways that neither of us anticipated. Along the way other scholars were invited to contribute: some have withdrawn, and others have contributed, although not always in the form that was originally envisaged. The result is neither a jointly authored book nor an edited collection. Each of the chapters is, to varying degrees, a collaboration by or with us. Apart from Iain McCalman's preface, the only chapter that is independently authored is Nick Mansfield's (Chapter 4), and it too draws on our work. Having said this, the views contained in each of the chapters are the responsibility of those listed as their authors. We would like to thank all those who participated in this project during its lengthy gestation: Michael Davis, Ian Dyck, Nick Mansfield, Iain McCalman and Jim Walvin.

Conducting the research for this book and devising a theoretical framework for the various chapters has been a fascinating new departure for both of us. It has taken us separately and jointly to new methodologies, understandings and some unlikely places. There have been times when our apparent obsession with cemeteries and books relating to the rituals to death has incurred some quizzical looks and bantering comments from our partners and children. We thank them for their forbearance.

Our initial interest in this project arose from a belief that historians of British reform movements had devoted little attention to monuments and that this was a symptom of a weakness in the writing of modern British history: a disregard for artefacts of cultural production and their relation to public memory. As we note in Chapter 1, a comparison with France and the United States gives Britain a less prominent place in the study of public memory than its rich heritage of public memorials would justify. There are many 'earth-mounds and monumental stone heaps' that deserve attention. We hope that, with our collaborators, we have gone some way towards redressing the balance. The range of artefacts of public memory in this book is limited, and we are conscious that there are many monuments and movements that we have not included, but our hope is that we have pointed the way for further research.

Paul A. Pickering and Alex Tyrrell

Notes on Contributors

Michael T. Davis is a Research Fellow, School of History, Philosophy, Religion and Classics, University of Queensland, Brisbane.

Nicholas Mansfield is Director of the National Museum of Labour History, Manchester.

Iain McCalman is a Professor of History and Federation Fellow, Humanities Research Centre, The Australian National University, Canberra.

Paul A. Pickering is a Reader in History and Senior Research Fellow, Humanities Research Centre, The Australian National University, Canberra.

Alex Tyrrell is a Reader in History, La Trobe University, Melbourne.

James Walvin is a Professor of History, University of York.

Preface

Iain McCalman

During the mid-1960s a now nearly forgotten British film called 'Morgan: A Suitable Case for Treatment' regularly did the rounds of Australian University campuses. For many of us, its screening became a sacred annual event. The film's hero, Morgan, played by a youthful David Warner, is represented as a neurotic working-class Londoner, descended from a long line of East-End battler stock. Morgan, however, proves to be both a troubled soul and hopeless failure at life. He is a sad disappointment to his long-suffering mother ('the last unreconstructed Stalinist') because his squeamishness prevents him from engaging in the bloody socialist politics of his forebears. At the same time, he has been left by his beautiful socialite wife because he is too fey and idealistic to cope with the brutalities of the middle-class boardroom and bedroom.

Always teetering on the brink of madness, Morgan consoles himself by indulging in Walter Mitty-style fantasies of swinging through the treetops as Tarzan of the Apes. He also makes regular pilgrimages to the grave of Karl Marx at London's Highgate Cemetery to commune with the spirit of the famous European revolutionary. In one of the film's most memorable scenes, Morgan one day experiences a moment of redemption while gazing wistfully as usual at Marx's memorial. Suddenly, he has a vision of the German philosopher's craggy, bearded bust metamorphosing into that of a titanic African gorilla. Buoyed with inspiration and hope, Morgan beats his skinny chest in front of this spectre of the great socialist primate, and, for a flickering moment, we believe that this young man's dream of a socialist paradise springing up on Britain's green and pleasant soil might somehow come to pass. But it is not to be. After a series of increasingly insane adventures, the film ends on an elegiac note as Morgan sees out the rest of his days working quietly in the garden of the lunatic asylum where he is an inmate. The scene closes with a glimpse of the fruits of Morgan's latest labours – a flowerbed designed in a hammer and sickle motif. Morgan has bequeathed to posterity his own idea of how a humane socialist society should venerate itself.

Despite its surface quirkiness, 'Morgan' carries a deeply serious message: not least because – like this wonderfully original book by Paul Pickering and Alex Tyrrell – it interrogates the neglected themes of memorialisation in the Anglo-Celtic popular imaginary. To explore such a subject properly, as Pickering, Tyrrell and their fellow contributors show, is to open up a plethora of new lines of historical investigation – into the workings of social memory, the psycho-social trajectories of nostalgia, the cultural particularities and global commonalities of signposting the

xi

past, and the flux of human fashion in dealing with mortality and immortality. The various chapters range widely in terms of subject matter: from Nick Mansfield's consideration of the banners and emblematic flags recorded in the National Museum of Labour History's recent survey to Alex Tyrrell's forensic explication of the 'campo santo' that the Preston teetotallers created for themselves in the heart of a mid-Victorian cemetery. Other chapters tell a story of struggle. For the Scottish Martyrs of the 1790s and the Chartists of the 1840s and '50s public memorialisation was carried through only in the face of determined opposition from political and social elites. The book also embraces what is nowadays called 'the new British history' by taking account of events in the wider British world. In the concluding chapter, Alex Tyrrell and James Walvin weigh the commemoration of the anti-slavery 'saints' with the representation of the slaves themselves. By posing the question 'whose memory is it?', this chapter addresses the often uneasy relationship between heritage and history and highlights, as do other contributions, the ways in which commemorations and de-commemorations of the dead press urgently on the politics of the living.

Who among us can forget watching those television news broadcasts depicting the dramatic de-pantheonisations of our day, when Gulliver-like statues of Lenin or Saddam were tumbled to the ground by crowds of chanting Lilliputians? Or who could fail to wonder at the amoeba-like adaptability of capitalism when these same statues were quickly reassembled and sold to newly-built theme parks? Here, these patched monoliths now entertain where they once intimidated or inspired. Licking ice-creams, former Soviet citizens look on the political icons of their past now transmogrified into objects of curiosity and nostalgia.

But how much worse a fate not to be memorialised at all. It is saddening to learn from this book that so many generations of men and women reformers in Britain have had neither their struggles nor their lives commemorated. For a long period, this fate was shared by even a globally famous historical figure like Thomas Paine, the fount of popular democratic theory in modern America, Britain and France. Paul Pickering here perceptively explains why William Cobbett embarked on the tragi-comical adventure of secretly digging up Tom Paine's bones from their resting place in an American farm and transporting them to Britain in 1819 for intended reburial. But memorials, like books, can miss their moment. Just as those who wished to erect a memorial to the victims of Stalin in the *glasnost* days of the Soviet Union found their endeavours overtaken by the rapidity of political change, so, too, Cobbett discovered that Paine's bones had become too controversial a subject in post-Waterloo Britain to risk the solemn community ritual of reburial and commemoration. As a result, Paine's bones became relics without a resting place. For a good part of the nineteenth century they rattled around in a sack which was dragged to successive British labour meetings, before they gradually succumbed to the depredations of domestic pets and souvenir hunters. Indeed, so effective was the conservative vilification of Paine during his own age that modern Britons and Americans were still resisting memorials to his achievements as late as the 1980s – apparently his mildly deist views on religion had pushed him beyond the boundaries of commemorative respectability.

Eventually, even Paine overcame the resistance of conservative British burghers. Towns like Thetford and Lewes, where he was born and worked, now carry proud memorials to 'the great reformer of mankind'. Other reformers of his era have been less fortunate. The band of ragged London ultra-radicals led by 'Captain' Arthur Thistlewood and Doctor Watson, who tried most strenuously to implement Paine's republican ideals during the late Georgian years, remain unmemorialised to this day. None of their names feature on the Reformers' Memorial first erected in London's Kensal Green Cemetery in 1885 and then extended in 1907.

In part, these ultra-radicals incurred the odium of both colleagues and foes because they were prepared to countenance, and attempt, armed insurrection. While many of their reformer colleagues believed in the necessity of violence as a mode of self-defence or of last resort, most were reluctant to imperil the ideals and achievements of the larger reform movement by indulging in what they thought of as grandiloquent and futile adventures. Radicals of Paine's era were also especially disadvantaged because for most of their active political lives Britain was engaged in fighting a counter-revolutionary war. It was, moreover, a new type of conflict, the prototype of what we now call 'total war'. Reformers found themselves confronted by a situation where symbols, relics and markers of domestic political allegiance – past and present – had suddenly become a matter of urgent contemporary policy. When, for example, the British government funded a Committee of Monuments in 1802 to commemorate the heroes of the recent conflict with Revolutionary France, Pitt was also quietly opening up a new front on the domestic political battlefield. The successes of the French Revolutionary armies had convinced him that the British state must undertake a comparable mobilisation of mass patriotic sentiment or perish; and so the manipulation of British popular memory became a propaganda necessity. Erecting memorials was the counterpart of hiring graphic artists like Gillray to idolise patriotic British tars and make radicals look like Jacobinical traitors.

As a result, during the first decade of the new century, a good deal of both state and private money was directed into producing public memorials that deified war heroes like Lord Nelson. In fact, 'the hero of Trafalgar' was given a massive state funeral in Westminster Abbey against his own written wish. So carefully contrived was the state pageantry at his funeral in 1805 that the eight common sailors who carried his coffin, outraged at the manipulative symbolics of the event, gave vent to their feelings in a small graveside rebellion. Suddenly, and apparently spontaneously, they grabbed the bloody ensign draped over Nelson's coffin, ripped it to pieces and divided the shreds of cloth among themselves as mementos of the naval commander they had loved. And of course in the aftermath of Waterloo when the Whigs had regained sufficient respectability to commemorate their own wartime heroes, they took care to muffle any suggestion that these statesmen might have shared the ideals of Britain's Gallic enemies.

Not so, the London ultra-radicals: it was their open adoption, in the first decade of the century, of emblems such as the *bonnet rouge* and the tri-colour that brought upon their heads the full force of a nervous post-war Tory government. Poverty, drink, a barrage of legislative repression and the unlovely attentions of spies, informers and provocateurs eventually goaded these ragged reformers into making several abortive attempts at armed insurrection. The penalty of failure was high; it included strangulation on the gallows or a lifetime of exile on one of the remotest continents on earth. For a few, punishment did not stop with death: their bodies and memories were ritually desecrated. Given the half-superstitious importance with which the British common people invested the process of laying the body to rest after death, the denial of a proper burial became an ultimate and deliberate indignity.

On 1 May 1820, five leading London ultra-radicals were hanged, then decapitated, outside Newgate gaol. These 'Cato Street' conspirators – named after the stable where they were caught – had allowed themselves to be lured into a pathetic plot to assassinate the British Cabinet. The day after the execution, prison authorities refused a petition to deliver the men's bodies to their wives for proper burial. Instead, the five corpses were covered in quicklime and stashed in a shallow trench under a passage that connected Newgate gaol and the Old Bailey. Their only memorial consisted of five sets of initials scratched on the adjacent wall by some nameless gaoler. Knowing that oblivion is more potent even than vilification, the state took care to ensure that the Cato Street conspirators were not even accorded an 'anti-memorial' of the type bestowed on infamous London predecessors like Sweeney Todd or Guy Faux. Sadder still than being forgotten by one's friends is to be forgotten by one's enemies.

As it happens, the only leading figure among the Cato Street conspirators who died in circumstances of sufficient comfort and respectability to attract a memorial proved to be the government provocateur who orchestrated the attempted coup, one George Edwards. But then Edwards knew all about commemoration: he was a modeller of statues who, among other achievements, produced several busts of Tom Paine for his erstwhile radical colleagues. After the trial of the conspirators, at which Edwards did not appear, the Home Office eventually spirited him to South Africa, where he changed his name to Parker and became a model of respectability. He died in comfortable circumstances in November 1843, leaving property valued at £500. He is buried with a headstone at Green Point on the fringes of Cape Town.

Poverty and unrespectability were thus the two other handicaps, along with extremism, that militated against the commemoration of London's early nineteenth-century ultra-radicals. Those among them who managed to die natural deaths, many in the 1830s and '40s, were almost all buried in unmarked paupers' graves. Not a few of them lie somewhere in the vast overgrown acreage of Kensal Green Cemetery. And, although several attempts are recorded of their former comrades trying to raise subscriptions for headstones, all such efforts foundered on the collective poverty of the circle.

Sadly for them, too, these ragged artisans and down-and-out petty professionals failed to catch the later waves of nostalgia by which a percentage of their contemporaries came posthumously to be remembered. As detritus of an earlier rougher age, where lower- and middling-class occupations often shaded into criminality and vice, they failed to participate in the great reformation of social values and behaviour that came to mark most of their Victorian counterparts. Lacking any legacy of sobriety or self-improvement, they remained an embarrassment to the radicals who succeeded them – those men and occasional women who contributed the names that did eventually make it onto the Reformers' Memorial at Kensal Green. London's ultra-radicals remain unforgiven to this day.

This wonderful book reminds us of the stark truth that to be without a memorial is often to be lost to history. Yet it shows us also that the work of remembering is far from over. I am consoled to think that, thanks to historians like Paul Pickering and Alex Tyrrell, some of these broken shards of memory might some day be reconnected. One day Morgan may once again beat his chest at Highgate Cemetery.

Bibliographical note

A full statement of the sources of this book will be found in the notes at the end of each chapter. The literature relating to commemoration, monuments and public memory continues to flourish. Works of a theoretical or comparative nature that informed the project are primarily listed in the notes to Chapter 1.

Chapter 1

The Public Memorial of Reform: Commemoration and Contestation

Paul A. Pickering and Alex Tyrrell

'The genuine heroes of the times that have been', wrote William Godwin in an *Essay on Sepulchres* (1809), 'were the reformers, the instructors, and improvers of their contemporaries.'[1] His train of thought was provoked by a visit to Westminster Abbey where he had searched 'in vain for the tombs of almost all the great men that have adorned our annals'.[2] There was no shortage of funerary monuments in the Abbey, but for the most part they commemorated the men who had presided over the unreformed *ancien regime*, and these were not the 'heroes' he had in mind. In making a case for the commemoration of truly 'great and excellent' men, Godwin adopted a surprisingly spiritual (even romantic) stance for one who would come to be known as an oracle of reason. 'His heart', he wrote, 'must be made of impenetrable stuff who does not attribute a certain sacredness to the grave of one he loved … '. Similar feelings, he believed, would be evoked by the memorials of those who had laboured to benefit mankind. The time had come to 'mark the spot, whenever it can be ascertained, hallowed by the reception of all that was mortal of those glorious beings; let us erect a shrine to their memory; let us visit their tombs … '.[3]

Godwin's remarks are a good starting point for anyone who is interested in commemoration and memorials of British reformers. Until very recently, and not only in Britain, scholars have given surprisingly little attention to memorials of this sort – so little that the very notion of someone like Godwin creating a 'shrine' to the embodiment of his ideals has been cursorily dismissed from consideration. In a widely received work that has investigated the meaning and significance of the cultural artefacts of collective belief Benedict Anderson has challenged his readers to imagine 'a tomb of the Unknown Marxist or a cenotaph for fallen Liberals' without entertaining 'a sense of absurdity'. It could not be otherwise, he writes: 'neither Marxism nor Liberalism are much concerned with death and immortality.'[4] This collection of essays argues to the contrary that no such act of imagination is required. It will show that Anderson's readers need only give a new meaning to an old adage: '*Si monumentum requiris, circumspice*'. Memorials of this sort are all around us, because radicals and reformers of all stripes have waged long and bitter campaigns to commemorate their ideals and the heroes who upheld them. Like those who are imbued with the sense of nationality that Anderson describes so persuasively, liberal and radical reformers have shown 'a strong

1

affinity with religious imaginings';[5] they too have felt a need for sacred sites of memory.

Godwin's use of the term 'instructors and improvers' also points to one of the themes that frequently appears in this collection of essays. Reformers have described their memorials as object lessons for the beholder; the messages are meant to create and reinforce the appropriate mentality for a reformed society. This belief led Godwin to make an unwarranted assumption about the mentality and prior knowledge of the viewer. 'The object of a monument', he insisted, 'is to mark the place where the great and excellent of the earth repose, and to leave the rest to the mind of the spectator.'[6] Like most of those who have planned monuments, Godwin seems to have had no doubt that the spectator would respond in the way that was intended. 'The affectionate recollection and admiration of the dead', he predicted, would 'act gently upon our spirits and fill us with a composed seriousness, favourable to the best and most honourable contemplations'.[7] Few modern scholars would share his faith; they envisage a more active role than the one expected of a mere 'spectator'. As Melissa Dabakis has written in her recent study of the representation of labour in American sculpture, 'Ultimately, it is the viewer, standing before the monument ... who completes the memory process.'[8] This in turn raises important questions for the historian. Is there only one reading of a monument? Is it not inevitable that multiple readings will be created as viewers bring a wide variety of experiences to bear on the interpretation of what they see? Are the readings ever completed, or do they change over time and, as often happens, in new locations?

These challenges were immediately presented to the authors of this chapter when they stood before two recently refurbished monuments in London's first great metropolitan cemetery at Kensal Green (see Figure 1.1). Nothing, certainly not the brief reference in the official leaflet, had prepared them for their first sight of these splendid monuments nestling in an unconsecrated corner of the cemetery. The two columns rise side by side, dwarfing many of the surrounding tombstones; the lustre of their restored granite seems to emphasise the weather-beaten and dilapidated condition of other monuments in the vicinity. One column, the oldest, is dedicated to the father of British socialism, Robert Owen. Raised in 1879, two decades after Owen's death, it summarises his labours for education, factory reform, international arbitration and reconciliation of 'the interests of capital and labour'. The other column, the Reformers' Memorial, is a much more remarkable commemoration. First erected in 1885, it offers itself as a history of British reform as, line by line, it sweeps the eye of the beholder through the names of 85 British radicals and reformers.[9]

The Memorial provides few clues as to its genesis. The first 46 names (inscribed on two sides) were selected in 1885 by the principal organiser and benefactor of both monuments, Joseph W. Corfield. Little is known about him apart from the fact that he was an active member of the co-operative movement and the South Place Institute, a one-time Unitarian Chapel that became the centre of a heady mix of progressive theology and politics in London. Shortly after the erection of the Memorial, the congregation embraced secularism, turning itself into the South Place Ethical Society.[10] Speaking at the unveiling of the Memorial in August 1885,

Fig. 1.1   The Robert Owen Memorial and the Reformers' Memorial, Kensal Green Cemetery, London.

Corfield told the 'assemblage' that 'it was intended, as far as possible, to inscribe the name upon the column of any social or political advocate who had won attention in society during the present century.'[11] According to the first historian of the monument, W.H. Brown, Corfield deliberately left two sides blank for additions by later generations.[12] Appropriately his daughter, Emma Corfield, was the first to contribute to this permanent work-in-progress. In 1907 she selected 24 names for the third side of the column. Since then the names of a further eleven individuals have been added to the pediment of the fourth side at the instigation of the co-operative movement. There is space for more.

Under the symbol of two clasped hands, the monument summons up the memory and inspiration of a great army of reformers united by the transcending belief that 'a far happier and more prosperous life is within the reach of all men.' The list is impressive. It includes the names of reformers associated with the era of the American and French Revolutions: Joseph Priestley, Thomas Paine and Thomas Spence. There are well-known heroes of the socialist, co-operative and trade union movements: Robert Owen, Abram Combe, G.J. Holyoake, George Odger and Alexander Macdonald. Radicals who campaigned for universal manhood suffrage and the reforms caught up in the Chartist movement occupy a prominent place: Major Cartwright, William Cobbett, Samuel Bamford, Henry Hunt, Richard Carlile, William Hone, Thomas Wooler, William Lovett, and David Williams. There are Christian Socialists: F.D. Maurice, Charles Kingsley, E.V. Neale and J.M. Ludlow. Nineteenth-century Liberals who were once household names are commemorated there: John Stuart Mill, W.J. Fox, George Thompson, Ebenezer Elliott and Charles Bradlaugh. The inscription gives special emphasis to the victorious campaigns for freedom of the press and universal manhood suffrage, but the range of reforms that are commemorated is much wider. For example, there is a scattering of names from the worlds of education, literature and progressive ideas: Joseph Lancaster, Harriet Martineau, William Howitt, John Ruskin, William Morris, Herbert Spencer and Richard Congreve. Middle- and working-class reformers predominate, but all classes are represented. Women take their places alongside the men – 16 in all – evoking by their names the memories of a galaxy of social reforms including those that were specifically concerned with discrimination against women: Elizabeth Fry, Lady Noel Byron, Frances Wright, Sarah Martin, Mary Carpenter, Frances Power Cobbe, Barbara Bodichon, Josephine Butler, Beatrice Webb and others. Rising above the distinctions of ideology, factional loyalty, personality, class and gender, this is a memorial that seeks to be inclusive according to the standards of the late Victorian/Edwardian era. It gives voice to a Lib-Lab history of reform; it brings women into public recognition; and, unlike the adjoining monument which hails 'Robert Owen Of New Lanark, Born At Newtown, N. Wales', as 'one of the foremost Englishmen', it is British not English. Two reformers (James Deans and Sir William Maxwell) are specifically identified as Scots.

In other respects the story of the monument is obscure. The names were apparently engraved on the stone in no particular order, sometimes even bringing together in death reformers who were antipathetic to each other in life – Richard Cobden and Ernest Jones, for example. Although the names go back to the seventeenth century and range forward to salute the reformers at the turn of the twentieth century, chronology plays no part in the order in which they appear. Nor do gender, class, or cause. Thus Lady Noel Byron follows Charles Kingsley; Major Cartwright follows John Stuart Mill; William Lovett follows Richard Carlile and

Richard Cobden is followed by Robert Cooper. In the case of some of the names added by Emma Corfield (and more recently) there are hints to help the viewer, undoubtedly in recognition that time had already begun to dim the public memory of the individuals concerned. 'John Bellers 1696' is the only name to which a date is attached; Lloyd Jones was 'an earnest worker with Robert Owen'; Charles Howarth was 'one of the Rochdale Pioneers'; Mary Lawrenson was a 'Pioneer Of The Women's Co-operative Guild'; and Sir William Maxwell was 'Past President Of The Scottish Co-operative Wholesale Society Limited And Past President Of The International Co-operative Alliance'. For the most part, however, the identification of individuals is taken for granted, a misguided assumption of everlasting prior knowledge that has been all too common on the part of those who erect memorials.

Moreover, like all historical accounts, the Reformers' Memorial offers only a partial view of the past. The apparent inclusiveness does not stand careful scrutiny. As early as 1925, W.H. Brown was suggesting that the 'omissions are as curious as some of the inclusions.'[13] Despite Emma Corfield's action in adding the names of several female reformers, women are under-represented; apart from William Morris there is no one who was influenced by Marx and Engels and, although the Memorial was inaugurated in 1885 by Patrick Lloyd Jones, a Dublin-born radical, there are few names with any Irish connection. The names of Wolfe Tone, Robert Emmet, Daniel O'Connell and Charles Stuart Parnell are nowhere to be found. Despite Corfield's links to the cause of secularism, William Godwin is not listed (nor is his more famous partner, Mary Wollstonecraft). Furthermore, within walking distance of the Memorial are buried several men who surely could also claim a place in a history of British reform: J.C. Loudon, J.B. Smith, Dr John Epps, George Birkbeck, Thomas Duncombe, Joseph Hume and Feargus O'Connor. No wonder that Brown described it as a 'very incomplete ... Who's Who'.[14]

A consideration of the Reformers' Memorial raises many of the issues that are discussed in this collection of essays. It was erected towards the end of what *The Times* had called the 'Monument mania' of the nineteenth century, an era when there was a general belief that the great and the good should be commemorated in this public form. Initially seen as a means of commemorating those of distinguished social and political rank, the public monument was democratised after the 1832 Reform Act when radicals and reformers challenged conservatives and patricians for the right to salute their heroes in this way and proclaim the values that they represented. As the relative obscurity of this cemetery site suggests, the outcome was not always an unqualified victory. The heroes of the Establishment and political conservatism were always more likely to be honoured in central public locations. Even in those cases where reformers were accorded a more central site, with the passage of time their memorials, like those of many conservatives, have sometimes been thrust into oblivion by removal to less conspicuous sites and even outright destruction. They are usually taken for granted by passers-by. Scholars have ignored them or brushed them aside with remarks about their pretentious banality and ugliness.

Although ancient, medieval and early modern memorials have long been the subject of distinguished historical works, it is only recently that historians have started to treat modern monuments as artefacts of public memory that merit serious consideration. G.L. Mosse's study of political symbolism and mass movements in Germany was an important innovation when it appeared in 1975,[15] but ten years later Maurice Agulhon regretted that public statuary remained a 'little studied topic' and concluded that 'visual symbols of power of the modern period are less studied, probably because they are presumed to be less important'.[16] Similar comments continue to appear in historical writings. In 1997 Kirk Savage complained that there is still 'relatively little scholarship on monumentality in the nineteenth century',[17] but his lament was losing its force at the time when he wrote, and since then the relevant historiography has become ever more impressive in its scope and intellectual richness. To mention only two recent examples, K.S. Inglis has written a masterly history of the war monument in Australia, and with the recent publication of *Funerals, Politics And Memory In Modern France, 1789–1996*, Avner Ben-Amos has given the iconography of death a prominent place in the history of French political life.[18]

Several approaches to writing the history of modern memorials emerge from this burgeoning historiography. Fundamental to these is the study of 'collective memory' or 'social memory', terms that are derived from the writings of the French sociologist, Maurice Halbwachs.[19] Reacting against the prevalent belief in the early twentieth century that memory is an activity of the individual, Halbwachs argued that it is 'a collective function'. We call 'recollections to mind by relying on the frameworks of social memory', he wrote; we are members of society, and we do not independently create our own memories.[20] Halbwachs saw these 'frameworks' as essential to the existence of the groups to which we belong – family, class and religion, for example. Without a shared memory the group would lose its unity of outlook. Halbwachs's writings have a special importance for the historian of public monuments. The collective memory he describes is not an abstraction: to a great extent its 'frameworks' are iconic and spatial in their genesis and characteristics. It is located in persons, events and places that groups associate with their past. 'A society first of all needs to find landmarks', Halbwachs wrote,[21] and one of his most important case studies took the form of an inquiry into the emergence of the Holy Places as a 'legendary topography' for Christians.[22] For Halbwachs the term 'legendary' did not imply a lack of epistemological significance; quite the contrary. As a site of memory the places associated with the events of Christ's life and death validated some of the most widely held beliefs of medieval Christianity. They had a pedagogic role, and they were associated with important collective rituals and practices.

As Halbwachs describes it, collective memory has some of the characteristics of a distorting mirror in the view it affords of the past; departures from reality are important, even necessary, parts of its construction.[23] Where reality conflicts with socially constructed belief, it is the former that is found wanting and needful of change – a change that can require spatial alterations. His account shows the Crusaders rebuilding Jerusalem in such a way that the Holy Places would match the narrative of early Christian history that their forefathers had constructed in western

Europe over many centuries. As a site of memory the real Jerusalem that they had conquered was unacceptable.

An important anthology of studies of the collective memory of political events edited by James W. Pennebaker, Dario Paez and Bernard Rimé in 1997 seeks to 'celebrate' and 'extend' the work of Halbwachs and other pioneers such as Lev Vygotsky, F.C. Bartlett and Karl Mannheim.[24] Drawing on a 'wide range of ideas across several disciplines in psychology, sociology, anthropology and political science', Pennebaker and his colleagues provide significant theoretical and empirical support for the contention that collective memory is socially constructed. For the student of what they call the 'emerging research topic of collective memory' they also add one important issue to the agenda: time.[25] When are monuments built? What factors impinge upon the chronology of commemoration?

Historians are intrinsically interested in what Tom Griffiths has called 'seasons of memory' and 'waves of nostalgia',[26] but rarely have these phenomena been studied systematically in relation to monuments. By calculating the date of the erection of every monument in the United States in the hundred years prior to their study, Pennebaker and Banasik conclude that monuments 'were erected either immediately after an event, or in 20 to 30 year cycles thereafter'.[27] These findings are directly relevant to several of the chapters in this volume. After presenting their findings, Pennebaker and Banasik go on to explore two related questions: why does it often take 20–30 years to erect a monument? And, why does monument making tend to continue in 20–30-year cycles? In seeking to answer these questions, the authors offer several interconnected hypotheses. First, they suggest that events have their greatest impact on people between the ages of 12 and 25, a time of 'tremendous emotional and physiological variability' and 'identity formation', but also a period during which young individuals are least likely – socially and financially – to be able to engage in commemoration: 'Soon after a potentially memorable event, this group does not have the economic or political clout to establish monuments. Around 25 years later, when the affected cohort is, on average, over 40 years of age, they are now in the position to openly acknowledge their own past ... '.[28]

Second, Pennebaker and Banasik suggest that the memory cycle reflects the time needed to achieve sufficient psychological distance – in the case of a traumatic event – and for a 'consensus narrative' to emerge.[29] The assumption in the latter case is that monuments reflect consensus. This view is also advanced by Kirk Savage in his study of Civil War monuments in the United States. Although his book is predicated on a recognition that public space is a 'representational battleground, where many different social groups fight for access', Savage insists that monument makers seek closure. 'Public monuments were meant to yield resolution and consensus', he insists.[30] For some of the radical monument makers studied in this volume, however, consensus was the furthest thing from their minds, and the fruits of their labour were meant to stand as permanent symbols of defiance and opposition.[31] Moreover, the notion of closure implies that memorials are exclusively about the past. Many memorials were about the future.

The analysis of collective memory, drawing broadly on the work of Halbwachs, has much in common with cultural anthropology, especially the form that has been eloquently advocated by Clifford Geertz. Where Halbwachs wrote of 'the frameworks of social memory' that hold society and groups together, Geertz writes of a 'cultural frame' of social order, the component parts of which are similar to the collective rituals, practices and spatial icons identified by Halbwachs. The 'master fictions' that Geertz sees as expressing and justifying the values of social and political hierarchies are also similar in many respects to the 'collective memories' that result from the pressure exerted by society on individuals.[32] People, Halbwachs writes, feel an obligation as members of groups to construct the events of the past in a touched-up form to 'give them a prestige that reality did not possess'. In the works of both scholars, the written and spoken word is no longer privileged as the source of memory and culture. Halbwachs's 'framework' is embedded in localities and artefacts that are imbued with social meaning: Geertz's 'frame' consists of 'stories, ceremonies, insignia, formalities, and appurtenances'.[33]

The lines of inquiry opened up by Halbwachs and Geertz have proved fruitful for the study of public memory and public memorials. Historians have described memorials and sites of memory as 'a type of speech' that articulates a sense of the past in which 'origin myths' and teleological 'narratives' provide a focus of group loyalty. Following the example of social anthropologists who borrow metaphors from the dramatic stage and religion, historians refer to 'performative memory' and a 'dramaturgy' of public life that portrays 'mythic narratives' through memorials that are 'catechisms in stone' erected on 'sacro-secular political sites' which serve as a 'pedagogical space ... to teach the people the new civic virtues'. Those who visit these sites go on a 'funerary pilgrimage', and take part in ritual performances that mobilize the group.[34]

The importance that Halbwachs attached to 'the localization of memories' has been given added force by writings on the social and political culture of the modern city. Historians have referred to the importance of 'the public sphere', a concept that was developed by Jürgen Habermas and refined in critical reviews by other scholars.[35] For Habermas the story of 'the public sphere' is one in which the liberal bourgeoisie that emerged in western Europe during the eighteenth and nineteenth centuries began to emancipate itself from the controlled public knowledge of the *ancien regime* and learned to think thoughts that were 'directed against the authorities'.[36] This was a process 'in which the state-governed public sphere was appropriated by ... private people making use of their reason' to establish 'a sphere of criticism of public authority'.[37] These people had their own institutions and places of resort – the financial, commercial and professional institutions of western European cities – and they created others such as the coffee house. They appropriated or infiltrated the cultural institutions that had developed under royal and aristocratic patronage such as the world of letters, the reading room, the theatre, the museum, the concert and the salon. Wrested from courtly and aristocratic control, the public sphere became the domain of public opinion.[38] Habermas does not mention it, but this would become the world in which the public memorial provided a rallying point for groups that stood outside and in opposition to constituted authority and established hierarchies.

Habermas's emphasis on the importance of urban culture has been taken further by scholars who have focused more sharply on the topography of the city and the social significance of its architecture including its monuments. Like Halbwachs, they see a landscape that has been shaped to accord with the beliefs of those who have taken possession of it:. national and civic elites, other social and political groups, architects and town planners. Historians who practise this 'historical geography of ideas' are concerned with 'spaces of knowledge production and consumption';[39] borrowing a metaphor devised by French scholars, they explore the city to take notice of its *architecture parlante* and deconstruct its social messages.[40] The outcome is an image of the nineteenth-century city that to a great extent validates Habermas's model of an emergent liberal bourgeois 'public sphere', but with a crucial difference. The liberal bourgeoisie did not have things all its own way; the city was a landscape of contestation and negotiation between different groups. As Geoff Eley pointed out in an important extension of Habermas's model of public life, 'the public sphere was always constituted by conflict'; there were 'competing publics ... at every stage'. Liberals and radicals competed against each other as well as against the conservative establishment.[41]

More recently, this notion of multiple and competing public spheres has been usefully examined by a sociologist, John Roberts, in relation to an episode in nineteenth-century British radical politics. Drawing on the work of the 'Bakhtin circle', especially V.N. Voloshinov, Roberts posits the existence of what he calls a 'proletarian public sphere' which by the middle of the nineteenth century had become a 'powerful form of resistance to the fetishistic idiosyncrasies of capitalist space'.[42] Although he does not discuss monuments, Roberts describes how the massive Chartist demonstrations in London's Hyde Park in 1855 'indelibly inscribed a working class public sphere at this royal park'.[43] Although his argument has some force, 'class' would seem to be less useful as a category, even in relation to his own example, than he asserts. What he describes as a 'working class' or 'proletarian' public sphere is perhaps better understood as an independent, oppositional, or alternative public sphere. Something similar to this has been detected in the transformation of Trafalgar Square from what one historian has called an 'emblem of empire' into 'the country's foremost *place politique*' where demonstrations were held that were 'most often anti-imperialist'.[44]

Several streams of historical inquiry intersect at this point to indicate the importance of the public memorial in modern history. The city emerges as a monument in its own right. It is a world of 'spatial politics' (Rosalyn Deutsche's neatly apposite term),[45] and, as Ben-Amos emphasises, politics necessarily involves 'the manipulation of symbols' for the pedagogic purposes of social control.[46] Memorials take their place among these symbols. They define civic virtue and provide sources of inspiration for the future. The aspiration of those who erect them has been well summarised by Paul Shackel in his study of the making of the American landscape: 'Those who control the past have the ability to command social and political events in the present and the future.'[47] Scholars have used Gramsci's notion of 'hegemony' to describe the part played by the constructed landscape in the 'public sphere'; dominant classes and regimes build memorials to consolidate their ascendancy over the hearts and minds of those they rule.[48] Applying a notion that resembles Halbwachs's depiction of a legendary topography, the contributors to Eric Hobsbawm and Terence Ranger's collection of essays on 'invented traditions' have shown the care that regimes of varied political persuasion have bestowed on sites of memory to establish continuity with perceptions of the past in ways that express the values of the present.[49] Thus in recent writings conservatives are shown using monuments and their attendant rituals to reinforce traditional ideals of hierarchy; reformers use them to voice 'oppositional histories'; and new regimes of all sorts employ them as ideological barriers of 'unequivocal demarcation' between past and present.[50]

The proliferation of public monuments as a means of recruiting the dead for political narratives (Thomas Laqueur's words)[51] was urged on and given shape by the special place of death in nineteenth-century European culture, an area of research that has attracted much attention from recent historians. 'Death and dying', writes Thomas Kselman, 'have become fashionable topics in recent years',[52] and, together with Michel Vovelle, James Curl, Pat Jalland and other historians,[53] he has shown that during the nineteenth century there was a cultural shift in attitudes to the dead. There was a 'celebration of death', to use Curl's term, involving expensive rituals and lavish displays of artefacts and paraphernalia of all sorts.[54] New cemeteries were endowed with monuments that exemplified a 'new funerary art'.[55] Thus it was not only the difficulties that they encountered in obtaining other sites that induced reformers to place some of their public memorials in cemeteries;[56] nineteenth-century cemeteries were designed as places of public resort where memory was combined with edification, and some impressive memorials were placed there by preference.[57] As Roy Porter has pointed out, even in the case of private funerary monuments (the vast majority), 'tombstones have their stories to tell', and some of these stories belong to the public sphere.[58]

It will be evident that the history of sites of memory has emerged as an area of inquiry in which French scholars and those who write on French history have acquired a special expertise. K.S. Inglis has paid tribute to a French 'enterprise which might be called iconographic history', a pursuit that has given rise to 'a broader French project, *Les Lieux de Mémoire* ... committed to the interpretation of monuments and other texts as bearers of collective memory'.[59] The doyen of the broader project is Pierre Nora,[60] who has drawn on and developed the ideas of Halbwachs. His influence is seen in several of the essays in this volume, but the writings of Maurice Agulhon have a special significance. In his works is to be found one of the key terms for the historian of public memorials – 'statumania'. There too can be found a chronology of the rise of the modern public monument. 'Every regime', Agulhon writes, 'has its own Pantheon (in the literal as well as the figurative sense) and places statues of the appropriate notables in public squares.' In France for the most part these were kings and saints during the *ancien regime*. A start was made on honouring great men during the Enlightenment, but statumania was closely associated primarily with revolutionary regimes after 1789. The 1830 revolution occupies a crucially important place in Agulhon's chronology: it was followed by 'the first great surge of the French national statumania' when statues of great men were erected as 'motionless visual messages'. Conservatives too had their sites of memory, but, as described by Agulhon, statumania in France was a phenomenon especially favoured by secular, optimistic regimes; they sought to use public places for the pedagogic purposes of an ideology of liberal humanism.[61]

Agulhon's pioneering researches into statumania have been followed up by other scholars of French history, notably William Cohen, author of a study of statues in the provinces, and Avner Ben-Amos in his magisterial survey, *Funerals, Politics and Memory in Modern France, 1789–1996*.[62] As a consequence, nineteenth-century French history has set something like a benchmark for this form of study. Despite Kirk Savage's lament on the paucity of research, American scholars, including Savage himself, have revealed important aspects of a similar phenomenon in the United States after its Civil War,[63] and Germany too has been well served by Mosse's analysis of the symbols and rituals of modern German history.[64]

British historians, however, have lagged behind. A comment by Agulhon indicates that possibly the reason for this weak historiography is that Britain has less to offer the historian. 'French history', he writes, 'has been richer in symbolic struggles than has British history.'[65] This is an inadequate explanation. It may well be the case, as Sean Wilentz claims, that France, more than any other western nation, has been 'self-conscious – some might say pompous – in the propagation of political rituals and symbols',[66] but the deficiency in British historiography owes more to the lack of interest by modern historians than to the materials with which they have to work. The opportunities were demonstrated as far back as 1871 when the Rev. Charles Rogers completed a pioneering project that was intended to list and describe the monuments of Scotland with contextual data. Rogers saw these monuments (most of them were created during the nineteenth century) as 'milestones in the pathway of civilization', and appropriately he modelled his research procedures on the great social inquiries to which the Scottish Enlightenment had given birth, the old and new *Statistical Accounts of Scotland*. Thus, he not only toured much of Scotland in search of information but also wrote to the entire parish clergy and schoolmasters to seek their assistance. The outcome was a remarkable two-volume work of reference that deserves to be much better known.[67] Recently Jo Darke has provided a further indication of what can be done in her reference to the British Isles as 'a great open-air gallery of sculpture and stonework' with a 'kaleidoscopic collection of statues and equestrian figures, obelisks and classical columns, inscribed stones, carved crosses and other monumentalia'.[68] Many of these are symbols of power and struggle.

The story of statumania in nineteenth-century Britain and France was remarkably similar in its chronology and in some, though not all, of its characteristics. In neither country were there many statues and monuments in public places before the nineteenth century. In both cases those of a non-religious nature were principally of royal personages.[69] In the eighteenth century, however, Westminster Abbey was already assuming many of the characteristics that would later be associated with the Panthéon; in 1711 Joseph Addison wandered there surveying 'the tombs of the great' and 'the epitaphs of the beautiful'.[70] The turn of the nineteenth century was a time of importance for the history of the public monument in Britain as well as France. As Linda Colley has pointed out, the British government kept a close watch on the public displays of the French during the war era and devised its own versions.[71] The emulation applied to monuments. Napoleon's great military memorials are well known; less well known is the decision by the British Government to set up a Committee of National Monuments in 1802 and vote £40,000 for the commemoration of British war heroes.[72] Scotland had its counterpart in the form of the monuments that were built and projected for the Calton Hill in Edinburgh in memory of Nelson and the Scottish war dead.[73]

These were only the beginnings. In 1838, *The Times* regretted to see that within a circumference of thirty miles there were no more than seventeen statues in London, but it noted that this was an improvement on twenty years earlier when there had been half that number, most of which were of monarchs.[74] The change came in with a rush. Lord Lauderdale detected a similar wave of statumania in Britain to the one that Agulhon sees sweeping over France after the 1830 Revolution. In 1833 he complained that 'it is one of the absurd fashions of the present day that leads people to think if their relation dies, that they have a right to draw upon the purses of all who were acquainted with the deceased, for a supply to build a monument.'[75] Even the name that was given to this phenomenon was similar in both countries. Agulhon quotes a reference in 1842 to '*La Manie des statues*'; *The Times* for 12 August 1850 headlined 'The Monument Mania'.[76] On both sides of the Channel voices of concern were raised that the concept of the public monument was being trivialised. In 1903, the *Dépêche de Toulouse* recoiled from the indiscriminate display of frock coats, pants and shoes that was to be seen on pedestals across France.[77] In Britain, Coventry Patmore had previously voiced his misgivings more pithily: 'Shall Smith Have A Statue?'[78]

Worse still for conservatives was the prospect that the proliferating public monuments would be politicised by their opponents. The bitterness of the contests between conservatives and reformers for the control of public space reached a degree of intensity in France that far exceeded developments in Britain – *dépanthéonisation*, the term that splendidly describes attitudes and practices in France,[79] had no British counterpart. Nonetheless, British liberals and radicals showed that they were fully aware of the benefits of using memorials to control public spaces where they could extol their ideals. The Whigs took the lead, and by 1816 they were marking out a section of London as their own site of memory. In that year a statue was unveiled in Bloomsbury Square showing Charles James Fox, dressed as a Roman senator holding Magna Carta and looking down Bloomsbury Place towards Russell Square, the site of a statue of the fifth Duke of Bedford.[80] Other Whig luminaries were commemorated on a grand scale during the decades that followed. Earl Grey of Reform Bill fame stands on a magnificent Doric column, 135 feet high in Newcastle upon Tyne. He is hailed as the 'Champion of Civil and Religious Liberty' who 'safely and triumphantly attained … the great measure of Parliamentary Reform'.[81] The first Earl of Durham ('Radical Jack') is commemorated on a hilltop site in County Durham by a Temple of Theseus that was opened in 1844 during an impressive ceremony to which many travelled by special railway excursions.[82] The chronology of statumania and its politicisation occurred unevenly across Britain. London and Edinburgh were abreast of developments in

France, but the new industrial towns showed little interest until much later. Birmingham was an especially destitute example. When Karl Friedrich Schinkel, Privy Counsellor for Public Works in Prussia, visited the town in 1826 he found 'nothing here of any value to me'. Apart from some 'ugly churches', the city was embellished only by 'an awful bronze statue of Nelson in the Market-place notable only for a large ship's bow and [the admiral's] missing arm'.[83] Likewise when J.G. Kohl visited Birmingham in 1844 he too was surprised to find that the town still had only this one statue. Leeds and Birmingham, he believed, were 'the most ... ornamentless towns in England'.[84] The 1850s, when statues were erected to honour Sir Robert Peel, seem to have been the crucial decade for statumania in the industrial towns.[85] Peel had been a Conservative prime minister, but the memorials honoured him as a reformer; in a self-sacrificing gesture he had placed nation above party and safeguarded the people's bread. In 1859, there was an even more striking development: Birmingham consolidated its reputation as a centre of movements for radical change by honouring two of its own best-known and most controversial sons. The first was Thomas Attwood, the leader of the Birmingham Political Union during the 1830s. A statue was erected to show him addressing one of the great meetings that were held in Birmingham during the agitation for the First Reform Bill. In his left hand he carried a scroll bearing the word 'Reform'. A Roman fasces (the emblem of unity and law) carried the words 'Liberty, Unity, Prosperity'.[86]

Later that year the sense of change in Birmingham was strengthened when a committee embarked on the task of erecting a statue in honour of another recently deceased fellow-townsman, Joseph Sturge. Described by one historian as 'the compleat reformer',[87] Sturge had participated in so many movements for radical reform that the committee made it clear from the outset that the statue they had in mind would be a public statement that defied convention. In the words of the Rev. J.A. James, Sturge had been a man of religious principle, and his statue would function as 'a kind of open-air preacher'. It would stand forth as a perpetual symbol of defiance, one that could never be silenced by 'summonses from the police' and 'the condemnations of the magistrates'.[88] The statue still stands in Birmingham showing Sturge, hand on bible, commending to passers-by the message of 'Charity', 'Peace' and 'Temperance' (carved in letters of gold on the pedestal) that he did so much to promote in his lifetime. At his feet drinking fountains gave water to those whom Sturge had laboured to save from the curse of intoxicating drink.[89] Speeches delivered in support of the fund-raising appeal emphasised the need to persevere with Sturge's campaigns for reform.

For many years after its inauguration in 1862 Sturge's statue continued to fulfil a preaching function. In 1864: John Bright invoked it as something like a text for one of the rousing speeches that he gave to his constituents in Birmingham: he told them that he never passed the statue without hoping that the people of the town would draw from it the inspiration that would lead them to adopt Sturge's principles on the 'public questions' of the day.[90] The public question of the day that Bright had in mind on that occasion was the American Civil War, and the speech provided an example of the way a memorial could be given a new reading. Suppressing any reference to Sturge's consistent opposition to all wars, Bright invoked the memory of Sturge's labours for the abolition of slavery to justify the aggressive stance that he himself was taking on behalf of the Northern states. Sixty years later, the statue was given a meaning more in keeping with Sturge's opinions. In the aftermath of the First World War, a metal plate was added to honour the man who had 'laboured to bring freedom to the negro slaves, the vote to British workmen and the promise of peace to a war-torn world'.[91] The statue's subsequent experience has been typical of many. It has been moved to a less conspicuous site, its fountains are dry, and it has been vandalised.[92]

Birmingham's nineteenth-century experience further exemplifies themes that will be developed in this collection of essays. As the committee that raised funds for the erection of Sturge's monument acknowledged, up to that time public statuary had customarily been reserved for 'Warriors and Statesmen, Kings and Rulers of Men'.[93] It was a novelty for a town to commemorate one of its own citizens, especially one of humble birth who had challenged the established beliefs and power structures of the day. Knowingly and unapologetically, both the Attwood and Sturge committees made very few concessions to the conventions of statuary that reflected the values of the landed gentry. The new civic heroes were to stand forth clothed as they had appeared in life and not, as was often the case with contemporary statues, in the attire of ancient Greece and Rome with its resonances of traditional taste and order.[94] Thus there was little need to read the inscriptions on these statues to see their most basic theme. At a glance the reformer's statue proclaimed the values of a modernising radical creed. By the end of the century there were similar statues, busts and monuments all over Britain. Bright's statue, for example, stands in Rochdale, and in Manchester Richard Cobden was only one of a galaxy of Anti-Corn Law League leaders to be honoured in this way: J.B. Smith, George Wilson, Sir John Potter, C.P. Villiers and John Bright.[95]

The essays in *Contested Sites: Commemoration, Memorial and Popular Politics in Nineteenth Century Britain,* exemplify the importance of many of the themes discussed above for the making of an oppositional public memory in modern Britain. They range over several well-known reform movements, campaigns and individuals – from the Scottish Martyrs, and Tom Paine to anti-slavery campaigners, teetotalers and the Chartists. The sites of memory do not encompass the wide range of those in Nora's volumes, but they include statues and other forms of memorial as well as plaques, tombstones and banners. The collection embraces a wide variety of reformers, including the working-class radicals who were absent from Habermas's model of the public sphere. Like the Reformers' Memorial at Kensal Green it is not a comprehensive examination: there are many absent causes and individuals who might have found a place. Rather, again like Corfield's monument, the collection is intended as a work-in-progress that will open up the study of oppositional commemoration in British popular politics and point the way to further research. It will suggest that, in addition to providing an important means of contesting public space, memorials have fulfilled important functions within popular radicalism: from expressions of group identity to sources of inspiration. As Stan Newens, a stalwart of many progressive causes and a long-serving Labour Member of the European Parliament, has written recently in relation to the Reformers' Memorial in Kensal

Green, the 'purpose of a memorial is to remind us of what we owe to those who went before us and to engender respect for their endeavours'. Like Godwin, Newens recognises that radical monuments are as much about the future as about the past. 'Hopefully', he continues, the Reformers' Memorial will encourage 'later generations to cherish and defend their achievements and inspire those with social ideals to dedicate themselves to their realisation'.[96]

The age of statumania has passed, and across the world many of its exhibits either do not exist or have fallen into neglect. Some monuments have been moved to different and less conspicuous sites,[97] some have been destroyed:[98] and in various countries feminists, race reformers and other groups have contested the definition of public memory that they offer.[99] As in the case of the Soviet Empire where there has been a clearance of ideological artefacts,[100] the end of the British Empire resulted in the repatriation or removal of imperial icons from Ireland and former colonies.[101] Lack of interest has been widespread, endorsing Jay Winter's summary of the place that many monuments occupy in the public sphere – a 'trajectory of decomposition, a passage from the active to the inert'.[102] One reason for the lack of interest during much of the twentieth century was that the celebration of death lost much of the fascination it had held for the Victorians, and its appurtenances were seen as distasteful objects to be avoided or carefully confined. With few exceptions such as Highgate and Père Lachaise, cemeteries ceased to be places of public resort, and their memorials were ignored and neglected.[103]

Monuments continued to be built during the twentieth century; two world wars amply kept the tradition alive. After the First World War, Lord Edward Gleichen deplored their 'alarming extent' in London and called for the appointment of a central authority that would 'pull down the bad statues, as well as those erected to comparative nonentities'. This would leave the way clear for the rearrangement of the survivors in dignified ways that would commemorate 'great movements and great men'. Gleichen conceded that he would have to wait until the millennium for this to happen, and that it was more likely that monuments would continue to be built to the accompaniment of cheap jibes from the few who took much notice of them.[104] And so it has gone on. In the 1980s, there was even an abortive project for a grandiose pyramid-like structure that would have commemorated the Battle of Britain as the central feature of a Docklands site where London would be shown forth as the 'New Jerusalem' of private enterprise.[105] On a less ambitious scale, statues and other memorials of politicians and dignitaries have also gone on being created, and, as the recent decapitation of a statue of Margaret Thatcher has demonstrated, they have retained their controversial power.[106]

The oppositional memorial has been another survivor, and there have been controversial attempts at contesting received images of the past by commemorating groups that were previously seen as peripheral or lacking in merit. The recent creation of the Staffordshire 'Shot at Dawn Memorial', a statue that honours military deserters who were executed during the First World War, has been an especially striking use of a public monument to reshape history in a way that would previously have been unthinkable.[107] In Scotland, where important monuments were created in the nineteenth century as expressions of national identity, time-hallowed episodes in the national memory continue to be cherished. One example is a Highland Clearances Memorial complete with a Wall of Descendants.[108] This memorial is likely to evoke painful images of a far distant past that have strong resonances in the present day.[109] Perhaps it is not surprising that this upsurge of feeling has been accompanied by an attempted *dépanthéonisation* of one of the traditional villains of this tragedy, the first Duke of Sutherland. In 1994, an unsuccessful campaign was waged to remove the statue of the Duke from the place it has occupied on a 100-ft pillar on Ben Bhraggie, near Golspie. Comparisons were made with the removal of statues in the former Soviet Empire, but opinions were divided, and there were those who wished to retain the statue precisely because it served 'to remind people of the iniquities that took place and of the continuing absurdity of how land is held and who has power over it'.[110]

Monuments, like most other aspects of modern life, have also become contested sites of gender. Middle-class culture during the Victorian era did not easily accommodate women in the public sphere, and by the end of the nineteenth century very few of them had been commemorated by monuments.[111] The change was slow in coming. Contemporary attitudes could permit the erection of a drinking fountain at the Royal Exchange in 1879 to honour motherhood in the form of a woman with two children, and in 1893, it was a further sign of the times with reference to both gender and class when a statue was erected to 'The Housemaid'.[112] To modern eyes these are examples of gender stereotyping; they foreshadowed much of the commemoration of women in the twentieth century that now seems to exemplify what has been called 'contributionism' – images of nurses on war monuments, for example. The criticism is still made that women are inadequately represented.[113]

Other attempts at reforming the concept of the memorial as a site of public memory have been more resourceful, not to say fanciful. Pressing on from democratisation to popularisation, Birmingham has commemorated the comedian Tony Hancock by an unconventional representation, and in Dundee a public walkway with verse engraved on the pavement has been created to lead visitors into the scenes described by William McGonagall, the world's worst poet – a 'legendary landscape' that surpasses any envisaged by Halbwachs.[114]

It is easy to be facetious about such memorials, but it may well be that the public monument of popular amusement is the way of the future, and that didactic memorials such as the ones discussed in this volume are becoming redundant. If this is so, one of the contributory factors is likely to be a sharp decline in respect for historical and general knowledge together with a loss of the nineteenth-century notion of the public sphere as the rallying point for what the historian Trygve Tholfsen has called 'the Religion of Improvement'.[115] Consider the following two statements about what should happen when the person commemorated by a monument has passed beyond living memory. The first was offered in Montrose in September 1859 when a statue was unveiled in honour of Joseph Hume, who had represented the constituency as its radical MP. There was a great procession consisting of the Masonic lodges, friendly societies and contingents from nearly every trade and profession in the town. Many members of the general public attended, there were bands of music and businesses closed. Evidently there was little need to justify the monument to people such as these; it could be taken for granted that they knew Hume's merits. The principal speech was delivered by one of the burgh councillors who preferred to look into the future. The Town Council, he promised, would preserve the statue 'in all its pristine beauty and truthfulness to future eyes', so that those 'yet unborn', including 'many a child of obscurity', would ask what sort of man was commemorated and be prompted to draw lessons from his personal and public life.[116] The ceremony was a classic example of what may be called the pedagogic impulse in nineteenth-century civic life. Conservatives and reformers could agree on at least this much: the memorial was an ideal medium for conveying the virtues of private and public life.

In October 2000, a very different attitude was displayed to public monuments. The Mayor of London, a quintessentially late twentieth-century oppositional figure – 'Red' Ken Livingstone – touched off a major controversy by calling for the removal of the statues of Generals Havelock and Napier from Trafalgar Square. Many of the responses were predictable. A Conservative Party spokesman denounced 'Britain-bashing from the left', and the regimental secretary of Havelock's former regiment wrote that Livingstone was 'consigning our history to oblivion', a process that must surely end with Nelson himself being 'ripped' from his column.[117] They misunderstood their opponent: Livingstone rested his argument, not on ideological or historical considerations such as those that had characterised *dépanthéonisations* elsewhere in Europe, but on public ignorance – an ignorance that he evidently thought should not be disturbed. 'I think that the people on the plinths in the main square in our capital city should be identifiable to the generality of the population', he argued.[118] Claiming to speak on behalf of 'ordinary Londoners', Livingstone freely admitted that he did not have a 'clue' who the generals in question were, but this did not matter: 'it is time to look at moving them and having figures on those plinths that ordinary Londoners would know.' His comments threw the floodgates open for suggestions of statues not only of such people as Lady Thatcher but also of 'Posh' Spice, David Beckham, Richard Branson and Barbara Windsor, the 'cheeky cockney matriarch' of the 'Carry On' films and the soap opera, 'EastEnders'. It seemed that Coventry Patmore's question, 'Shall Smith have a statue?' was about to be answered.

Doubtless much of this banter was provoked by an incorrigibly controversial politician, but Livingstone had raised an important question. The Victorians had a very keen sense of why public monuments should be erected for the benefit of future as well as present generations. The monument of a man such as Hume embodied a metanarrative of reform that drew on memories of the past and was projected into the future; it had immense relevance at the national, local and personal levels of daily life.[119] There is no such metanarrative in the postmodern world, a place where history itself, so we have been told, has reached its end. There is no modern 'statumania', and we seem to have little idea of what should be done with the public memorials that we have inherited from a past that has ceased to live in the minds of most people. Yet, as is pointed out in this volume and elsewhere, new narratives can be told in old places of memory, and monuments can have a second life. We are also living in an era when suppressed histories such as those of the Highland Clearances and transatlantic slavery can be revealed in ways that are unmistakably relevant to the present day. Perhaps it is too early to terminate the history of the memorial of reform.

Notes

1   Godwin, W. (1809), *Essay on Sepulchres. Or, A Proposal For Erecting Some Memorial of the Illustrious Dead in All Ages, on the spot where their remains have been interred,* New York: M. & M. Ward, p. xiv. This little-known pamphlet is not among Godwin's collected works.
2   Ibid., p. 47f.
3   Ibid., p. 34, 44–5.
4   Anderson, B. (1991), *Imagined Communities. Reflections of the Origin and Spread of Nationalism,* London: Verso, pp. 9–10.
5   Ibid.
6   Godwin, *Essay on Sepulchres,* pp. 75–6.
7   Ibid., p. 47
8   Dabakis, M. (1999), *Visualizing Labor in American Sculpture: Monuments, Manliness, and the Work Ethic, 1880–1935,* Cambridge: Cambridge University Press, p. 5.
9   A full list of the names on the monument is provided in the second edition of W.H. Brown's booklet (see note 12 below) reprinted with an Introduction by Stan Newens MEP, London, 1998.
10 See Royle, E. (1980), *Radicals, Secularists and Republicans: Popular Freethought in Britain, 1866–1915,* Manchester: Manchester University Press, p. 42.
11 *Co-operative News,* 29 August 1885, p. 791.
12 Brown, W.H. (1925), *Pathfinders: Brief Records of Seventy-four Adventurers in clearing the way for free public opinion,* Manchester: Co-operative Union, p. 7.
13 Ibid., p. 8
14 Ibid.
15 Mosse, G.L. (1975), *The Nationalization of the Masses. Political Symbolism and Mass Movements in Germany from the Napoleonic Wars Through the Third Reich,* New York: Howard Fertig.
16 Agulhon, M. (1985), 'Politics, Images and Symbols in Post-Revolutionary France' in Wilentz, S. (ed.), *Rites of Power. Symbolism, Ritual and Politics since the Middle Ages,* Philadelphia: University Of Pennsylvania Press, pp. 188, 191.
17 Savage, K. (1997) *Standing Soldiers, Kneeling Slaves: Race, War and Monument in Nineteenth-Century America,* Princeton, NJ: Princeton University Press, p. 215.
18 Inglis, K.S. (1998), *Sacred Places: War Memorials in the Australian Landscape,* Melbourne: Miegunyah Press; Ben-Amos, A. (2000), *Funerals, Politics and Memory in Modern France, 1789–1996,* Oxford: Oxford University Press.
19 Halbwachs, M. (1992), *On Collective Memory,* trans. and ed. by L.A. Coser, Chicago, IL: University of Chicago Press. Halbwach's influence can be seen in recent works on public memory by Paul Connerton, James Fentress and Chris Wickham which provide some of the basic concepts used by historians of public monuments. Connerton offers the 'implicit rule that participants in any social order must presuppose a shared memory'. 'Our memories', he adds, 'are located within the mental and material spaces of the group.' Fentress and Wickham write that 'much memory is attached to membership of social groups of one kind or another'. See Connerton, P. (1989), *How Societies Remember,* Cambridge: Cambridge University Press, pp. 3, 37; Fentress, J. and Wickham, C. (1992), *Social Memory,* Oxford: Oxford University Press, p. ix.
20 Halbwachs, *On Collective Memory,* pp. 182–3.
21 Ibid., p. 222.

22 Ibid., pp. 191–235.
23 Ibid., p. 182.
24 Pennebaker, J.W., Paez, D. and Rimé, B. (eds), (1997), *Collective Memory of Political Events: Social Psychological Perspectives*, Mahwah, NJ: Lawrence Erlbaum Associates, p. x; Mannheim, K. (1928), *Essays of the Sociology of Knowledge*, London: Routledge & Kegan Paul; Bartlett, F.C. (1932), *Remembering: A study in experimental and social psychology*, Cambridge: Cambridge University Press; Vygotsky, L.S. (1971), *The psychology of art*, Cambridge, MA: MIT Press.
25 Pennebaker et al., *Collective Memory*, p. x.
26 Griffiths, T. (1995), *Hunters and Collectors: The Antiquarian Imagination in Australia*, Cambridge: Cambridge University Press, p. 7.
27 Pennebaker et al., *Collective Memory*, p. 12.
28 Ibid., pp. 12–17.
29 Ibid., p. 13.
30 Savage, *Standing Soldiers*, pp. 3–4. See also Meskimmon, M. (2003), *Women Making Art: History, Subjectivity, Aesthetics*, London and New York: Routledge, pp. 60–68.
31 See also Dabakis, *Visualising Labor*, p. 4.
32 Geertz, C. (1985), 'Centers, Kings and Charisma: Reflections on the Symbolics of Power' in Wilentz, *Rites of Power*, pp. 30, 33.
33 Ibid., p. 15.
34 The quotations, which are offered only as a sample, are taken from the following: Inglis, *Sacred Places*, p. 7; Fentress & Wickham, *Social Memory*, p. 128; Connerton, *How Societies Remember*, p. 72; Pickering, P. A. and Tyrrell, A. (2000), *The People's Bread*, London: Leicester University Press, Chap. 9; Darrian-Smith, K. and Hamilton, P. (eds) (1994), *Memory and History in Twentieth-Century Australia*, Melbourne: Oxford University Press, p. 2; Agulhon, 'Politics, Images and Symbols in Post-Revolutionary France', p. 178; Laqueur, T. (2001), 'In and Out of the Panthéon', *London Review of Books*, 23 (18), September, p. 6; Ben-Amos, *Funerals, Politics and Memory in Modern France*, pp. 32, 92.
35 Habermas, J. (1989), *The Structural Transformation of the Public Sphere*, Cambridge: Polity Press; Calhoun, C. (ed.) (1992), *Habermas and the Public Sphere*, Cambridge, MA: MIT Press.
36 Habermas, *The Structural Transformation of the Public Sphere*, p. 25
37 Ibid., p. 51.
38 Ibid., pp. 31–43.
39 Philo, C. (1999), 'Edinburgh, Enlightenment and the Geographies of Unreason' in Livingstone, D.N. and Withers, C.W.J. (eds) (1999), *Geography and Enlightenment*, Chicago, IL: University of Chicago Press, p. 373.
40 Markus, T.A. (1982), 'Introduction', *Order in Space and Society. Architectural Form and its Context in the Scottish Enlightenment*, Edinburgh: Mainstream Publishing Company, p. 7.
41 Eley, G. (1992), 'Nations, Publics and Political Cultures: Placing Habermas in the Nineteenth Century' in Calhoun (ed.), *Habermas and the Public Sphere*, p. 306.
42 Roberts, J. M. (2001), 'Spatial Governance and Working Class Public Spheres: The Case of a Chartist Demonstration at Hyde Park', *Journal of Historical Sociology*, 14 (3), September, p. 309. Voloshinov, V.N. (1973), *Marxism and the philosophy of language*, New York: Seminar Press.
43 Roberts, 'Spatial Governance', p. 326.
44 Mace, R. (1976), *Trafalgar Square. Emblem of Empire*, London: Lawrence and Wishart, pp. 7, 15.
45 Deutsche, R. (1996), *Evictions: Art and Spatial Politics*, Cambridge, MA: MIT Press, pp. 21–2, refers to the neoclassical monuments in nineteenth-century American cities as instruments for tightening 'social control' by providing models of 'order, timelessness and moral perfection'.

46 Ben-Amos, *Funerals, Politics and Memory in Modern France*, p. 3

47 Shackel, P.A. (2001), *Myth, Memory and the Making of the American Landscape*, Gainesville: University Press of Florida, p. 3. The importance of idealised visions of the past in landscapes has been endorsed by Rosemary Mitchell. She quotes C. Delheim's statement that the Victorians saw the past as 'a visual, rather than a verbal faculty, cultivated in the landscape more often than in the library'. See Mitchell, R. (2000), *Picturing the Past. English History in Text and Image, 1830–1870*, Oxford: Oxford University Press, p. 16.

48 See, for example, Cohen, W. (1989), 'Symbols of Power: Statues in Nineteenth-Century Provincial France', *Comparative Studies in Society and History*, 31, p. 495.

49 Hobsbawm writes that 'Buildings and monuments were the most visible form of establishing a new interpretation of German history' after 1870. See Hobsbawm, E.J. (1992), 'Mass-Producing Traditions: Europe 1870–1914' in Hobsbawm, E.J. and Ranger, T. (eds), *The Invention of Tradition*, Cambridge: Cambridge University Press, p. 275.

50 Connerton, *How Societies Remember*, pp. 7, 15.

51 Laqueur, 'In and Out of the Panthéon', p. 3.

52 Kselman, T.A. (1993), *Death and the Afterlife in Modern France*, Princeton: Princeton University Press, p. 3.

53 Vovelle, M. (1983), *La Mort et L'Occident de 1300 à Nos Jours*, Paris: Gallimard; Curl, J.S. (1972), *The Victorian Celebration of Death*, Newton Abbot: David and Charles; Jalland, P. (1996), *Death in the Victorian Family*, Oxford: Oxford University Press.

54 Curl, *The Victorian Celebration of Death*, Chap. 1.

55 Vovelle, *La Mort et L'Occident de 1300 à Nos Jours*, p. 632.

56 Ben-Amos, *Funerals, Politics and Memory in Modern France*, p. 89.

57 This point has not been given sufficient weight by Maurice Agulhon. He excludes cemeteries from his analysis on the grounds that they belong to a traditional category. See Agulhon, M. (1978), 'La "statuomanie" et l'histoire', *Ethnologie Française*, 2/3, pp. 145–6.

58 Porter, R. (1990), 'Preface' in Barnard, S.M., *To Prove I'm Not Forgot. Living and Dying in a Victorian City*, Manchester: Manchester University Press, p. x.

59 Inglis, *Sacred Places*, p. 7.

60 Nora, P. (1984), *Les Lieux de Mémoire*, Paris: Gallimard. Broadly conceived though it is, Nora's project has been criticised as a work of 'pantheonization' that adopts highly selective criteria for the definition of memory. Describing Nora as one of the 'foremost barons' of the Académie Française, Sudhir Hazareesingh has attacked *Les Lieux de Mémoire* for consecrating 'a particular form of ideologized memory' that excludes the unsavoury aspects of French history such as the treatment meted out to workers, Algerians, Jews and women. See Hazareesingh, Sudhir (2003), 'Guard dogs of good deeds. Remembering badly and forgetting well: history and memory in modern France', *Times Literary Supplement*, March, pp. 12–13.

61 Agulhon, 'Politics, Images and Symbols in Post-Revolutionary France', pp. 179, 185, 191, 193. See also his 'La "statuomanie" et l'histoire', pp. 147, 154: '*La Monarchie de Juillet, c'est précisément, ... la première grande invasion de la statuaire publique*'.

62 Full details of Cohen and Ben-Amos's writings are provided in notes 18 and 48 above.

63 See Savage, *Standing Soldiers*, p. 8.

64 For full details of Mosse's *The Nationalization of the Masses*, see footnote 18. See also two articles on modern German identity and memory by Koshar, R.J. and Koonz, C. in Gillis, J.R. (ed.) (1994), *Commemorations: the Politics of National Identity*, Princeton, NJ: Princeton University Press.

65 Agulhon, 'Politics, Images and Symbols in Post-Revolutionary France', p. 199.

66 Wilentz, 'Introduction' in his *Rites of Power*, p. 5.

67 Rogers, C. (1871), *Monuments and Monumental Inscriptions in Scotland*, London: Charles Griffin & Co., vol. 1, pp. ix–xi. The brief references, of variable quality, to monuments in N. Pevsner's series (itself a *lieu de mémoire*), provide a useful starting

point for England. See Pevsner, N. (1957), *The Buildings of England*, Harmondsworth: Penguin.

68 Darke, J. (1991), *The Monument Guide to England and Wales*, London: Macdonald Illustrated, p. 9.

69 For France see Agulhon, 'Politics, Images and Symbols in Post-Revolutionary France', p.190. For Britain see *The Times*, 1 September 1838.

70 Read, B. (1982), *Victorian Sculpture*, New Haven: Yale University Press, p. 85. See also Addison, J. (1937), 'Westminster Abbey' in Eliot, C.W. (ed.), *English Essays from Sir Philip Sydney to Macaulay*, New York: Harvard Classics, p. 80.

71 Colley, L. (1992), *Britons. Forging the Nation, 1707–1837*, New Haven, CT: Yale University Press, p. 216.

72 Whinney, M. (1964), *Sculpture in Britain, 1530–1830*, Harmondsworth: Penguin.

73 See Chapter 2 below.

74 *The Times*, 1 September 1838. Darke, *The Monument Guide to England and Wales*, p. 29, states that London's first non-royal public statues date from 1809 and 1816.

75 Lord Lauderdale to William Allen, 30 December 1833, William Adam Papers, National Register of Archives, Scotland, Bundle 406.

76 Agulhon, 'La "statuomanie" et l'histoire', p. 148. See also *The Times*, 12 August 1850 (first published in the *Spectator*).

77 Cohen, 'Symbols of Power', p. 495. See Whinney, *Sculpture in Britain*, p. 361 for B.R. Haydon's complaint in 1812 about the proliferation of 'boots, spurs, epaulettes, sashes, hats and belts' badly sculpted in marble.

78 Patmore, C. (1898), *Principles in Art Etc.*, London: G. Bell, p. 204.

79 Agulhon, 'La "statuomanie" et l'histoire', p. 147. '*Dépanthéonisation*' describes the removal or destruction of the physical remains and statuary of great men who are no longer deemed worthy of veneration in public places.

80 Penny, N.B. (1976), 'The Whig Cult of Fox in Early Nineteenth-Century Sculpture', *Past and Present*, 70, February, pp. 96–100. See also Chapter 7 in this volume for references to Fox's memorial in Westminster Abbey where he is depicted dying in the arms of Liberty, praised by one of the slaves who had benefited from the abolition of the slave trade. According to Gleichen, E. (1928), *London's Open Air Statuary*, London: Longman's, Green & Co., p. 175, the Bloomsbury monument of Fox was paid for by the surplus raised for the Westminster Abbey monument.

81 Pevsner, *The Buildings of England*, p. 246.

82 Darke, *The Monument Guide to England and Wales*, pp. 229–32. See also *The Times*, 30 August 1840.

83 Schinkel, Karl Friedrich (1993 edn), ' *The English Journey': Journal of a Visit to France and Britain in 1826*, Bindman, D. and Riemann, G. (eds), New Haven, CT: Yale University Press, p. 126.

84 Kohl, J.G. (1968, first edn 1844), *England and Wales*, London: Frank Cass, p. 11.

85 Darke, *The Monument Guide to England and Wales*, p. 13 refers to 'a flood of feeling in the northern towns' after Peel's death. The Peel statue in Birmingham was originally surrounded by a railing depicting 'large clusters of wheat-ears'. See Dent, R.K. (1973, first edn 1878–80), *Old and New Birmingham*, Wakefield: E.P. Publishing, vol. 3, pp. 558–9.

86 *Birmingham Journal*, 11 June 1859. See also Dent, *Old and New Birmingham*, vol. 2, pp. 351, 561.

87 Temperley, H. (1972), *British Antislavery, 1833–1870*, London: Longman, p. 72

88 Richard, H. (1864), *Memoirs of Joseph Sturge*, London: S.W. Partridge, pp. 576–9.

89 The Sturge statue project provides an early example of divided opinions over the merits of creating a monument of civic utility in preference to a statue. There was a proposal that Sturge should be commemorated by the building of an additional wing of the General Hospital: *Birmingham Journal*, 27 August 1859.

90   Smith, G.B. (1881), *The Life and Speeches of the Right Hon. John Bright, M.P.,* London: Hodder & Stoughton, vol. 2, p. 131.

91   The plate still exists.

92   During the Second World War the statue was provided with its own air-raid shelter in the form of an encasing brick-built structure: photograph in the possession of Alex Tyrrell.

93   *Birmingham Journal,* 24 December 1859.

94   Darke, *The Monument Guide to England and Wales,* pp.13, 29 refers to Sir Joshua Reynolds's influential belief that contemporary clothing was not suitable for a statue in comparison with the timeless dignity of classical garb. Angus B. Reach, on the other hand, poked fun at the 'metallic falsehoods' and 'granite lies' of classical clothing and speculated on how archaeologists of a distant future would interpret the statuary of nineteenth-century Britain: they would imagine that Pitt, Fox and Canning addressed Parliament in togas. See *Douglas Jerrold's Magazine,* July–December, 1846, p. 537.

95   Gleichen, *London's Open Air Statuary,* p. 192 described the statue raised to Cobden in Camden Town as 'About the cheapest statue on record, and one of the worst'.

96   S. Newens, Introduction to *Pathfinders,* p. ii.

97   The statue of Joseph Sturge is one of these.

98   The destruction of the Hunt monument in Manchester and the monument erected to commemorate Queen Victoria's visit to Dundee in 1844 are examples.

99   See, for example, the references to feminist opposition to war memorials in Inglis, *Sacred Places,* pp. 466, 468. For references to racial feeling see Shackel, 'The Robert Gould Shaw Memorial: Re-defining the Role of the Fifty-Fourth Massachusetts Volunteer Infantry' in his *Myth, Memory and the Making of the American Landscape,* and Savage, K., 'The Politics of Memory: Black Emancipation and the Civil War Monument', Gillis (ed.), *Commemorations,* Chap. 7.

100 The *Guardian Weekly,* 12–18 July, 2001 carried an article describing a project to make the famous 'Worker and Woman Collective Farmer' sculpture the figurehead of a huge shopping mall in Moscow.

101 Read, *Victorian Sculpture,* p. 40.

102 Quoted by Alimental, E.A.T., 'Introduction' in Shackel (ed.), *Myth, Memory and the Making of the American Landscape,* p. xii.

103 Nunhead Cemetery provides an excellent example of changing attitudes to public cemeteries during the twentieth century. The Southwark Local Library contains a collection of news cuttings from the 1980s deploring the overgrown and vandalised condition of the cemetery. Since then the restorative care of the London Borough of Southwark and the Friends of Nunhead Cemetery has transformed this situation.

104 Gleichen, *London's Open Air Statuary,* p. xv and xvi.

105 Theo Crosby, the designer, offered this as a belated response to what he saw as the error made after the Second World War when the building of hospitals and schools was preferred to the erection of monuments. See Wright, P. (1989), 'Heritage and Danger: The English Past in the Era of the Welfare State' in Butler, T. (ed.), *Memory, History, Culture and the Mind,* Oxford: Blackwell, p 151.

106 Gary Younge's article, *Guardian Weekly,* 11–17 July 2002, on the decapitation revisited several of the issues raised by Coventry Patmore's 'Shall Smith have a statue?'.

107 Ibid., 13–19 September 2001.

108 *Scots: The Journal of the Scots Heritage Society,* 17, 2002, pp. 18–22.

109 Another example is the cairn that the inhabitants of Gigha in Argyll erected in July 2002 to mark their acquisition of the island after a controversial struggle. See *Scotsman,* 24 July, 2002. A senior minister in the Scottish Executive participated in the ceremony.

110 Withers, C.W.J. (1996), 'Place, Memory, Monument: Memorializing the Past in Contemporary Highland Scotland', *Ecumene,* 3, p. 332.

111   The exception that seems to prove the rule is the Sinclair Monument erected in
      Edinburgh to honour Catherine Sinclair (1800–64), a novelist and philanthropist.
      Birrell, J.F. (1980), *An Edinburgh Alphabet*, Edinburgh: James Thin, The Mercat Press,
      p. 47. See also Rogers, *Monuments and Monumental Inscriptions in Scotland*, vol., 1,
      p. 11. Florence Nightingale's statue in Waterloo Place, London was erected in 1915, five
      years after her death. See Gleichen, *London's Open-Air Statuary*, pp. 19–20.
112   Read, *Victorian Sculpture*, p. 211.
113   Inglis, *Sacred Places*, pp. 466–8, provides some interesting Australian examples of
      feminist protests.
114   Malcolm Robertson provided the reference to Tony Hancock. For McGonagall, see
      BBC News, 24 June 2002.
115   A survey completed during the sixtieth anniversary of the Battle of Britain, for example,
      showed that 10 per cent of Britons aged 18 to 24 believed that it had occurred in 1815
      and a further 11 per cent thought it had occurred in 1066. See *Daily Mirror*, 15
      September 2000. For 'the religion of improvement' see Tholfsen, T.R. (1976), *Working
      Class Radicalism in Mid-Victorian England*, London: Croom Helm, p. 140.
116   *Brechin Advertiser*, 27 September 1859. See also *Dundee Courier*, 28 September 1859.
117   *Guardian*, 19 October 2000.
118   Ibid.
119   For Hume see Chapter 2 in this volume.

Chapter 2

Bearding the Tories:
The Commemoration of the Scottish
Political Martyrs of 1793–94

Alex Tyrrell with Michael T. Davis[1]

Ninety feet high and rising to a commanding height on the slopes of the Calton Hill in Edinburgh, the obelisk known as the Scottish Political Martyrs' Monument points like a finger of rebuke over a delinquent city. It commemorates an episode that has acquired a special place of infamy in Scottish history. In 1793 and 1794, at the time of the French Revolution and the outbreak of war between France and Britain, the five men whose names are commemorated on the monument were put on trial in Edinburgh, found guilty of various charges of sedition and sentenced to transportation to Botany Bay for 14 years.[2] Throughout Lowland Scotland they and other 'Friends of the People' who favoured extending the parliamentary franchise

Fig. 2.1   An early twentieth-century view of Edinburgh showing the obelisk erected in honour of the Scottish Political Martyrs (centre).

had drawn inspiration from the early stages of the French Revolution. Their rapidly multiplying societies and their Conventions of reformers had aroused the fear and resentment of the privileged and the propertied, giving rise to a conservative reaction of which these state trials were only the best known examples. Four simple inscriptions decorate the monument. One of these is a list that names the five men: Thomas Muir, Thomas Fyshe Palmer, William Skirving, Maurice Margarot and Joseph Gerrald. Another inscription names those responsible for the erection of the monument and gives the year of the laying of the foundation stone: 'The friends of parliamentary reform In England and Scotland. 1844'. The third inscription quotes from the speech that Muir threw in the face of his judges: 'I have devoted myself to the cause of the People. It is a good cause – It shall ultimately prevail – It shall finally triumph.' The fourth inscription is William Skirving's defiant statement of his belief in an ultimate vindication: 'I know that what has been done these two days will be re-judged.'

The appeal by Muir and Skirving to opinion beyond the court attracted sympathy from the outset. It was not only the harshness of the sentences that aroused concern. The coarse jocularity with which Lord Braxfield, the presiding judge, conducted the trial and the blatant partiality of the jury he had personally selected aroused such a sense of shock that there were protests in Parliament. For two decades after the Martyrs' trials there was little opportunity to voice dissent in Scotland, but memories were long.[3] Educated young men – some were Whigs with a passion for constitutional propriety and civil liberty; others called themselves radicals and were disciples of Jeremy Bentham – carried this sense of shock into their years of maturity and eminence.[4] Working men who also called themselves radicals but took their creed from Major Cartwright, William Cobbett, T.J. Wooler and other advocates of manhood suffrage invoked the names of Muir and his associates on the banners that they carried in Edinburgh and Glasgow during the campaign for the 1832 Reform Bill.[5] It was at this time that Peter Mackenzie, a Glasgow radical, set out to consolidate the sense of continuity with the heroic past by writing the first major biography of Muir. Years later Mackenzie would refer to how, as a young man, he had fallen under the spell of the Martyrs' tragically noble story and dedicated himself to their memory with 'something like chivalry and devotion'.[6] Deeply moved by Muir's prophecy that future generations would endorse his stance, Mackenzie tried to give it effect as part of the great change that was sweeping across the nation at the time of the Reform Bill. He expressed the hope to the Lord Advocate, Francis Jeffrey, that Edinburgh or Glasgow would soon be adorned with a monument to the memory of the Martyrs, and he urged the idea strongly in his biography of Muir.[7] A few years later he even went on a 'pilgrimage' to visit Muir's grave in Chantilly.[8] Conservatives might complain about the use of the term, and sticklers for the truth pointed out that three of them were English, but by then the five felons were firmly established as 'the Scottish Political Martyrs'.[9] It was a time to act on the adage: 'The traitors of one age were the patriots and martyrs of another.'[10] The monument that was inaugurated in 1844 was the fruit of this conviction.

Over the years, the Martyrs and Lord Braxfield have remained part of Scottish public memory to such an extent that modern historians have warned readers against seeing them as people of folklore.[11] Knowledge of the monument has fared less well. In 1981, one of Muir's biographers doubted that 'many people today know or care whom the monument commemorates'.[12] A similar statement could have been made about the attitude of historians to almost any of the modern monuments in British cities. In recent years, however, there has been a change; memorials and other manifestations of public memory are now major themes of scholarly inquiry. 'Every regime has its own Pantheon', writes Maurice Agulhon, 'and places statues of the appropriate notables in public squares'; they merit scholarly inquiry.[13] This essay will attempt to rescue the Martyrs' Monument from neglect and misunderstanding by demonstrating its important symbolic role in the political struggles of the second quarter of the nineteenth century and relating it to the phenomenon that Agulhon has called the 'statumania' of that era.[14] The essay will conclude by showing how a monument of one era may be divested of its original meaning and rebranded for use in another era by a new generation.[15]

Edinburgh provides an exceptionally clear example of a growing interest in public monuments during the early nineteenth century. The building of the New Town provided an ideal opportunity for creating an *architecture parlante*, an opportunity that was used by the civic elite to such an extent that the result has been described as a monument in its own right.[16] The choice of classical Roman and Greek architecture together with mathematically logical forms of town planning spoke volumes for a mentality that was pervaded by the rational ideas of the Scottish Enlightenment. According to a recent historian, Thomas Markus, the intention was to create in Edinburgh 'a zone of order, luxury and visible status for the permanent use of the ruling elite'. There was to be an almost total contrast with 'the density, social mix and increasing squalor of the Old Town'.[17] Markus does not make this point, but it should be noted that the New Town elite was also proclaiming the triumph of a conservative polity in the aftermath of the French Revolution. This was the polity defended by William Pitt the Younger, the Prime Minister whose name was carried as an icon far into the nineteenth century by Tories who celebrated his memory in their Pitt Clubs as 'the pilot that weathered the storm' during the French Revolution and the Napoleonic Wars.

There is no mistaking the political message of the *architecture parlante* that the Edinburgh Tories adopted. In the form of a statue on a magnificent 132-ft high pillar that was modelled on Trajan's column in Rome, Henry Dundas, Lord Melville, dominates the skyline at the eastern end of the urban grid of the New Town. 'Harry IX', as he was nicknamed, Melville was the great friend of William Pitt, and he ruled Scotland as a personal fiefdom in the interest of Pitt's version of Toryism. Melville's nephew was the Attorney General who prosecuted the Martyrs, and, when the ferocity of the sentences was challenged, Melville himself publicly endorsed the procedures of Braxfield's court.[18] The location of Melville's monument gave rise to some debate when it was planned, but the prominence it was to be accorded was never in doubt: the Calton Hill, the Castle Esplanade and Arthur's Seat were considered as sites before the centre of Saint Andrew's Square was finally selected.[19] Thus, when the citizens of Edinburgh looked up to Melville on his column, they were reinforcing the lessons they had learned about the Tory ascendancy of those days. In death as in life Melville was destined to tower over the city. And, if anyone missed the political significance of this monument, there were further object lessons nearby in the form of two statues at important street intersections. One of these was of George IV, the monarch who gratified Sir Walter Scott and the Tories by accepting their invitation to visit Edinburgh in 1822. The other statue was of none other than William Pitt himself.[20] It was all very similar to the process that Avner Ben-Amos has described with reference to nineteenth-century France: by means of statues and street names (there are interlocking Pitt and Dundas Streets in the New Town), the Edinburgh Tories were making the city 'a pedagogical space' for the propagation of their own 'civic virtues'.[21]

John Lowrey, an architectural historian, has described the place that the Calton Hill was meant to occupy in this depiction of Edinburgh as an urban stage for the celebration of the political ideals of Pitt and Melville. Unlike their contemporaries in the United States who appropriated Greek architecture to the ideals of 'political liberty, republicanism and revolution', Edinburgh's elite conceived its urban utopia in a context of 'empire and conquest'.[22] Created as the 'Modern Athens', the city would have the Calton Hill as its Acropolis. The remnant of a huge volcanic cone, the Hill is a commanding eminence that overlooks much of the urban area, and, when it was linked to the New Town by major street developments in the early nineteenth century, it became the focal point of much of the civic elite's sense of Edinburgh as Scotland's capital city. There, on a site crowned by buildings in classical architecture that called the Parthenon to mind, Edinburgh could proclaim Scotland's share in the defeat of the French and show itself forth as a city where the highest ideals of the Enlightenment had triumphed. The Nelson Monument celebrated Britain's naval power, and the National Monument was intended to commemorate the Scots who died in the British armed forces during the French Wars.[23] The Observatory, the Playford monument, the Dugald Stewart monument, the Robert Burns monument and the Royal High School all pointed to Scotland's and Edinburgh's intellectual and cultural greatness during these years. At a time when an older sense of Scotland's separate identity seemed to be disappearing, the New Town and the Calton Hill were intended to give Edinburgh, in Lowrey's words, 'an identity for itself within the British imperial state'.[24] Thus, although the Secretary of the National Monument Committee saw the project he was promoting as a manifestation of the 'friendly rivalship' between the three kingdoms of the British Isles in which they could exhibit their 'primaeval greatness', he was insistent that this would not damage the Union: 'the more completely the three countries are amalgamated, so much the better'.[25] It would be hard to find a more fitting example of the sense of national identity that Linda Colley has seen emerging from the long wars against the French: there was a strong sense of Britishness but one that accommodated differences between Scots and English.[26]

Except for the National Monument, which ran out of money after a few pillars were erected, these structures were in place when the 1832 Reform Act and the Burgh Reform Act brought the Tory ascendancy to an end. With the benefit of hindsight we know that the Calton Hill project came to an end then too. The National Monument was never completed, and no more major buildings were erected on the summit, but this was not anticipated at the time. The Calton Hill was seen as an unfinished project, and there were occasional attempts to complete it.[27] For several years during the 1830s and 1840s, it was used as the venue for an interesting example of Scottish statumania when one of the local sculptors, Robert Forrest, set up a studio and exhibition for his works within the embryonic National Monument.[28] Referring to 'a treat of no ordinary kind', the *Scotsman* urged its readers to pay a visit to Forrest's statuary as a civic and national duty: 'Every individual in Edinburgh, young and old, should see this exhibition, in order to assure themselves that Scotland can produce Sculptors as well as Greece and Rome.'[29] Forrest's collection steadily expanded to include Sir Walter Scott, Lord Byron, Elizabeth Tudor, Napoleon, Robert the Bruce, Marlborough and Wellington.[30]

In the new set of circumstances created by the political changes of the 1830s, questions inevitably arose as to the likelihood that the public places of Edinburgh would feel the force of the reformers' zeal. How would the Whig MPs and the radical Town Councillors who now dominated the politics of Edinburgh imprint their visions and their national narratives of progress on the face of the city? Would new gods and a different set of heroes be worshipped on the slopes of Edinburgh's Acropolis? Even before the downfall of the Tory political ascendancy, the Whigs had obtained control of the National Monument project and converted it from a Pantheon of conservative military virtues into a Parthenon where 'Scotland's civil as well as military achievement' would be celebrated.[31] During the 1830s a wide variety of reformers began to stake out their claims to a share of the Calton Hill. In 1833, anti-Annuity Tax demonstrations sometimes commenced there; in 1835, Daniel O'Connell addressed a large meeting on its slopes; and by the end of the decade radical working men had started to hold meetings there.[32] In 1834, when Earl Grey, the Prime Minister whose government had brought in the 1832 Reform Act, paid a triumphal visit to the city, the celebrations climaxed in a great banquet that was held in the grounds of the Royal High School. The venue was a temporary pavilion, but the ubiquitous Thomas Hamilton, the architect who had created the Royal High School and the adjacent Robert Burns memorial, designed it on a spectacular scale. With their sumptuous decorations and their flamboyant gaslights – Lord Cockburn referred to a scene like one from the *Arabian Nights* – these specially constructed pavilions were novelties in the world of political agitation and they attracted considerable attention.[33] The way the future might develop was there for all to see. As the *Scotsman* had tartly warned the conservatives when the Pitt monument was erected, 'The decoration of our city by works of art is yet only begun.'[34]

The audacity of those who planned the Martyrs' Monument can only be appreciated if it is related to this context of political change during the 1830s. As William Cohen has pointed out with reference to nineteenth-century France, the choice of location for a monument is important, not least because it can be used to confront opponents by denying them a monopoly of a public space to which they attach ideological significance.[35] From the outset the planners saw the Calton Hill as 'undoubtedly the most appropriate place' to honour the memory of those whom they considered to have been unjustly convicted as felons. The site that they had in mind was one on the summit of the Hill where, if they had had their way, they would have placed a massive obelisk alongside the other monuments and thrust it into the heavens above the city. They commissioned Thomas Hamilton as their architect and described the obelisk as one that would be a tasteful addition to the Hill,[36] but, above all, they intended to commemorate the political victims of Pitt, Melville and the Tories. Commanding the skyline above the Melville column and the other statues below, it would proclaim the great change that had come over Scottish politics during the 1830s.[37] In 1837, one of the speakers at a public meeting could not have been more blunt about the intention. The Martyrs' Monument, he said, would rise up on the Calton Hill in stark contrast with the three statues in the New Town that personified 'vice between tyranny and corruption', that is, the statue of George IV, flanked by the Pitt statue and the Melville column. Honouring the 'faithful avenged', it would stand alongside the other monuments that had been erected on the Calton Hill to commemorate a man of science, a philosopher and 'our own immortal Burns, himself a political martyr'.[38]

It is scarcely surprising that such a project was resisted throughout its planning, but, bold though it was, and condemned though it might be as an innovation that smacked of foreign influences, there was something that was peculiarly British in the reformers' vision of the role of the public monument. Unlike in France, where each change of régime in the nineteenth century was accompanied by a clearing and replacement of statues, the planners had no desire to monopolise the streetscape. William Tait envisaged visitors to Edinburgh turning their gaze to the Martyrs' Monument after 'the humiliating monuments' of Toryism had 'glared on their eyes'.[39] Thus Melville, Pitt and George IV would remain in place to be challenged in daily combat by the Martyrs. Just as in Parliament where the proponents of divergent points of view took their turns in debate across the chamber, so would these political statements in metal and stone share the public space between them. This battle of monuments would respect the values of British constitutionalism.

Although the idea of the Martyrs' Monument seems to have been first mooted by Peter Mackenzie, and one of the *Scotsman's* correspondents made a similar suggestion in 1833,[40] everyone agreed that the driving force behind the project came from Joseph Hume, one of the best known of the radical MPs in Westminster.[41] After a false start as a Tory, Hume dedicated a long career in the House of Commons to the advocacy of an advanced political programme that owed much to the ideas of Jeremy Bentham's variety of radicalism. He has been described as 'in a sense, the creation of James Mill', Bentham's confidant, whom he had first met as a school-boy at Montrose Academy.[42] Unimpressive intellectually – even the sympathetic *Schoolmaster and Edinburgh Weekly Magazine* saw him as a humourless plodder who had never 'uttered a perfect sentence'[43] – Hume was famous for the robust constitution and capacity for sustained hard work that he placed at the service of a strenuous programme of reforms which included the extension of the franchise, free trade, repeal of the Combination Laws, and a variety of schemes for promoting 'the march of mind'. Above all, he was the scourge of those who benefited from the 'Old

Corruption' that oiled the wheels of the political establishment, earning himself a reputation as a fanatic who was obsessed with wasteful forms of government expenditure. Nonetheless, although Hume's relationship with Whig Cabinet ministers was often strained during the 1830s, he was careful to keep up his links with them. In 1836 and 1837, at the time when he was making the Martyrs' Monument one of his projects, he was trying to work with the Whigs and at the same time retain contact with those whose radicalism went further than his own.[44] Seen from his point of view, the monument offered an ideal medium of co-operation for a wide spectrum of those who saw themselves as reformers. At the same time as it celebrated some of the best-known martyrs of radicalism, it could be presented to the Whigs as a means of asserting their vision of themselves as champions of civil and religious liberty.[45] There was little to chose between Hume and some of the Whigs when they recalled their memories of the state trials in 1793 and 1794. At that time Hume had been in Edinburgh as a student at the University, and, according to his own testimony, he had never forgotten his sense of shock on learning what had been perpetrated in the name of the law.[46] Henry Cockburn, Francis Jeffrey and Lord Holland were Whigs who uttered similar sentiments. Writing to Hume in March 1837, Holland summarised this point of view by referring to 'the disgust and abhorrence' he had always felt for the arbitrary trials of men who, as he put it, had called for the sort of reforms that the Whigs were implementing in the 1830s.[47]

Hume's attention was drawn back to the Martyrs when Mackenzie sent him a copy of *The Life of Thomas Muir.* He was immediately attracted to the idea of a monument; it chimed in with his interest in using public places for national education. Many years later, he would be accorded a place of honour in Samuel Smiles's *Duty* because of his agitation on behalf of public access to the Tower of London, Hampton Court and other places of historical interest.[48] Rewriting and expounding the nation's recent history by means of public monuments could be seen as an extension of this project. In his reply Hume welcomed Mackenzie's suggestion of a monument, and explained that the proposal was similar to one with which he was already involved: in a few weeks, he was to participate in the inauguration of a monument in London to honour the memory of Major Cartwright.

Hume's letter to Mackenzie deserves to be better known, for it sets out the reasons for the interest that radicals of this era took in public monuments. As he explained, a monument had a utility that went beyond the pious commemoration of the illustrious dead. Together with ceremonies such as the public dinners that were held to inaugurate them, monuments provided an opportunity to promote ideas of reform. Concerned by what he saw as the Tories' stranglehold on the statumania of the age, Hume wished to upset the convention that public memorials were for 'conquerors and statesmen, who have been successful in their career, though often of questionable utility to humanity and good government'. The time had come to erect 'statues in honour of the honest, virtuous, and unfortunate martyrs in the cause of liberty'. Scots, he told Mackenzie, would derive a further benefit that would extend far into the future; a monument honouring those who had been condemned for their reforming opinions in 1793 and 1794 would be 'a beacon to future governments to avoid acts of tyranny and oppression such as these excellent and virtuous men suffered'.[49]

Hume took up the idea of the memorial with his customary energy. Speaking from the chair at the dinner to inaugurate the Cartwright statue on 20 July 1831, he toasted the memory of the Scottish Martyrs and launched a subscription list.[50] There the matter remained until the end of 1836 when Hume resumed the subject by calling a public meeting in London.[51] By then the statumania of the age was in full flood, and the minds of reformers turned easily to thoughts of monuments. It was a decade when reality melted easily into fantasy. In 1833, with the encouragement of some nobles and gentlemen, Richard Trevithick sent a proposal to William IV for 'a gilded conical' column that would rise a thousand feet above London (five times the height of Nelson's Pillar) to celebrate the 'glory of the British Constitution and the passing of the Reform Bill'. Hollow and made of cast-iron, this monument would have allowed visitors to reach the summit in an elevator that was worked by atmospheric pressure.[52] Five years later, when R.M. Beverley heard that Joseph Sturge, the Quaker anti-slavery abolitionist, had succeeded in overthrowing the Apprenticeship system that had retained elements of slavery in the British West Indies, he too could not restrain an instinctive flight of fancy towards a monument:

> They are going to erect some huge monument to the Conqueror of Waterloo at an immense expense – to commemorate a victory which has eminently failed in all it's [*sic*] political intentions – but why not erect some colossal something to Joseph? Let us have him in bronze striding over the rail-road, at the entrance into Birmingham, higher than the Church steeples, & with a broad brim 30 feet in diameter … .[53]

Thus, when Hume discussed his idea of a Martyrs' Monument with his circle of associates, their aspirations can be seen as modest only if they are judged against these extremes. He told Colonel Thomas Perronet Thompson that only the difficulty of finding a suitable site was holding him back from erecting a monument in honour of Queen Caroline, George IV's injured spouse, whose cause the radicals had championed in 1820.[54] As for the Scottish Political Martyrs, he thought they would need two monuments, one in Edinburgh and one in London. Writing to Francis Place, Thompson welcomed the idea of a monument to the Scottish Political Martyrs but wished to see them honoured in London rather than in Edinburgh as the commencement of a nation-wide campaign to commemorate reformers. A London monument with a damning inscription, he wrote, would 'beard the monuments which the Tories are erecting every day to the objects of their worship'. It would be 'the grandest move against the enemy, that God or the devil has put into the hearts of the Radicals yet'. Other places that had suffered from Tory misrule would follow suit, and in due course Thompson looked forward to seeing a Peterloo monument.[55]

During the winter of 1836–37, Hume achieved much for the projected Martyrs' Monuments. He set up a committee in London with himself as Chairman and fifty members who included Francis Place and a string of radical MPs: Dr Bowring, George Grote, J.T. Leader, Sir William Molesworth, Daniel O'Connell, Colonel Perronet Thompson, Thomas Wakley and others.[56] Much of this membership was merely titular,[57] and Hume had to rely heavily on his own great energy. Meanwhile, prompted by this 'chosen band of reformers in the sister kingdom', a committee came into existence in Edinburgh which organised a public meeting where resolutions were passed condemning the 'rancorous tory persecution' of the Martyrs and calling for the erection of a monument to 'form an enduring record of their deeds, and an encouragement to the men of future times to emulate their heroic example'.[58] The committee included the names of some members of the Town Council, but in practice most of the work seems to have fallen to William Moffat and William Tait. Moffat had a personal interest in promoting the cause of the Martyrs, having attended the trials of Muir and Palmer in 1793 as their confidant and legal agent. He named his son Thomas Muir Moffat, and in 1834 he publicised the fate of his friends and his own subsequent sufferings in *The Tory Persecution of some of the Original Members of the Scottish Association, for Obtaining Parliamentary Reform*.[59] Moffat conceded that Hume was 'the Lynch pin of the Machine' for raising money for the Martyrs' Monument,[60] but he was actively involved in fund raising and maintained close contact with Hume on issues regarding the progress of the scheme.[61] William Tait's contribution was especially important in rousing and sustaining interest in Edinburgh. He was the publisher of *Tait's Edinburgh Magazine,* a widely read publication that was characterised by its Benthamite radicalism. *Tait's* launched the movement in January 1837 by publishing an article on the Martyrs.[62]

From the outset it was agreed that money from London was to supplement the contributions raised in Edinburgh,[63] where an obelisk was to be created that would be as high as Cleopatra's Needle.[64] A letter that Tait wrote to the Lord Provost of Edinburgh in January 1837 summarised the early plans that were devised for the Edinburgh monument. Making it clear that he was acting in co-operation with like-minded people in London, Tait explained that a nation-wide subscription was being raised. Reformers of all opinions (presumably a reference to the inclusion of Whigs) were to be approached for their financial support, and it was anticipated that there would be a good response. There were plans for a 'handsome Obelisk', and the outcome would be 'an ornament' to its locality. A site of forty to fifty square feet would be needed, the most suitable locality for which would be the Calton Hill. If the Town Council granted the land, Tait anticipated that the scheme would go ahead rapidly.[65]

Predictably, there was strong opposition. Defeated but not chastened by the political changes of the decade, the Edinburgh Tories, or Conservatives as they now preferred to call themselves, were not prepared to allow Joseph Hume to write his version of recent history on the civic landscape they had created. Through their local mouthpiece, the *Edinburgh Evening Post*, they used this issue as their opening shot for a campaign that they waged against Hume and his local allies during 1837 and 1838. In a racy and pungent style that would have won the admiration of William Cobbett, the arch-polemicist of the early nineteenth century, they depicted Hume's character as an 'unwholesome compound of impudence, absurdity, hatred of his country and its institutions, presumption, ignorance, and vulgarity'.[66] He was the very epitome of 'The Modern Radical':[67]

> But times and seasons to the rads
> No good will e'er convey,
> The Church and Laws, and King and Lords,
> By them are swept away.
> And though the gaol and workhouse hold
> More rads than e'er before,
> There's Roebuck, Hume and Molesworth left,
> To discontent the poor.
> Like red-hot ranting radicals,
> All of the modern time.

When Hume lost his Middlesex seat in the 1837 election, the *Post* was enraged to see him brought back to Parliament as the MP for Kilkenny thanks to the patronage of the one person in public life that conservatives hated even more – Daniel O'Connell. Hume had become the 'illiterate hanger-on of an Irish vagabond's popish following'.[68]

Hume's proposal for a Martyrs' Monument took its place in the *Post's* syllabus of errors; it was exactly the sort of thing that would appeal to a 'great Hume-Bug' who was intent on honouring traitors, fools and madmen as the first instalment of a radical reform that would destroy the most valued institutions in the British polity and society.[69] The Conservatives were particularly angered by what they saw as the determination of the local radicals to use Edinburgh as a forum for promoting Hume's political ideology.[70] Thus, when the Town Council made him a freeman in August 1837, the *Post* condemned those who had attached the reputation of the city to 'the sneerer at religion, and the spoliator of the English and Irish Church, the advocate of voluntary church principles, the advocate of vote by ballot, household suffrage, annual parliaments, the expulsion of the Bishops from the House of Peers, and the supporter of the reform or degradation of the peers'. Such a Town Council no more represented respectable opinion in Edinburgh 'than the prating of a parrot represents the speech of the human race, or the acts of a monkey the intellect of a man'.[71] History was inextricably intertwined with present-day politics in the columns of the *Post,* and the proposed monument provided the Conservatives with an opportunity to smear Hume's local allies by associating them with images from the past – a past of dark sedition and imminent revolution that required repression. Just as the Martyrs had been condemned for their admiration of the French Reign of Terror,[72] so were their modern defenders to be seen as 'orators of the Muir, Palmer, Tom Paine, and Thunder and Lightning Schools' who would only be restrained by 'the treadmill, or a course of the shower-bath – the water at zero'. Their proposal for a monument would 'turn the stomach of a badger'.[73] As for Councillors Russell and Maclaren, two of Hume's principal local allies, the *Post* looked forward to the day when, like Muir and Palmer, they too might be 'compelled to cross the seas for the good of their country'.[74]

This was all part of the cut and thrust of a debate that was often conducted with an eye to its jocular qualities, but there was an underlying sense of menace. The Whigs were in decline by 1837, and in one of his speeches Hume referred to the possibility that the Tories might return to government. Sir Robert Peel's reformulation of old Toryism as a new conservatism was too recent to be reassuring, and one of the reasons Hume offered for promoting the idea of a monument was the need to remind people of the sort of repression that they could expect from the Conservatives.[75] There is no doubting the reality of this fear during the 1830s; reformers of a wide variety of opinions shared it, and they expressed it in private communications as well as public utterances.[76] Like the Conservatives, they looked back to the past, and their arguments were no mere excursion into antiquarianism. In the 1830s Peter Mackenzie was not only Muir's biographer, he was also vindicating the memory of a more recent batch of Scottish martyrs, three of whom had been executed and others transported in 1820 for their participation in the 'Radical War' that culminated in the 'Battle' of Bonnymuir. As a youth, one of the executed men had corresponded with William Skirving in 1793.[77] Thanks to Mackenzie's efforts the survivors in New South Wales obtained a free pardon,[78] but he could still take visitors on something like a *via dolorosa* to see the birthplace of one of these rebels, the condemned cell, the gallows, the battle site of Bonnymuir, the graves of two of the executed men, and a monument that had recently been erected to honour them.[79]

There seemed to be no escape from the dark shadows of the 1790s. In 1834, Hume was in the forefront of the campaign that condemned the transportation of the Tolpuddle Martyrs to New South Wales; they were victims, he told the House of Commons, of 'one of the gagging acts passed to put down discussion in the height of Mr. Pitt's power'.[80] Similarly, for Henry Cockburn and Francis Jeffrey, the repression of 1793 and 1794 was a present-day reality in the form of legal precedents that had never been overturned. Cockburn, who made a study of Scottish sedition trials, noted anxiously that in 1817 and 1820 judges had referred with respect to the precedents set by the trials of 1793–94: 'whigs', he wrote, 'felt as if the days of Braxfield had come back, or might do so.'[81] Like other Scottish Whig lawyers, Cockburn had little respect for the Martyrs and their ideology of reform – he saw their radicalism as foolish posturing that had discredited the more moderate reforms for which Whigs were working[82] – but he was repelled by what the Tories of the Melville era had done in the name of the law. The monument he wished to see would be one that rebuked bad judges instead of celebrating brash radicals.[83]

In the short run, Tait made good progress in his dealings with the Town Council. He was in close contact with the radicals there, especially the strong group of Dissenters for whom the idea of an established church was so repugnant that, together with other 'voluntarists' in Scotland and England, they campaigned against the legal requirement to pay church rates.[84] The concept of martyrdom came readily to their minds, for Tait was one of those who earned the title 'church rate martyr' because of the strength of his convictions. In 1833, in a demonstration that began on the slopes of the Calton Hill, he had been given a hero's welcome on his release from prison after refusing to pay the Annuity Tax which supported the clergy of the Church of Scotland in Edinburgh.[85] Thus he quickly received provisional approval from the Town Council for the monument, and, together with the Superintendent of Works, he visited the Calton Hill to choose a suitable site. They found one on the north-eastern extremity, and all seemed to be set for a swift and triumphant conclusion.[86]

Unexpectedly, however, there were difficulties, and the project was not resumed until 1842. Tait did not give reasons when he referred to this delay in a letter to the Town Council,[87] but they may be surmised. The original proposal that there should be a monument in London as well as Edinburgh had never been relinquished, and the committees in the two cities experienced difficulties in making an apportionment of funds. Moreover, the Edinburgh committee's first choice of a design was too ornate for Hume and his London associates.[88] More importantly, Hume found it impossible to maintain his links with the broad spectrum of reformers to whom he had looked for support when he launched the monument project. In February 1838, he had a major disagreement with Perronet Thompson, and he argued with the Whigs over Lord John Russell's famous statement that the 1832 Reform Act represented 'finality'. As William Moffat pointed out in a letter to one of the monument's subscribers: 'In these times of general distress, as well as the apathy and division of both Whigs and Radicals, it has been found a very uphill proceeding to raise money for deserving worth.'[89] There was also the problem posed by the emergence of the Chartist movement. At a time when there was a very real fear of revolution, and Chartists were making the same tragic journey to Her Majesty's penal colonies, it would have been difficult if not foolhardy to promote the idea of raising a monument to the Martyrs of the 1790s. In the 1820s and 1830s, Hume had enjoyed the respect of William Lovett and other radical artisans with whom he co-operated in several of their campaigns[90] – he even flirted with Chartism[91] – but his relationship with them was often an uneasy one. He preferred household suffrage to manhood suffrage, and his support for the New Poor Law earned him a reputation as an advocate of the hated theories of Thomas Malthus.[92] His association with Daniel O'Connell also alienated those Chartists who endorsed Feargus O'Connor's opposition to 'The Liberator'.[93] Hume intervened on behalf of gaoled Chartists, but he could not bridge the deep gulf that had opened between working-class Chartists and middle-class radicals.[94]

The Martyrs' Monument took its place in this story of class tension. In 1837, before the People's Charter appeared, there was a rowdy confrontation that helped to set the pattern for the next few years. When Hume called a meeting in the Crown and Anchor in London in February 1837 to launch the project, Feargus O'Connor, Henry Vincent, the Rev. Arthur Wade and other future Chartists arrived to challenge his right to appropriate the memory of the Martyrs to his current political programme. Vincent praised Thomas Paine and looked forward to the day when Britain would become 'a democratic republic'; Wade said that 'the best Whig was not equal to the worst Radical'; and O'Connor proposed an amendment demanding universal suffrage, a policy that Hume saw as impractical and extreme. The meeting plunged into uproar in the face of O'Connor's accusations that Hume was acting on behalf of the Whig government.[95] The point at issue went beyond the monument; other questions were being asked. Why was Hume concealing the Martyrs' belief in universal suffrage and annual parliaments? Was it possible to speak of these men as if they were a band of brother reformers? Were there not suspicions that Margarot had been a spy for Pitt and Melville?[96]

Francis Place's letters voiced his despair at what was happening at this time. He worked hard, apparently with some success, to save Margarot's reputation, but for the rest he recorded a story of failure. He was appalled by O'Connor's intervention at the Crown and Anchor meeting and subsequently recorded his sense of outrage in a bitter description that mingled derogatory Irish and West Indian stereotypes. O'Connor, Place wrote (he even included a sketch), had the forehead of a 'Carrib' and a skull 'in the shape of a soda water bottle with the neck part forwards ... with a couple of lips which when in motion moved as much upwards as downwards [and] formed a huge potatoe trap out of which flowed a torrent of fulsome praise, abuse and nonsense'. Place believed, and it is difficult to disagree with him, that Hume was not the man to overcome this crisis; too many working men had been alienated by his apparent duplicity with respect to the Martyrs' support for male suffrage.[97] Not surprisingly, the project ground to a halt during the years between 1837 and 1842.

When it was resumed in 1842, the Tories were back in power, and the search was on for some means by which a broad coalition of reformers could be re-established. 1842 was the year when Joseph Sturge and other 'moral radical' Dissenters launched the Complete Suffrage movement and accepted the full programme of the People's Charter. Their hope was to forge an alliance with working-class radicals who were prepared to break with O'Connor's leadership. Complete Suffrage Associations were set up in many cities throughout Britain. One of the most impressive of these, the Edinburgh Complete Suffrage Association, took a keen interest in the trials and punishment of political prisoners.[98] Sturge's religious-based form of radicalism was different from Hume's Benthamism, but there was sufficient tolerance of differences to allow for a measure of co-operation. One of his biographers describes Hume as 'rudderless' at this time, offering 'scattergun' opposition to the Conservative Government.[99] His resumption of the monument project as a means of summoning up memories of past Tory injustices seems to fit easily into this pattern.

On 4 January 1842, Hume wrote to Tait suggesting that they should resurrect the idea of a Martyrs' Monument. He had evidently been attempting to pursue the project in London but had failed to find a site. Hume admitted that he had been disappointed by the response to his appeal, but the London committee had raised £800 of which he proposed to give £300 for a Calton Hill monument, if the Edinburgh Committee would raise £200 in addition to the £300 it had already raised.[100] Accordingly, Tait returned to the Town Council in July, reminding it of his approach in 1837 and the tentative agreement on a site. The obelisk would be built according to a plan devised by Thomas Hamilton, he added, and, if the Council agreed, work would commence promptly. He and his associates would accept any site on the Calton Hill, but they would prefer one that was to the right of the stair on the western side.[101] Close to the other monuments, this was a position that could easily be viewed from many parts of the city. On 26 July 1842, by a majority of 15 to 4, the Town Council voted to grant a site, as far as lay in its power and subject to its approval of the design of the monument.[102]

This was not the victory it seemed. As Lord Cockburn pointed out, the Conservatives were not the only opponents; 'several good whigs' disliked the idea of this monument, and the opposition was stronger than the size of the majority indicated.[103] In addition to political considerations, there were aesthetic misgivings.

Cockburn, the ever-vigilant defender of Edinburgh's public environment, voiced some of these. For him the design of the obelisk was 'abominable', and he was uneasy about the idea of endowing the Calton Hill with political monuments that would be 'discordant' for those who promenaded there.[104] A few years later, in his famous *Letter to the Lord Provost on the best ways of spoiling the beauty of Edinburgh,* he would describe the Calton Hill as 'the glory of Edinburgh ... adorned by beautiful buildings, dedicated to science and to the memory of distinguished men'.[105] The caveat that the Council had attached to its approval provided abundant ammunition to use against the Monument, and the wheels ground slowly over the next two years. Two weeks after the Town Council made its decision, the Treasurer, Sir William Drysdale, opened a sustained campaign of obstruction by moving successfully that the matter should be delayed while the Councillors perused the reports of the trials of the Martyrs 'so as to be enabled to judge of their innocence or guilt'. The Council minutes do not record the outcome of this bizarre attempt at a re-trial, but for the rest of the year Drysdale succeeded in postponing a discussion of the matter, until on 6 December 1842 he moved that the application for a site be rejected outright. [106]

Drysdale did not succeed, and the Council endorsed its earlier decision, but he had made his point. The Councillors, he argued, had been correct to enter the caveat in which they expressed a doubt about their powers. The city had fallen into bankruptcy, and its property could not be alienated without the agreement of the creditors. Moreover, under statutes and contracts that regulated the development of that area of Edinburgh, all public buildings on the Calton Hill needed the approval of the Governors of George Heriot's Hospital, the Lord President of the Court of Session, the Lord Justice Clerk and the Lord Chief Baron. Wisely, the Councillors submitted the proposal to their Law Committee, which upheld the substance of Drysdale's argument. The applicants would have to approach two heads of the law courts or at least seek the approval of Heriot's Hospital. For good measure the Law Committee recommended that the Councillors should not sanction the monument unless they were perfectly satisfied that it would be ornamental to the Hill and the city. The Council accepted the report and sent a copy to Tait.[107]

In the meanwhile the Conservatives kept up the pressure, and as before they adopted the poetic mode. In January 1843, *Blackwood's Edinburgh Magazine* – *Tait's* and *Blackwood's* were political and commercial rivals[108] – regaled its readers with a wickedly humorous fantasy, *The Martyrs' Monument. A Monologue,* in which it mocked the radicals and Town Councillors of Edinburgh as fanatics who were prepared to wage a war of statues in the destructive French style:[109]

> Were I a chosen Councillor – a tetrarch of the town,
> I'd drag from off their pedestals these Tory statues down;
> I'd make a universal sweep of all that serves to show
> How vilely the aristocrats have used us long ago.

As the *Monologue* continues, the monuments of Nelson, Pitt, George IV and 'Royal Charles' come tumbling down and are replaced by memorials of violent radicals and criminals: Thistlewood, Hatfield, Ings, 'the good DESPARD', Papineau, Jack Cade, and the body-snatchers, Burke and Hare. Even Sir Walter Scott does not escape the iconoclasm of the Town Council:

He always back'd the cavalier against the Puritan,
And sneer'd at just fraternity, and the equal rights of man.

Accordingly Scott is ousted from the incomplete spire that was then rising in his honour above Princes Street. Thomas Paine takes his place.

Place him within your Gothic arch, the only fit compeer
Of those whose martyr monument the Council seek to rear.

The obstacles and opposition would have daunted lesser men than Tait and Hume, but in November 1843 Tait was able to inform the Town Council that he had secured the agreement of the Governors of Heriot's Hospital.[110] The Council again voted in favour of the site subject to its earlier caveat and with the proviso that another design should be submitted for approval.[111] Matters now proceeded rapidly. Thomas Hamilton prepared plans for Tait, giving him a choice between a decorated obelisk rising to a height of 60 feet and a simpler version that would rise higher. The Lord Provost's Committee conducted a meeting of inspection on the Hill on 30 January 1844, and on 12 February it reported in favour of a site on the south-east angle of the Hill just north of the bell tower of the Royal High School. This was a site that would be visible from the eastern approaches and other parts of the city, and it would not interfere with the other buildings on the Hill. Tait was told he could proceed if he obtained the endorsement of a fine arts panel consisting of Sir William Allen, Montagu Stanley and Horatio McCulloch.[112] On 19 February 1844, he was able to report that he had obtained favourable opinions from all three. Hamilton's design, they believed, was 'chaste, simple and elegant'. Although Allen would have preferred a site near the Robert Burns memorial, he had been impressed by the 'simplicity and grandeur' of the proposal. Stanley too had been impressed by the 'innate simplicity and purity of design' which would enrich that part of Edinburgh. Both of them made it clear that they would not have accepted a Gothic design. 'Florid Gothic', Stanley wrote, would clash with the Grecian buildings nearby, and it would be 'very inappropriate to the stern simplicity of a Scottish martyr'. The Town Council then granted the site and indicated its preference for an obelisk.[113]

Seven years after the idea had been launched the way now seemed clear for the erection of the Monument in the immediate neighbourhood of the other buildings on the Calton Hill. The triumph was short-lived. The Town Council's records are silent at this juncture, but other sources indicate that Tory property owners in the neighbourhood intervened decisively and carried the day by threatening a legal interdict.[114] In the face of this threat and the further delays that could ensue, the Monument Committee opted for second best. On 11 July 1844, it purchased a plot in the Old Calton Burial Ground, and on 7 August it invited every citizen 'who loves liberty and detests persecution' to attend the laying of the foundation stone. This was a good outcome, the *Scotsman* believed: the monument would be seen 'towering over every monument or building in the vicinity, the symbol of the victory of liberal principles over the old Tory persecuting spirit'.[115] Admittedly, the new site was lower on the Hill than the one that the Town Council had been prepared to grant; nonetheless this was still a commanding eminence.[116]

On 21 August 1844, the great day came when the monument was inaugurated by the ceremonial laying of its foundation stone. Lord Cockburn believed that the event was 'felt all over Scotland', and he rejoiced in the thought that it was enough to make Braxfield 'start from his grave',[117] but as a dramaturgy of triumph it too was something of a second best. Much was made of the harmony of their co-operation, but the division between those who called themselves reformers was proclaimed for all to see.[118] The ceremonies began with the assembling of four hundred members and supporters of the Edinburgh Complete Suffrage Association at the Centre Meadow Walk, an arrangement that deliberately entailed a long march through the city streets. According to instruction, the marchers were dressed in black clothes and carried no banners, a phenomenon that puzzled the reporter of the *Edinburgh Evening Courant* who was used to colourful processions, but which was entirely consistent, not only with respect for the dead, but also with the puritanical religious ethos of the Complete Suffrage movement.[119] At the City Cross seven Town Councillors joined the procession and, observed by large crowds, they headed it for the rest of the way to the Old Calton Burial Ground where Hume and the monument committee were waiting. There was no officiating clergyman, but the usual rituals were performed in laying the foundation stone. Hume placed a sealed bottle containing several documents under the stone;[120] Masonic ceremonies were performed; and Gerrald's prayer on the night he was arrested was read out. Immediately, however, one of the disadvantages of this site was made evident: the trustees of the burial ground had limited the numbers to be admitted, and in any case the space was too small and cramped to serve as a gathering point for rallies. While Hume delivered an address, a larger crowd gathered to hear other speakers higher up on the Hill.

The speeches again pointed up the differences between reformers. The 'ill-fitting whiggism' that has been seen as the hallmark of Hume's political opinions was much in evidence that day.[121] He dwelt on his memories of the events of 1793–94 and welcomed the fact that there would soon be a standing repudiation of the monuments that the Tories had erected 'in every street', but he warned his listeners that the 'full and fair representation of the people' was unlikely to come in his lifetime. In other words, he stopped short of endorsing the demands of the Complete Suffragists. Instead, he expressed gratitude for the subscriptions given by reformers of a very different sort: Lord Holland, the Dukes of Bedford and Norfolk and the Earls of Essex and Leicester. Meanwhile, higher up on the Hill, three thousand people were treated to a very different performance. Patrick Brewster, the minister of Paisley Abbey Church, who had once earned a reputation as a Chartist firebrand and retained strong democratic opinions, addressed them. John Dunlop of Brockloch, the president of the Edinburgh Complete Suffrage Association, also spoke.

Later that day, with Hume still uneasily trying to present himself as a man for all seasons, the same divisions appeared again. The Committee and subscribers entertained Hume at a dinner that was presided over by Sir James Gibson Craig, one of the local Whig MPs. Thomas Babbington Macaulay, the other Whig MP for Edinburgh, declined to be present.[122] Priced at half a guinea, the dinner was obviously intended for a select attendance, and Gibson Craig's 'sedative' speech made it clear that he and other subscribers to the Monument were celebrating Whig traditions of reform. Two of the toasts were to 'The memory of Charles James Fox' and the 'Health of Earl Grey'.[123] That evening, at what Lord Cockburn called a 'cheap soirée',[124] the Complete Suffrage Association organised a much more animated celebration with Dunlop of Brockloch in the chair. Two Dissenting ministers – William Marshall and Dr John Ritchie – denounced the Corn Laws and called for Complete Suffrage. Skirving's son was also present to invoke the memory of the Martyrs. There was even a toast to 'Mr O'Connell, and the Political Martyrs of Ireland', indicating once again that this monument was no mere gesture to the past. 1843 had been 'The Repeal Year' when O'Connell had promised to bring an Irish Parliament into existence again, and he had been arrested after one of his 'Monster Meetings' was officially banned. At the time when the Martyrs' Monument was inaugurated, O'Connell's conviction by a Protestant jury in Dublin was being tested on appeal by the House of Lords.[125]

Appropriately, some of the speakers at the soirée returned to the theme that they were engaged in an ongoing struggle for freedom that was commemorated by sacred sites and monuments. In his speech, Dr Ritchie took his listeners to the Political Martyrs' Monument by way of what was almost a Cook's tour of some of the sacred sites of Protestant martyrology. He had, he said, stood at Smithfield; he had visited the place where Patrick Hamilton and George Wishart had been executed during the Scottish Reformation, and he had visited the bloody sites of Covenanting history including Magus Muir, Priesthill and Cameron's grave at Airsmoss. Now he hailed this new site as one where the democratic principle in church and state would be honoured.[126] Dunlop of Brockloch saw it as important that the Martyrs' Monument would stand near the Robert Burns memorial, and he invoked the memory of Burns's experiences as a radical in 1793.[127] In a characteristically fiery speech, Brewster also drew attention to the political symbolism of the monuments that were massing on Edinburgh's skyline. He spoke of the monument that was being erected to honour Sir Walter Scott and denounced its 'rich tracery and magnificent proportions' as symbols that were appropriate to 'a man who had never shown himself favourable to the liberties of the people'. The Robert Burns memorial on the Calton Hill was of much 'greater interest' to radicals, Brewster added, not least because of 'the recent Tory demonstration in honour of the memory of that poet'. He was referring to the Robert Burns Festival over which the Earl of Eglinton had presided in Ayr. The Earl is best known for the medieval tournament that he had organised in 1839, and he has been seen as a figure of ridicule, but a serious intention underlay the great dramaturgical displays on which he bestowed so much care and money. The tournament was intended to promote a revival of the aristocratic spirit of the feudal past in reaction to the reforms of the decade.[128] Likewise, with Robert Burns cast in the unlikely role of the loyal peasant poet, Eglinton conducted the Burns Festival in 1844 as the celebration of a traditional organic society in which everyone knew his place.[129] This was too much for Brewster. Reciting some of Burns's best-known poetic declarations in favour of political reform, he insisted on restoring Burns and his memorial to the world of radicalism.[130] Hume's reaction pointed up the difference between the two men; cutting Brewster short, he remarked that these comments showed 'just how differently the same subjects may be viewed by different individuals'.[131]

Hume's expression of tolerance for a diversity of opinion was wasted on the local Conservatives. The dreaded legal interdict, it soon transpired, had not been averted, and on 27 January 1845 the Lord Ordinary, Lord Robertson, upheld the complaints of some of the proprietors of the Old Calton Burial Ground, who included the trustees of the late William Blackwood, the owner of *Blackwood's Magazine*. Their plea that the monument was an inappropriate structure for such a place presented two lines of argument to the Court. One was that plots could be sold only for the purposes of burial. The other expressed 'detestation of the conduct of convicted criminals, and the impropriety of perpetuating their memories by any testimonial so placed'. Announcing his decision, Robertson loftily dismissed any thought of political considerations: the question before his court was 'one of novelty'. The monument, he ruled, did not conform to the uses normally made of burying places in Scotland, and therefore it was out of place in this burial ground.[132] His Lordship could have seen the error of his opinion by taking a very short walk to the nearby Greyfriars Kirkyard where there was another 'Martyrs' Monument' – one commemorating those who had been executed for their illegal Covenanting beliefs in the seventeenth century.[133] The Monument Committee had also informed Robertson that it could meet the other objection; it planned to have interments in the hollow pedestal at the foot of the obelisk.[134] The intention was to exhume Muir's remains at Chantilly for reburial in a cavity of the monument, but these plans came to nothing despite Moffat's best efforts. In June 1845, advice was received from France that Muir's grave could no longer be found.[135]

Robertson's judgment was appealed to the Court of the First Division, and on 4 March, five weeks later, everyone was back in court again. For Francis Jeffrey, one of the judges who heard the appeal, this must have been a profoundly satisfying moment. According to Lord Cockburn, his friend and biographer, he had been present at Muir's trial and could never mention it 'without horror'.[136] Now he had an indirect opportunity to repudiate it. In a judgment that Cockburn described as 'singularly beautiful',[137] Jeffrey spoke of a new age, one in which many changes had been made, and he pointed to 'the lapse of time as a material element in estimating the danger of political monuments'. Lord Fullerton's judgment was more forthright. He rejected the argument that those who owned plots in the burial ground had any right to be offended by the sight of such a memorial. If their sensitivities were 'so combustible as to rise into a flame at the sight of this monument, he thought it was they who should be chargeable with carrying political feeling into a burying-ground.' The court was divided, but these opinions carried the day, and the interdict was recalled.[138] This was not the full legal rehabilitation of the Martyrs that some had desired, but their story could be left to find its way into folklore.

All that was needed now was the completion of the monument, and in September

1845 this was achieved. A flag was hoisted, and the coping stone was set in place. Modelled on Cleopatra's Needle, the monument was 90 feet high and could be seen from many parts of the city.[139] When the inscription was added, there was something for everyone except the Tories. The project was attributed to 'the friends of parliamentary reform', leaving Whigs and Complete Suffragists to provide their own interpretations in their different ways. Lord Cockburn marvelled at the restraint of the planning committee in withstanding the temptation to insert its own interpretation of the monument's symbolism; he would have liked to see an inscription that robustly condemned the Martyrs' judges.[140]

Eventually even Lord Cockburn's aesthetic objections were overcome when he saw the obelisk erected on its site: 'nothing', he wrote, 'that sticks up without smoking seems to me ever to look ill in Edinburgh. This pillar adds to the general picturesqueness of the mass of which it is a part.'[141] The monument became an accepted feature of the Edinburgh skyline, acquiring familiarity over the years but losing the political impact that its planners had desired: it stood apart from the monuments further up the hill, and its brief inscription required supplementary knowledge that the casual observer was unlikely to possess. When the German novelist, Theodore Fontane, visited the Calton Hill in 1859 and was struck by the appearance of the buildings as 'a hall of fame for the Scottish people', he did not comment on the Martyrs' Monument.[142] Later in the century, Robert Louis Stevenson would revisit the story of the Martyrs in his *Weir of Hermiston,* but he did not mention their memorial either there or in his *Edinburgh: Picturesque Notes* where he described the 'field of monuments' on the Calton Hill.[143] The passing of the years was producing a situation where few would know or care about the nature of the commemoration.

Over the years Hume had not abandoned the idea of erecting a monument to the Martyrs in London, but, although he eventually succeeded, the outcome was less happy than in Edinburgh. The project was so thoroughly lost in the mists of obscurity that a recent historian has mistakenly described the idea as 'scrapped'.[144] It could have been otherwise; for a brief moment in 1842 Hume, like the Edinburgh committee, came very close to enjoying a complete triumph. The Marylebone Vestry of which he was a member granted him a site near Regent's Circus, and at the end of December a start was made on digging the foundations. Immediately, however, the project encountered strong opposition. There was the usual mockery to contend with. A caricature was produced that displaced the Martyrs and showed a resplendently vain statue of Hume dominating the Circus. *The Times,* no friend of the project, also reported that someone obtained access to the site and erected a long pole 'surmounted by a blood-red cap of liberty' (a slaughterman's cap). More importantly, a motion was introduced in the Vestry to block further building work. Then, suddenly, the matter was taken out of the Vestrymen's hands by the Commissioners of Woods and Forests, who insisted on their jurisdiction in the matter and forbade the monument as 'objectionable'.[145] Hope flickered again when it was reported that the Duke of Bedford would allow the monument to be erected in Bloomsbury Square, but this too came to nothing.[146]

There the matter remained until 1851 when Hume, again like the Edinburgh

Fig. 2.2   The Scottish Martyrs' Monument in Nunhead Cemetery, London.

committee, found another site – one in a burial ground. In the almost complete absence of documentary evidence this is an outcome about which little can be said conclusively. It was a time when Hume was involving himself heavily in a variety of projects that were more 'scattergun' and 'rudderless' than ever. For example, he was taking the lead in a scheme to raise a 'Poor Man's Monument' as a tribute to the recently deceased Sir Robert Peel.[147] This was also the time when Hume was promoting the Little Charter of parliamentary reform, a political programme that foundered in the face of public apathy and disunity among radical reformers.[148] There can have been little interest in his attempt to create a second Martyrs' Monument. As for public opinion in general, there was the Great Exhibition to think about. Unfortunately, no evidence seems to have survived to shed light on how Hume overcame these problems, and, *mirabile dictu*, no newspapers seem to have carried reports of the inaugural ceremony, but eventually in February 1851 he completed his task. Another obelisk – 33 feet high and made of granite – was erected in Nunhead Cemetery.[149]

This obscure south London site could not bear comparison with Regent's Circus, but from Hume's point of view, as a radical who wished to create public places of rational instruction and recreation, there was something to be said for the outcome. Nunhead was one of the new-model cemeteries that urban reformers were creating in the mid-nineteenth century as public places for honouring the dead and edifying the living.[150] It was designed, so the planners announced, to be a place of 'extensive ornamental Gardens, studded with chastely designed Architectural Tombs ... with extended Galleries for Monuments, Tablets, Busts, etc. for both public and private characters'.[151] Standing just inside the entrance of the cemetery, the Scottish Martyrs' Monument occupies one of the most prominent sites, and to this day promenaders cannot ignore it. Nonetheless, only the *Illustrated London News,* in an article that was belatedly published in 1853, seems to have taken any notice. The article praised the 'courage' of the Martyrs and the 'perseverance' that Hume had displayed in their vindication, but it emphasised that these qualities were no longer needed now that the 1832 Reform Act had exerted its influence. The monument should be seen as one that celebrated other qualities: 'patience, humility and good will'. Those who contemplated it should feel grateful for their good fortune in being British and enjoying a degree of 'freedom and security ... beyond what revolutions and violence have ever secured to less steady and persevering nations'.[152] These sentiments resembled the ones that Lord Palmerston had recently uttered in June 1850 as the peroration of his famous Don Pacifico speech, where he had praised the British for standing forth in strife-torn Europe as a nation of cheerful self-improvers who were making the most of a liberal society.[153] Ironically, a monument that had been conceived as a polemic in stone to protest against a national injustice and warn future generations against the ever-present threat of oppression was now bearing testimony to a mood of national self-congratulation. The age of the Scottish Political Martyrs, Peterloo, the Radical War, the Reform Bill and 'the Condition of England Question' was giving way to the 'Age of Equipoise'.[154]

In the course of the twentieth century there have been attempts to revive interest in the commemoration of the Martyrs. Some of these have been associated with left-wing groups which saw the Martyrs as progenitors. In 1929, for example, the Calton Hill obelisk was the backdrop chosen by the Independent Labour Party for a memorial service in honour of Muir,[155] and in 1968, the Workers' Party of Scotland staged a commemorative meeting in the Old Calton Burial Ground where one of the speakers compared the struggles of the Martyrs to the 'courage and self-sacrifice [that] will always be required of those who fight for Socialism'.[156] A few years later, in 1976, the Edinburgh Central and North Labour Parties made an attempt at reviving this tradition, but their zeal was short-lived.[157] In this respect the Scottish radicals who were executed or transported in 1820 have been better served by posterity. Several memorials commemorate them, and an '1820 Committee' holds an annual ceremony at the monument in the cemetery where the executed men are interred. In May 2002, the Scottish First Minister rededicated one of these memorials in Stirling.

In very recent times, however, there has been a revival of interest in the commemoration of the Scottish Martyrs. The lead was taken in Australia. This was entirely appropriate, because the first monument to honour their principles and sufferings had been erected in Sydney, not in Edinburgh or London. When Joseph Gerrald, the only one of the five to be buried in New South Wales, died in 1796 and was interred at Farm Cove in Sydney, a tombstone was erected to salute him as 'a martyr to the liberties of his country'. This memorial seems to have been removed a decade later,[158] but in 1996, to honour the bicentenary of his death, Gerrald was honoured at a ceremony in Sydney's Botanic Gardens. One of the ministers in the New South Wales government unveiled a plaque and commented on the irony that a man who had been transported for expressing his support for democratic government had been buried 'within sight of the mother parliament of Australia'.[159]

Soon afterwards an even more ironic revival of interest took place in Scotland. The Calton Hill, and with it the Martyrs' Monument, were reinvented as symbols in the war of political ideas that broke out in Edinburgh over the siting of the new Scottish Parliament. The belief gained ground – even reaching Ian Rankin's apolitical fictional detective, John Rebus – that one of the reasons for the Labour government's rejection of the Calton Hill as a site was because it was 'a "Nationalist symbol"'.[160] The reference was to the decision of the Blair government in London and the newly devolved government in Edinburgh not to proceed with the plans drawn up by the Callaghan Labour government in the 1970s to use the Royal High School on the Calton Hill for the Scottish Parliament. They chose to build an entirely new parliament house near Holyrood Palace. The decision in favour of the Holyrood site has been defended for practical reasons, but critics preferred an explanation that relied on political symbolism. During the years of John Major's anti-devolutionist government, some of the advocates of a Scottish Parliament had kept vigil outside the Royal High School, as a consequence of which, so the Scottish First Minister was said to believe, the Calton Hill had become a discordant 'nationalist shibboleth'.

The debate did not end with the commencement of work on the Holyrood site. It has found its way into John Lowrey's recent article on 'Greek Revival Edinburgh' where reference is made to the belief that the Labour Party leadership in London and Edinburgh rejected the Calton Hill site because of its 'nationalist as well as national' symbolism.[161] This thesis has been pressed further in a book by David Black, a journalist who sees the rejection of the Calton Hill site by the 'New Labour' politicians as an indication of their intention to keep Scotland within a carefully controlled form of devolution and out of the hands of Scottish Nationalists. From a 'New Labour' point of view, the Royal High School was either 'the nationalist shibboleth', or, scarcely more acceptable, a survival from the 'Old Labour' era of the 1970s. By taking this attitude and going ahead with the Holyrood site by undemocratic means, 'New Labour', so Black argues, has trampled over the commonly held opinion that the Calton Hill has a special place in Scottish history as the 'outdoor Pantheon' of the nation.[162] This argument gains force, he continues, when it is remembered that the Martyrs' Monument and the Royal High School are near neighbours, and that the Monument, 'perhaps the single most evocative memorial' on the Hill, exhibits 'the democratic ideal at its most poignant'. Proclaiming 'the core principle of universal democracy', it 'reminds us that in Scotland political reform was achieved at great personal cost to those who championed it'. It would all be very different, Black believes, if those whom he calls 'the New Labour rebranders' would stand in front of 'this simple dignified memorial which still has the power to move us'. They would have no alternative other than to reproach themselves for the folly with which they have spurned the architectural symbols of Scotland's national identity.[163]

The dispute serves as a reminder that monuments can acquire new meanings with the passage of time – meanings that would have been unrecognisable to their planners. As this chapter has shown, the Martyrs' Monument in the Old Calton Burial Ground originated as a manifestation of the strong sense of British nationality that brought Scottish and English reformers together during the first half of the nineteenth century. It was erected to honour five men, three of whom were English;[164] paid for by funds that were raised in London as well as Edinburgh; provided with an inscription that proclaims the co-operation of Scottish and English reformers in attempts to reform the Parliament of the United Kingdom; and paired with a similar obelisk in London. Now, apparently, it is being transformed into a symbol of Scottish national identity. The controversy provides an excellent example of Ernest Renan's famous dictum that 'forgetting and … historical error are an essential factor in the creation of a nation'.[165] It is also an excellent example of the dictum of another French intellectual, Pierre Nora, the doyen of public memory studies: '*lieux de mémoire* thrive only because of their capacity for change, their ability to resurrect old meanings and generate new ones along with new and unforeseeable connections (that is what makes them exciting)'.[166]

Notes

1   Alex Tyrrell has researched and written most of this chapter. Michael Davis has provided primary sources and made additions to the text.
2   The story of the Scottish Political Martyrs has been told many times. See, for example, Ferguson, W. (1968), *Scotland: 1689 to the Present,* Edinburgh: Oliver & Boyd, pp. 248–59; Bewley, C. (1981), *Muir of Huntershill,* Oxford: Oxford University Press, and Brims, J. (1990), 'From Reformers to "Jacobins": The Scottish Association of the Friends of the People' in Devine, T.M. (ed.), *Conflict and Stability in Scottish Society 1700–1850,* Edinburgh: John Donald.
3   According to Lord Cockburn, (1852), *Life of Lord Jeffrey with a selection from his correspondence,* Edinburgh: Adam & Charles Black, vol. 2, p. 268, this was a time when spies noted the names of those who attended the dinners that were held to honour Charles James Fox.
4   Henry Cockburn and Francis Jeffrey are discussed below. See also Romilly, S. (1840), *Memoirs of the Life of Sir Samuel Romilly, written by himself with a selection from his correspondence,* 2nd edn, London: John Murray, vol. 2, p. 23. Romilly was in Edinburgh during the trials of the martyrs. A decade after their transportation he helped to destroy Lord Melville's political career by presenting the impeachment against him 'for crimes destructive of the welfare of his country'. See Anon., (1806), *The Trial by Impeachment, of Henry Lord Viscount Melville, For High Crimes and Misdemeanours, Before the House of Peers in Westminster Hall,* Edinburgh: J. Robertson, Oliver & Co., p. 152. A section from Romilly's diary was read to the Edinburgh Town Council during one of its debates on the application for a site for the Martyrs' Monument. See *Scotsman,* 27 July 1842. At the time of the Martyrs' trials, Romilly unsuccessfully defended James Belcher against charges of selling Thomas Paine's works in Birmingham. The case for the Crown was

presented by Spencer Perceval, a future Tory Prime Minister, and it was upheld by 'an unusually illiterate jury'. See Kentish, J. (n.d.), *An Approving Conscience: A Sermon Composed upon the Occasion of the Death of Mr James Belcher, and delivered in the New Meeting House, Birmingham, on Sunday, December 31st, 1809*, Birmingham: James Belcher & Son, pp. 20–21.

5 Bewley, *Muir of Huntershill*, p. 185. See also the description of the 'Reform Jubilee Procession' of the Edinburgh and Leith trades in *Johnstone's Monthly Register of Public Events and Monthly Scottish Lists*, August 1832; and Millar, W. (1832), *An Account of the Edinburgh Reform Jubilee*, no publisher.

6 Mackenzie, P. (1865), *Reminiscences of Glasgow and the West of Scotland*, Glasgow: John Tweed, vol. 3, p. 334.

7 Ibid., vol. 4, p. 402. See also Mackenzie, P. (1831), *The Life of Thomas Muir*, Glasgow: W.R. McPhun, p. 45, and *Scotch Reformers' Gazette*, 24 August 1844.

8 Mackenzie, *Reminiscences*, vol. 1, p. 98.

9 Various names were used to describe the five men whose names appear on the monument in the Old Calton Cemetery. The terms 'Scottish Political Martyrs' and 'Martyrs' will be used in this chapter.

10 Lord Fullerton, quoted by the *Edinburgh Evening Courant*, 6 March 1845.

11 Ferguson, *Scotland: 1689 to the Present*, p. 256. See also Devine, T.M. (1999), *The Scottish Nation, 1700–2000*, London: Allen Lane, p. 207. On Braxfield see Osborne, B. (1997), *Braxfield: The Hanging Judge*, Glendaruel: Argyll Publishing.

12 Bewley, *Muir of Huntershill*, p.188. This book contains several errors with respect to the history of the Martyrs' Monument.

13 Agulhon, M. (1985), 'Politics, Images and Symbols of Post-Revolutionary France' in Wilentz, S. (ed.), *Rites of Power. Symbolism, Ritual and Politics since the Middle Ages*, Philadelphia: University of Pennsylvania Press, p. 179.

14 Ibid., pp. 188, 191.

15 For a famous recent attempt at rebranding a monument see *Guardian Weekly*, 12–18 July 2001 which describes plans to place the famous 'Worker and Woman Collective Farmer' sculpture on top of a shopping mall in Moscow as 'a figure head for Russia's new capitalist ideology'.

16 Glendinning, M., MacInnes, R. and Mackenzie, A. (1996), *A History of Scottish Architecture from the Renaissance to the Present Day*, Edinburgh: Edinburgh University Press, p. 189.

17 Markus, T.A. (1982), *Order in Space and Society. Architectural Form and its Context in the Scottish Enlightenment*, Edinburgh: Mainstream Publishing Company, pp. 8, 17, 28.

18 Cockburn, H. (1970), *An Examination of the Trials for Sedition which have hitherto occurred in Scotland*, New York: Augustus M. Kelley, vol. 2, p. 137.

19 Fry, M. (1992), *The Dundas Despotism*, Edinburgh: Edinburgh University Press, pp. 313–14. The monument was completed in 1827 at a cost of £8000.

20 The statues attracted comment at the time. The *Scotsman*, 28 September 1833 saw the statues of George IV, Pitt and Melville as 'emblems to remind us of past degradation'. Anon., (1848), *The Topographical Statistical, And Historical Gazetteer Of Scotland*, Edinburgh: A. Fullarton & Co., vol. 1, p. 445 described the statue of Pitt as possessing 'considerable dignity', unlike that of George IV which suggests 'some particulars in the natural history of the kangaroo, which by no means contribute to sublimity of effect'.

21 Ben-Amos, A. (2000), *Funerals, Politics and Memory in Modern France, 1789–1996*, Oxford: Oxford University Press, p. 32.

22 Lowery, J. (2001), 'From Caesarea to Athens. Greek Revival Edinburgh and the Question of Scottish Identity within the Unionist State', *Journal of the Society of Architectural Historians*, 60 (2), June, p. 141.

23 According to Withers, C. (2001), 'Monuments' in Lynch, M. (ed.), *The Oxford Companion to Scottish History*, Oxford: Oxford University Press, p. 428, the National

Monument was intended to be a memorial erected on the Mound before a different plan was chosen involving the Calton Hill site.

24 Lowery, 'From Caesarea to Athens', p. 154.

25 Anon., (1819), *Report of the Proceedings ... With A View To The Erection of a National Monument*, Edinburgh: James Ballantyne & Co., p. 15.

26 Colley, L. (1992), *Britons. Forging the Nation, 1707–1837*, New Haven: Yale University Press, p. 6; Eastwood, D., Brockliss, L. and John, M. (1997), ' From dynastic union to unitary state: The European experience' in Brockliss, L. and Eastwood, D. (eds), *A Union of Multiple of Identities. The British Isles, c.1750–c.1850*, Manchester: Manchester University Press, p. 199, describe this attitude as one of 'cementing allegiance to the State of the United Kingdom' by letting 'traditional loyalties coexist in healthy competition like houses in a public school'.

27 For example, the *Ayr Advertiser*, 2 September 1847, referred to a new move to carry on 'the works, in imitation of the Pantheon, on the Calton Hill', but by then the unfinished monument had become a civic feature in its own right. The *Builder*, 7 August 1847, surmised that many in Edinburgh would not favour 'any further addition to the picturesque and majestic pillars by which their city has been so long surmounted'.

28 Anon. [1844?], *A Descriptive Account Of The Exhibition Of Statuary, National Monument, Calton Hill, By Robert Forrest, Sculptor*, Edinburgh: Edinburgh Printing and Publishing Company.

29 *Scotsman*, 6 July 1833.

30 Ibid., 25 May 1833; 27 May 1843. The Calton Hill narrowly escaped being endowed with statues of Robert the Bruce and William Wallace. Rogers, C. (1871), *Monuments and Monumental Inscriptions in Scotland*, London: Charles Griffin & Co., vol. 1, p. 6, refers to a statue of Bruce designed by George Cruikshank. Mackay, C. (1887), *Through the Long Day, or Memorials of a Literary Life during Half a Century*, London: W.H. Allen, vol. 1, pp. 374–5, refers to a large statue of William Wallace that the Scottish sculptor, Patrick Park, created in the hope that it would be erected on the Calton Hill. When objections were raised to the nudity of the statue, Park smashed it.

31 Cookson, J.E. (1999), 'The Napoleonic Wars, Military Scotland and Tory Highlandism in the Early Nineteenth Century', *Scottish Historical Review*, lxxviii, 1 (205), April, p. 74.

32 *Scotsman*, 14, 28 August 1833; Anderson, J. (1856), *A History of Edinburgh*, Edinburgh: A. Fullerton & Co., p. 447; Wilson, A. (1970), *The Chartist Movement in Scotland*, Manchester: Manchester University Press, pp. 51, 54, 57, 63 and 77.

33 Grant, J. (n.d.), *Old and New Edinburgh: Its History, Its People, and Its Places*, London: Cassell & Co., vol. II, p. 104; Cockburn, H. (1874), *Journal of Henry Cockburn, Being a Continuation of the Memorials of his Time, 1831–1854*, Edinburgh: Edmonstone and Douglas, vol. I, p. 66; Anderson, *A History of Edinburgh*, pp. 438, 440. For a description of one of these pavilions see Pickering, P.A. and Tyrrell, A. (2000), *The People's Bread. A History of the Anti-Corn Law League*, London: Leicester University Press, pp. 194–6.

34 *Scotsman*, 28 September 1833.

35 Cohen, W. (1989), 'Symbols of Power: Statues in Nineteenth-Century Provincial France', *Comparative Studies in Society and History*, 31, pp. 495, 502–3. Cohen describes the erection of the statue of a freethinker in juxtaposition to the Fourvière Cathedral in Lyon which had been built as an act of atonement for the sins of the Commune. Pierre Nora is surely wrong when he writes that statues and monuments to the dead 'could be placed elsewhere without altering their meaning'. See Nora, P. (1996), *Realms of Memory. Rethinking the French Past*, New York: Columbia University Press, vol. 1, p. 18.

36 William Tait to the Lord Provost of Edinburgh, 16 January 1837, Town Council Records, vol. 223, Edinburgh City Archives, City Chambers. Inglis, K.S. (1998), *Sacred Places. War Memorials in the Australian Landscape*, Melbourne: Miegunyah Press, p. 160 refers to the advantages of an obelisk as a public monument: 'it was easily and if need be

cheaply supplied, non-sectarian, traditionally recognizable as a symbol of death or glory'. On Hamilton see Fisher, I. (1965), 'Thomas Hamilton of Edinburgh: Architect and Town Planner (1784–1858)', unpublished PhD thesis, Oxford.

37   Paul Connerton refers to the tendency of supporters of a new regime to devise acts and artefacts of memory that provide an 'unequivocal demarcation' between the old and new orders: 'To pass judgment on the practices of the old regime is the constitutive act of the new order', Connerton, P (1989), *How Societies Remember*, Cambridge: Cambridge University Press, p. 7.

38   *Edinburgh Evening Post and Scottish Literary Gazette,* 25 March 1837; *Scotsman,* 25 March 1837. Mackenzie, *The Life of Thomas Muir*, p. 45 had similarly emphasised the desirability of using the monument to contest the Tory statuary in Edinburgh.

39   Tait, W. (1837), *Memoirs and Trial of the Political Martyrs of Scotland, Persecuted During the Years 1793 and 1794*, Edinburgh: William Tait, in British Library, Place Papers, Additional MS. 27816, ff. 330–47.

40   'Amicus Bonorum' in *Scotsman,* 3 July 1833.

41   The paucity of documentary material has obscured Hume's importance in British politics, but see Huch, R.K. and Ziegler, P.R. (1985), *Joseph Hume: The People's MP,* Philadelphia: American Philosophical Society; Chancellor, V. (1986), *The Political Life of Joseph Hume, 1775–1855,* London: Valerie Chancellor. Neither of these books mentions the Martyrs' Monuments in Edinburgh and London.

42   Halévy, E. (1972), *The Growth of Philosophic Radicalism,* New Jersey: Augustus M. Kelley, p. 309; Bain, A. (1967), *James Mill. A Biography,* New York: Augustus M. Kelley, p. 7.

43   *Schoolmaster and Edinburgh Weekly Magazine,* 16 February 1833; *Dictionary of National Biography,* vol. X, p. 961 attributes almost all the articles in this publication to Christian Isobel Johnstone.

44   Huch & Ziegler, *Hume,* pp. 96–102.

45   The monument that was erected to commemorate Thomas Hardy, the London counterpart of the Scottish Martyrs, offered a Whiggish reference to his death after he had seen 'a great part of his laudable and enlightened objects fulfilled by the Passing of the REFORM BILL', Place Papers, Additional MS. 27816, f. 240 undated newsclipping.

46   *Edinburgh Evening Courant,* 22 August 1844. Hume's later references to his attitude to the sentencing of the Martyrs in 1793 and 1794 must be balanced against his earliest foray into parliamentary politics as a Tory.

47   Cockburn, *Journal of Henry Cockburn,* vol. II, p. 95; Cockburn, *Life of Lord Jeffrey,* vol. 1, p. 58, Vassall Holland to Joseph Hume, 7 March 1837; *Morning Chronicle,* 13 March 1837.

48   Smiles, S. (1887), *Duty,* London: John Murray, pp. 317–18. See also Anon. (1855), *New Graves: A Chronicle of Death's Doings,* London: reprinted from the *Biographical Magazine,* pp. 15, 17; Joseph Hume to the Lord Provost of Edinburgh, 24 August 1844, 'Political Martyrs' Monument MS', Edinburgh Public Library. In this letter Hume refers to his success in facilitating public access to the Tower of London and the Scottish Royal Regalia. He wished to see the public right of access to the Robert Burns monument on the Calton Hill similarly extended.

49   Joseph Hume to Peter Mackenzie, 14 June 1831, *Scotch Reformers' Gazette,* 24 August 1844. For Cartwright's statue see Osborne, J.W. (1972), *John Cartwright,* Cambridge: Cambridge University Press, pp. 152–3.

50   Mackenzie, *Reminiscences,* vol. 4, p. 389.

51   British Library, Place Papers, Additional MS, 27816, f. 244, excerpt from the *Constitutional,* 20 December 1836.

52   Dickinson, H.W. and Titley, A. (1934), *Richard Trevithick. The Engineer and the Man,* Cambridge: Cambridge University Press, pp. 252–4; Harper, E.K. (1913), *A Cornish Giant. Richard Trevithick; The Father of the Locomotive Engine,* London: E. & F.N. Spon, p. 55.

53 R.M. Beverley, 26 June 1838, Sturge Papers (held by members of the Sturge Family). Dickson, N.T.R. (2002), '"The Church itself is God's clergy". The principles and practices of the Brethren' in Lovegrove, D.W. (ed.), *The Rise of the Laity in Evangelical Protestantism*, London: Routledge, p. 217, identifies Beverley as 'a lawyer and Anglican turned Dissenter, who was for a while associated with the Brethren'.

54 British Library, Place Papers, Additional. MS, 27816, ff. 314–18, T.P. Thompson to Francis Place, 5 March 1837.

55 Ibid., ff. 261–4, T.P. Thompson to Francis Place, 28 January 1837.

56 For the full committee list, see *Scottish Political Martyrs for Parliamentary Reform in 1793–4*, 25 February 1837, Scottish Record Office, GD/572/45/1 and 2.

57 At a committee meeting on 23 February 1839 attended by only six members in addition to Hume, a sub-committee was set up consisting of Hume, Alexander Galloway and [?] Rennie. See 'Minutes of Meeting of the Committee for Erecting Monuments to the Political Martyrs of 1793–4', 23 February 1839, 'Political Martyrs Monument MS'.

58 *Edinburgh Evening Courant*, 25 March 1837; Cockburn, *An Examination of the Trials for Sedition*, vol. 2, p. 248.

59 A copy of this publication can be found in the Dr Williams's Library, London, shelfmark 12.58(65). Another copy is located in the Dr Williams's Library, shelfmark 12.80, Rutt, J.T. (1832), *Life and Correspondence of Joseph Priestley*, London: R. Hunter, vol. 2, opposite p. 222. Muir expressed an early concern for Moffat's safety and the threat of persecution in Edinburgh following his trial. See National Library of Scotland, MS 98, f. 105, Muir to George Dyer, 16 April 1794.

60 Dr Williams's Library, shelfmark 12.58(65), William Moffat to John Towill Rutt, 25 February 1837.

61 Ibid., shelfmark 12.80. William Moffat to Rev. Hugh Hutton [Birmingham], 7 November 1838 (inserted on unpaged sheet, last folio in volume); Moffat to Hutton, 28 January 1839 (inserted opposite p. 222); Moffat to [Hutton?], 16 March 1839 (inserted on unpaged sheet, last folio in volume); National Library of Scotland, MS 3397, f. 3, Joseph Hume to M. Young, 11 September 1842.

62 Anon. (1837), 'Memoirs And Trials Of The Political Martyrs Of Scotland; Persecuted During The years 1793–4–5', *Tait's Edinburgh Magazine*, vol. 4, January. The *Wellesley Index To Victorian Periodicals, 1824–1900*, vol. IV, p. 513 attributes this article to Christian Isobel Johnstone, the editor.

63 In January 1842 Hume referred to a fund of £800 in London. See 'Political Martyrs Monument MS', Joseph Hume to William Tait, 4 January 1842. The *Scotsman*, 16 August 1837, referred to support given by Lords Holland and Brougham, Sir James Gibson-Craig, and the Lord Provost of Edinburgh. It also praised Dunfermline, Kirkcaldy, Leith and other Scottish towns for taking up the cause with 'heartiness and zeal'.

64 Joseph Hume to William Tait, 23 April, 1837, 'Political Martyrs Monument MS'.

65 Edinburgh City Archives, Record of Town Council, vol. 223, 31 January 1837, letter from William Tait to the Lord Provost, 16 January 1837.

66 *Edinburgh Evening Post*, 3 March 1838.

67 Ibid., 23 Sept. 1837.

68 Ibid., 7 October 1837. *Blackwood's Edinburgh Magazine*, September 1837, described Hume's defeat in Middlesex as the most gratifying result of the 1837 General Election.

69 *Edinburgh Evening Post*, 23 September 1837.

70 Ibid., 6 May 1837.

71 Ibid., 26 Aug. 1837. The *Post's* line of argument here was similar to the one advanced by Conservative Town Councillors and *Blackwood's Edinburgh Magazine*, May 1837 against the Town Council's petition to Parliament endorsing the Irish Corporation Bill and the English Church Rates Bill.

72   Muir claimed that he had tried to save Louis XVI's life.
73   *Edinburgh Evening Post*, 1 April, 1837.
74   Ibid., 11 February 1837.
75   British Library, Place Papers, Additional MS, 27816, f. 430, *Constitutional*, 21 February 1837.
76   For example, Francis Jeffrey anticipated in 1835 that 'perilous' times were approaching when 'the Tory sword would be the heaviest, and its conquests consequently the most bloody', Cockburn, *Life of Lord Jeffrey*, vol. 2, p. 274. In 1820, Jeffrey had defended another group of Scottish radicals who were sentenced to transportation to New South Wales (two others were executed). See Macfarlane, M. and A. (1981), *The Scottish Radicals. Tried and transported to Australia for Treason in 1820*, Stevenage: Spa Books, p. 7.
77, Mackenzie, *Reminiscences of Glasgow*, vol. 1, p. 138. Mackenzie directed part of his campaign to an exposure of 'the spy system' that he believed the Tories had used to entrap innocent men, Mackenzie, P. (1833), *Reply to the Letter of Kirkman Finlay, Esq. on the spy system*, Glasgow: Muir, Gowans & Co. See also Macfarlane, *The Scottish Radicals*, pp. 9, 15, 16.
78   Mackenzie, *Reminiscences*, vol. 4, p. 378. Mackenzie acted through two MPs, one of whom was Joseph Hume.
79   The Stirling Town Council blocked Mackenzie's initial attempt to erect the memorial in Stirling churchyard where two of the Radical War martyrs were buried. See Mackenzie, *Reminiscences*, vol. 4, pp. 374, 395.
80   *Hansard's Parliamentary Debates*, vol. xxii, 1834, col. 939 and vol. xxiii, 28 April 1834, cols. 114–15. Hume was one of the horsemen who led the great procession from Copenhagen Fields to present a monster petition to the Home Office. See Marlowe, J. (1974), *The Tolpuddle Martyrs*, Frogmore: Panther Books Ltd., p. 132.
81   Cockburn, *An Examination of the Trial for Sedition*, vol. 2, pp. 74, 86–7, 220–21.
82   Ibid., vol. 2, p. 43. Cockburn described the flaunting of French revolutionary symbols and styles of dress by the Martyrs and their associates.
83   Cockburn, *Journal of Henry Cockburn*, vol. 2, pp. 95–7.
84   For the dominance of Edinburgh Town Council by Dissenters and their close association with radicalism see Williams, J.C. (1972), 'Edinburgh Politics: 1832–52', unpublished PhD thesis, Edinburgh University, pp. 16, 51, 57.
85   *Scotsman*, 14 August 1833. See also Anderson, *A History of Edinburgh*, pp. 429–31. Williams, 'Edinburgh Politics', p. 151 refers to other Edinburgh anti-church rate 'martyrs'.
86   Edinburgh City Archives, Record of Town Council, vol. 237, William Tait to the Lord Provost, 23 July 1842.
87   Ibid.
88   'Political Martyrs Monument MS', Joseph Hume to William Tait, 14 September 1838 and 'Minutes of Meeting of the Committee for Erecting Monuments to the Political Martyrs of 1793–4', 23 February 1839.
89   Dr Williams's Library, shelfmark 12.80, William Moffat to [Rev. Hugh Hutton?], 16 March 1839 (inserted on unpaged sheet, last folio in volume).
90   Prothero, I.J. (1979), *Artisans and Politics in Early Nineteenth-Century London. John Gast and his Times*, Folkestone: Dawson, p. 271; Large, D. (1974), 'William Lovett', in Hollis, P. (ed.), *Pressure from Without in Early Victorian England*, London: Edward Arnold, pp. 120–21.
91   Epstein, J. (1982), *The Lion of Freedom: Feargus O'Connor and the Chartist Movement 1838–1842*, London: Croom Helm, pp. 263–4.
92   Hume was involved in the Leeds Household Suffrage campaign in 1841. See *Leeds Times*, 23 January 1841. See also Martin, L.D. 'Land Reform', in Hollis, *Pressure from Without*, p. 146.
93   Wilson, *The Chartist Movement in Scotland*, p. 105.

94 Epstein, *The Lion of Freedom*, p. 216. See also *Scotsman*, 23 January 1839, for William Tait's rebuke of Chartists who interrupted an anti-Corn Law meeting.

95 *Weekly True Sun*, 26 February 1837; *Edinburgh Evening Post*, 25 February 1837; *Scotsman*, 25 February 1837; Epstein, *The Lion of Freedom*, p. 42. *The Times*, 17 February 1837, described Hume's speeches at this time as 'half Radical, half Ministerial'. Although he mistakenly recalled that the meeting occurred in 1836, O'Connor was unequivocal that it was a 'party job': 'the object of that meeting was not for the purpose of shewing their devotion to the memory of the exiled patriots, but was merely convened for the purpose of elevating Whiggism ...', see *National Instructor*, 21 September 1850.

96 Place Papers, Additional MS, 27816, ff. 279–81, 289, Francis Place to Colonel T.P. Thompson, 13 and 16 February 1837.

97 Ibid., f. 299, Francis Place to George Grote, 21 February 1837.

98 For the Complete Suffrage movement see Tyrrell, A. (1983) 'Personality in Politics: The National Complete Suffrage Union and Pressure Group Politics in Early Victorian Britain', *Journal of Religious History*, xii, December. See also Tyrrell, A. (1987), *Joseph Sturge and the Moral Radical Party in Early Victorian Britain*, London: Christopher Helm, Chap. 10; Wright, L.C. (1953), *Scottish Chartism*, Edinburgh: Oliver & Boyd, p. 163.

99 Huch and Ziegler, *Hume*, p. 128.

100 'Political Martyrs Monument MS', Joseph Hume to William Tait, 4 January 1842.

101 Edinburgh City Archives, Record of Town Council, vol. 237, William Tait to the Lord Provost, 23 July 1842.

102 Ibid., 26 July 1842.

103 Cockburn, *An Examination of the Trials for Sedition*, p. 249.

104 Ibid.

105 Quoted in Cockburn, *Journal*, vol. 2, p. 324.

106 Edinburgh City Archives, Record of Town Council, vol. 237, 9 August, 6, 20, 27 September, 11 October 1842; vol. 238, 25 October, 22 November, 6 December 1842. Also see Drysdale, William (1842), *Substance of a Speech, delivered in the Town Council of Edinburgh, on the 6th December 1842 ... upon a Motion for Granting a Site for a Monument to Muir, Margarot, and others, convicted of Sedition in 1793–94*, Edinburgh: no publisher.

107 Edinburgh City Archives, Record of Town Council, vol. 238, 6 December 1842, 7 March 1843.

108 Oliphant, Margaret (1897), *William Blackwood And His Sons, Their Magazine And Friends*, Edinburgh: William Blackwood & Sons, vol. 2, p. 109.

109 Anon., (1843) 'The Martyrs' Monument. A Monologue', *Blackwood's Edinburgh Magazine*, January, pp. 126–7. The poem runs to 29 stanzas. Other newspapers joined in the controversy at this time. See n.d. [1843], 'The Scotch Martyrs and The "Times"' in *English Chartist Circular and Temperance Record for England and Wales*, no. 103.

110 Edinburgh City Archives, Record of Town Council, vol. 240, William Tait to the Lord Provost, 9 November 1843. Hume tried to employ newspaper pressure against those whom he described as the 'small party' in the Town Council who opposed the monument. See Mackenzie, *Reminiscences*, vol. 4, p. 391.

111 Edinburgh City Archives, Record of Town Council, 22 November 1843.

112 Ibid., vol. 241, William Tait to the Lord Provost, 19 January 1844; Minutes of Lord Provost's Committee 25 January 1844; Report of Lord Provost's Committee, 12 February 1844.

113 Ibid., William Tait to the Lord Provost, 19 February 1844, and decision in favour of granting the site by the Magistrates and Town Council, 20 February 1844.

114 *Scotsman*, 24 August 1844.

115   Ibid., 7 August 1844. Ben-Amos, *Funerals, Politics and Memory in Modern France*, p. 89, refers to the use of graveyard monuments by French radicals as a means of escaping the control of public space by hostile authorities.

116   *Edinburgh Evening Courant*, 22 August 1844.

117   Cockburn, *Journal*, vol. 2, p. 94; Cockburn, *An Examination of the Trials for Sedition*, p. 250.

118   The Chartists seem to have shown no interest. They were building their own monuments during these years. Wilson, *The Chartist Movement in Scotland*, p. 201 refers to the raising of funds for a monument to Dr John Taylor in Ayrshire. See also the essay on Chartist memorials in this volume by Paul Pickering.

119   *Edinburgh Evening Courant*, 22 August 1844. When Joseph Sturge stood as parliamentary candidate for Nottingham he entered the town in a procession from which 'meretricious adjuncts' had been deliberately excluded: Tyrrell, *Joseph Sturge and the Moral Radical Party*, p. 127. Wright, *Scottish Chartism*, p. 165, calls the procession of the Edinburgh Complete Suffragists to the Calton Burying Ground their largest demonstration in Edinburgh.

120   According to the *Northern Star*, 31 August 1844, the documents were newspapers of the day, Oliver and Boyd's *Almanack*, *Tait's Magazine* containing a record of the trial, a list of the Scottish subscribers to the monument and some coins of the realm.

121   Thomas, 'The Philosophical Radicals', p. 67.

122   Bewley, *Muir of Huntershill*, p. 188. Macaulay disapproved of the sentences, but did not admire the 'proceedings' of the Martyrs.

123   *Scotsman*, 24 August 1844; Cockburn, *Journal*, vol. 2, p. 94.

124   Cockburn, *Journal*, vol. 2, p. 94.

125   A *Scotsman* editorial, 21 August 1844, had pointed to the resemblances between the Scottish trials of the 1790s and O'Connell's trial.

126   (1844), *Speech of the Rev. John Ritchie, A.M., D.D., Delivered at the Complete Suffrage Banquet, Given in Honour of the Scottish Political Martyrs of 1793, At the Laying of the Foundation Stone of their Monument, by Joseph Hume, Esq., M.P.*, Edinburgh: Q. Dalrymple, p. 6.

127   On Burns's radicalism in the late eighteenth century see McIlvanney, L. (2000), *Burns the Radical: Poetry and Politics in Late-Eighteenth-Century Scotland*, East Linton: Tuckwell Press.

128   Anstruther, I. (1963), *The Knight and the Umbrella. An Account of the Eglinton Tournament 1839*, London: Geoffrey Bles. See also Tyrrell, A. (April 2003), 'The Queen's "Little Trip": The Royal Visit to Scotland in 1842', *Scottish Historical Review*, 82, 1 (213), April, pp. 67–9.

129   'The Burns Festival', (1844), *Blackwood's Edinburgh Magazine*, September, pp. 370–400.

130   The context of Brewster's remarks is ignored by Wright, *Scottish Chartism*, p. 166 who describes the attack on Scott as 'Entirely unprovoked'.

131   The preceding descriptions of the procession, the dinner and the soirée have been constructed from the *Edinburgh Evening Courant*, 2 August 1844; *Scotsman*, 24 August 1844; *Nonconformist*, 28 August 1844; and Cockburn, *Journal*, vol. 2, pp. 94–5. Brewster's remarks elicited hisses from some in the audience.

132   *Edinburgh Evening Courant*, 30 January 1845; Cockburn, *An Examination of the Trials for Sedition*, p.251, believed that the litigation was prompted entirely by 'political feelings'.

133   The Old Calton Burying Ground was not the venerable place described by the opponents of the Martyrs' Monument; there had been complaints about 'the practice of drying and bleaching clothes upon the graves', see *Scotsman*, 10 April 1833.

134   *Edinburgh Evening Courant*, 30 January 1845.

135 Dr Williams's Library, shelfmark 12.80, printed 'The Late Thomas Muir, Esq., Jr. Of Huntershill' (from the *Edinburgh Weekly Chronicle*, September 13, 1845) (inserted on unpaged sheet, last folio in volume).

136 Cockburn, *Life of Lord Jeffrey*, vol. 1, p. 58.

137 Cockburn, *An Examination of the Trials for Sedition*, p. 251.

138 *Edinburgh Evening Courant*, 6 March 1845; Anderson, *A History of Edinburgh*, pp. 504–5.

139 *Scotsman*, 1 October 1845.

140 Cockburn, *An Examination of the Trials for Sedition*, p. 252. Similarly, Lord Campbell saw the monument as a repudiation of an 'atrocious sentence' and trials that could not be read 'without amazement and horror'. Campbell, J. (1846), *The Lives of the Lord Chancellors and Keepers of the Great Seal of England*, London: John Murray, vol. 5, p. 612. Thomas Perronet Thompson had suggested a forthright inscription in 1837: 'In memory of the victims of unjust judges and political tyranny in the years 1792 and 1794', followed by the names and designations of the Martyrs and the words 'Transported among felons to New South Wales, for their advocacy of parliamentary reform, since happily triumphant'. The inscription that Peter Mackenzie devised in 1832 for the Radical War Martyrs' Monument in Thrushgrove had been similarly unrestrained. It referred to men who were 'Betrayed by Infamous Spies and Informers' and executed 'For The Cause of Reform Now Triumphant'. See Mackenzie, *Reminiscences*, vol. 4, p. 395.

141 Cockburn, *An Examination of the Trials for Sedition*, p. 252.

142 Fontane, T. (1998), *Beyond the Tweed. A Tour of Scotland in 1858*, London: Libris, pp. 71–2.

143 Stevenson, R.L. (1924), *Ethical Studies. Edinburgh: Picturesque Notes*, London: William Heinemann, p.176. Stevenson referred briefly to the Martyrs, but not to the Monument, in his explication of Raeburn's portrait of Braxfield in (1924), *Virginibus Puerisque and other essays in belles lettres*, London: William Heinemann, pp. 101–3. The standard late nineteenth-century reference work on Scottish monuments, Rogers, *Monuments and Monumental Inscriptions in Scotland*, vol. 1, p. 92, contains a brief reference to the Martyrs' Monument, but it mis-spells the names of Palmer and Gerrald.

144 Bewley, *Muir of Huntershill*, p. 187.

145 This episode is described in *The Times*, 2, 16 January 1843. Also see 31 October 1842, 15 November 1842, 21 November 1842, 20 December 1842; Westminster City Archives, T I/65, Marylebone Vestry Committee Minutes, ff. 102-3, 29 July 1842; f. 252, 19 November 1842; f. 260, 31 December 1842; f. 281, 7 January 1843.

146 *The Times*, 24 February 1843.

147 For Hume's part in the Peel memorial project – it was eventually transformed into a fund for donating books – see Huch and Ziegler, *Hume*, p. 149 and Read, D. (1997), *Peel and the Victorians*, Oxford: Blackwell, pp. 289–300.

148 Huch and Ziegler, *Hume*, pp. 146–50.

149 *Illustrated London News*, 26 November 1853.

150 Curl, J.C. (1972), *The Victorian Celebration of Death*, Newton Abbot: David & Charles, pp. 103–6.

151 Prospectus of the London Cemetery Company, n.d., facsimile held by the Southwark Local History Library.

152 *Illustrated London News*, 26 November 1853.

153 Quoted in Black, E.C. (1970), *British Politics in the Nineteenth Century*, London: Macmillan, p. 92.

154 Burn, W.L (1968), *The Age of Equipoise*, London: Unwin University Books, p. 16 refers to the years between 1852 and 1867 as a time when 'there was less of that single-minded vehemence which had characterized and perhaps nearly destroyed an earlier England.'

155   *Scotsman*, 23 September 1929. Also, see a printed circular (1929) *Independent Labour Party, Edinburgh and District Federation*, Edinburgh: no publisher, held in the Edinburgh Central Library.
156   Anon. (1968), 'Thomas Muir of Huntershill and the Scottish Martyrs. Commemoration Meetings arranged by the Workers' Party of Scotland', *The Scottish Vanguard: Journal of the Workers' Party of Scotland*, 2, p. 7. For a full summary of the meeting see ibid., pp. 6–9. Also see *Scotsman*, 2 September 1968; *Evening News* (Edinburgh), 8 August 1968; *Evening News* (Edinburgh), 11 July 1968; and a printed circular for the meeting held in the Edinburgh Central Library, shelfmark YDA 1864.968 [B33170].
157   *Edinburgh Evening News*, 20 July 1976.
158   Wilson, E. (1992), *The Wishing Tree. A Guide to memorial trees, fountains, etc. in the Royal Botanic Gardens, Domain, and Centennial Park, Sydney*, Sydney: Kangaroo Press, pp. 127–8.
159   *Sydney Morning Herald*, 23 April, 1996. The plaque briefly narrates Gerrald's biography and quotes his belief in the ultimate 'establishment of benevolence and peace'.
160   Rankin, I. (2000), *Set in Darkness*, London: Orion, p. 240. Rankin has also alluded to the Martyrs' Monument and the prosecution of the Martyrs in (2001), *The Falls*, London: Orion, p. 392.
161   Lowrey, 'From Caesarea to Athens', p. 157.
162   Black, D. (2001), *All The First Minister's Men. The Truth Behind Holyrood*, Edinburgh: Birlinn, especially Chaps 7–9.
163   Ibid., pp. 107, 115–16. The search for symbols relating to the Calton Hill's place in the quest for Scottish self-government continues. An article in the *Scotsman*, 29 October 2001, refers to the pressure on the National Museums of Scotland to house the Vigil Hut that was situated outside the Royal High School for almost five years after 1992 to raise signatures and otherwise promote the campaign for a Scottish Parliament.
164   This point was made at the time by the anonymous author of *The Political Martyrs*, February 1837, who wished to use the term 'British Martyrs' to acknowledge that three of them were English.
165   Renan, E. (1996), 'What is a Nation?' in Woolf, S. (ed.), *Nationalism in Europe, 1815 to the Present*, London: Routledge, p. 50. Reports in the *Scotsman*, 7 August 1844 and 1 October 1845, suggest that the London Committee contributed £600 of the £900 spent on the Edinburgh monument.
166   Nora, 'General Introduction: Between Memory and History' in *Realms of Memory. Rethinking the French Past*, vol. 1, p. 15. The Calton Hill's connection with the history of democracy in Scotland has received further endorsement in the form of a new monument. On 10 April 1998 a 'Democracie Cairn' was inaugurated there by 'the keepers of the Vigil for a Scottish Parliament'. The cairn contains stone from Paris ('used for defending democracy'), Auschwitz and Robert Burns's home in Mauchline. It quotes Burns's dismissal of rank as 'but the guinea's stamp' and Hugh MacDiarmid's admonition to his countrymen that 'the past and future's oors'. The cairn stands close to the site offered by the Edinburgh Town Council for the Martyr's Monument in 1844.

Chapter 3

A 'Grand Ossification':[1] William Cobbett and the Commemoration of Tom Paine

Paul A. Pickering

> Never will England be what it ought to be, until the marble of Pitt's monument is converted into a monument to the memory of Paine.
>
> William Cobbett[2]

In March 2001, the Mayor of New Rochelle, New York, launched a campaign to trace and return the skeletal remains of the republican heresiarch, Thomas Paine, to the upstate town where he spent the last decade of his life and where he was buried in 1809.[3] The immediate attention of the Citizen Paine Restoration Initiative, as it is called, was focused on Sydney, Australia. In 1987, a Sydney businessman had purchased a skull purported to be Paine's in London before taking it back to Australia where it was subsequently sold at an antiques fair. Since then the hapless skull has been the focus of a postgraduate paper (held appropriately in the 'Crypt' of Wesley College at Sydney University); it has been subjected, apparently, to DNA testing (in an attempt to prove that an heir to Paine resides in Australia's largest city), and has been the inspiration for an interdisciplinary doctoral thesis in religious studies and biochemistry.[4] The paper remains unpublished, the thesis marked 'not for loan', and the DNA results withheld. Although they doubt the Australian claim to a celebrated lineage, representatives of the Thomas Paine National Historical Museum are apparently keen to check the scientific results against samples of the brain stem that they hold at the Paine Museum in New Rochelle.[5] Even if they eventually succeed in obtaining the famous skull, the task facing the Restoration committee is likely to be fraught with difficulty: Paine's mortal remains have endured a fate that would be worthy of a medieval saint. The bones were lost not long after they were disinterred in 1819, and they are now almost certainly scattered far and wide: a rib is believed to be in France, a jawbone was reputedly in Brighton, a right hand in London, and sundry fingers, made into buttons, are strewn beyond recognition and restoration.

The disinterment of Paine's corpse by William Cobbett in 1819, and his subsequent removal of the remains to England captured the headlines at the time on both sides of the Atlantic and it has been noted in passing by many historians, including the numerous biographers of both men. Most historians have been quick to judge Cobbett's actions as rash and ill-conceived and to dismiss the whole episode, including his subsequent campaign to build a monument to Paine, as a fiasco and a farce.[6] The chorus of derision and humour orchestrated by Cobbett's many political opponents in 1819 still lingers. Few scholars have bothered to explore Cobbett's actions and motives, or to use the episode as a window into popular attitudes not only to Paine, but also to death and commemoration. In particular, the idea that physical remains can be used to create a site of public memory as an act of assertive pedagogy has been ignored. The 'fiasco', if that is what it was, deserves to be taken seriously. This chapter argues that Cobbett's actions were, paradoxically, both in tune with and a reaction against the dominant plebeian culture of the long eighteenth century; it suggests that whatever else he did wrong by digging up Paine, Cobbett erred principally in his timing: the radicals that he expected to enlist in his campaign to pay homage to Paine were either not interested or not yet alive to the oppositional potential of a political monument. The age when popular radicals built monuments had not yet dawned; by the time it had, Paine's bones were lost and there were other monuments to erect.

Shortly after midnight on a day late in September 1819, a strange party left New York on a 22 mile journey to New Rochelle. At the head of the group was William Cobbett. Aged in his mid-fifties, Cobbett was nearing the end of two years' self-imposed exile in the United States of America. A publicist and commentator of extraordinary ability, he had sought refuge in America in 1817 in the face of government hostility that would almost certainly have seen him imprisoned.[7] Accompanying Cobbett on his late-night journey was a well-known Manchester radical, William Benbow. A Grub Street publicist, physical force revolutionary and pornographer, Benbow was a veteran of the ill-fated Blanketeers march of Lancashire radicals on London in 1817 for which he had served the first of four prison terms.[8] Not long after his release Benbow had joined Cobbett in America where he helped in the preparation of the latter's famous *Political Register* from exile. On this night in September, however, Cobbett and Benbow carried neither pen nor pike; instead they brought shovels, as did the remainder of the company. Their destination was a farm in New Rochelle, Westchester County, that had been owned by Paine in the last years of his life.

It has been well documented that Paine's final years were unhappy ones. Spurned by the young republic that he had helped to forge (due to the heterodoxy of the *Age of Reason*), 'America's Godfather' had died impoverished, disenfranchised and friendless. His obituary in the New York *Post* concluded with clinical simplicity that he had 'lived long, done some good, and much harm'.[9] The obituary also indicated that Paine's dying wish to be buried among the Quakers, the religious brethren of his youth, had been refused and that he had been interred on his farm – 'the corner of a rugged, barren field' Cobbett later called it.[10] Paine's grave was marked by a simple stone identifying him as the author of *Common Sense*.[11]

Having reached their destination at the 'peep of day', the party dug up 'the coffin entire' and loaded it on a wagon for the return to trip to New York.[12] Within a few days, the bones and the coffin plate had been packed in a crate and loaded on the *Hercules* – without the knowledge of the captain it was later claimed[13] – as part of Cobbett's luggage in preparation for a triumphal return to England. As a consummate publicist with an acute sense of political dramaturgy, Cobbett was intent on orchestrating an expectant mood at home: Benbow was sent ahead on an earlier ship bearing letters heralding Cobbett's return and giving out tantalising hints as to the nature of his macabre cargo.[14] Cobbett's activities had also been brought to the attention of local officials in New Rochelle by curious inhabitants, but a 'sheriff's posse' was organised too late to intervene and the 'grave robbers' were not pursued.[15]

Cobbett's first account of his actions was contained in the *Political Register* of 13 November, two weeks after his departure from New York on 30 October. 'I have just done *here*', he told his readers, 'a thing, which I have always, since I came to this country, vowed that I would do, that is, *take up the remains of our former countryman*, PAINE, *in order to convey them to England!*'[16] At this stage his justification for his conduct fell into two parts. With a characteristic sense of self-importance Cobbett claimed, first, that he acted on behalf of 'the *reformers of England, Scotland* and *Ireland*' in response to what he described as the base treatment of Paine by those he called America's '*republican rulers*', a charge which he tinctured with a note of ethno-chauvinism. 'We will let the Americans see', he boasted, 'that we *Englishmen* know how to do *justice to the memory* of our former countryman'.[17] Even at this early stage, however, Cobbett also began to make the case that Paine, 'this child of the *Lower Orders*', should be commemorated in a way that was usually reserved for the political and social elite of the *ancien regime*: 'While the dead Boroughmongers, and the base slaves who have been their tools, moulder away under unnoticed masses of marble and brass', he predicted, 'the tomb of this "*Noble of Nature*" will be an object of pilgrimage'.[18] In private, Cobbett cherished high hopes that Paine's bones themselves would serve as a rallying point for reformers. As he told an American friend on the day following his trip to New Rochelle: 'I shall gather together the people of Liverpool and Manchester in one assembly with those of London, and these bones will effect the reformation of England in Church and State.'[19] Cobbett knew instinctively that which modern sociologists regard as axiomatic: that 'the dead can be used to mount an offensive on the legitimacy of a regime'.[20] At the very least, he had hit upon a way to confound a government bent on repression: whatever might be done to silence the living, Paine's bones would be beyond the reach of the law.

While Cobbett was in transit across the Atlantic, reports began to appear in the mainstream British press. On 20 November, for example, the London *Morning Advertiser* suggested that in the event of a storm the sailors 'who are proverbially superstitious' would be likely to 'relieve' Cobbett of his luggage and '*inter* the bones of the Atheist in the *sea*'.[21] It was wishful thinking. Cobbett arrived safely in Liverpool on Sunday, 21 November, although concern that there was fever on the ship prevented an immediate landing.[22] He could not have planned it better as the delay served merely to heighten the sense of expectation: the wait got the better of some who rowed alongside the *Hercules* in an attempt to confirm whether Cobbett 'had Tom Paine's remains with him'.[23] Friend and foe alike were on edge: the Town Crier of nearby Bolton was imprisoned for making an unauthorised announcement that Cobbett had arrived.[24]

The company were finally permitted to disembark on Friday, 26 November. Even the hostile press had to admit that an 'immense number of people' had gathered on the beach to meet the repatriated popular leader and that, moreover, he was cheered continuously during the 'considerable' walk from the docks to the Inn where he spent his first night on home soil for two years.[25] Among the crowd were many 'deputies' from radical organisations in many towns and villages. Dressed as a gentleman farmer (his preferred uniform for public performance), Cobbett acknowledged the plaudits of the crowd, but he did not address them. Again, it is hard to conclude other than that Cobbett was deliberately seeking to intensify the air of expectation. This was certainly the outcome. A large crowd reassembled on the following morning when Cobbett returned to the docks in order to undergo the 'usual inspection' at the Custom-house. After his large amount of luggage was meticulously searched, the final crate was opened and, 'sundry deeds and manuscripts removed', Cobbett informed the surrounding spectators, 'Here are the bones of the late Thomas Paine.' It was his first public statement in England for more than two years. According to a report in the *Morning Advertiser*, this 'intelligence caused a sudden and visible sensation and the crowd pressed forward to see the contents of the package'.[26] Some of Cobbett's opponents claimed that the crowd had stood in 'silent horror' as the Customs inspector proceeded to hold up a skull and several bones to exaggerated public scrutiny before passing the luggage in a perfunctory manner,[27] but other reports – from friend and foe alike – indicate that Cobbett made the most of the frisson of excitement that animated the crowd by declaring: 'How great must that man have been, when living, whose dry bones can create an agitation like this!'[28]

By this time opponents of reform had begun to attack Cobbett with a particular ferocity. According to Cobbett's own assessment, he was condemned in over 300 newspapers from John O'Groats to Lands End.[29] The metropolitan press especially, he complained, 'teemed with the most abominable calumnies, descending, at last, down to sheer execrations'.[30] The substance of these attacks was remarkably consistent although the tone varied from unctuous solemnity to scurrilous sarcasm. 'It is truly disgusting', editorialised the Whiggish *Morning Chronicle*, 'to hear that the corpse of the Author of The Age of Reason is to be hawked through the country, to stir up and inflame the unthinking multitude against the sacred truths of Christianity ... '.[31] *The Times*, denounced Cobbett for attempting a 'trick', 'the most disgusting, and, withal, the most laughable that was ever thought of', in an attempt to curry favour among the radicals he had deserted two years before: 'He pretends that he has pulled TOM PAINE'S carcass out of the earth by night ... The whole, we have no doubt, is a lie; but it is a lie so worthy of him who utters it, and so illustrative of the deep contempt which he entertains for the sottish understanding of those whom it is intended to deceive, that it is as good as a written volume of truth.'[32] In the columns of the London *Sun*, a self-appointed defender of the 'honest, the religious, and loyal part of the community',[33] Cobbett was systematically excoriated. Prompted, so it said, by its readers, it demanded 'to know why this fellow COBBETT was suffered to land the bones of his brother miscreant PAINE?' Raising the question of whether bones could constitute property – an issue that would loom large in their subsequent history – a correspondent went on to wonder if a 'spirited Magistrate' could not be found to intervene and 'stick ... up the Infidel's skeleton in

Surgeon's Hall among Traitors and Murderers'.[34] Assuring 'every lover of our Establishment in Church and State' of their determination to take Cobbett in hand, the editors opened their pages to anyone with a joke to make at his expense. Under the heading 'GRAND OSSIFICATION', one correspondent even scripted an elaborate mock funeral procession to convey 'the *Bones*' from Tyburn Turnpike to the 'Mausoleum that is to be erected by penny subscriptions (of which the great man is to be Treasurer)'.[35] In this fertile imaginative scene Paine was to be conveyed on a 'SUPERB NIGHT CART, Decorated with Cabbage Leaves, in Memorial of Tom's former Trade before he began Stay-making ... .' On the cart, the bones were to be suspended from a gibbet, together with a 'Farthing Candle ... in order to enlighten the world'. The mock ritual included many of the leading radicals of the day, such as Henry Hunt, Richard Carlile and Arthur Thistlewood, but the 'Chief Mourner' was the hapless Cobbett, 'supported by his Creditors'.[36]

Humour proved to be infectious: the taunts of the metropolitan newspapers echoed in the provincial press, as well as in pamphlet, poem, print and parliamentary debate. Cobbett was lampooned as the 'bone man', the 'resurrection man', the 'bone-raker', the 'bone-lecturer', the 'Importer' and the 'grave-robber'. One cartoon so amused Cobbett himself that he sent a copy to his son in America.[37] 'The Political Champion turned Resurrection Man' depicted Cobbett flying back to England on the wings of a 'diabolical monster'; in one hand he carries a quill and in the other, Paine's skull wearing a *bonnet rouge*. Following Cobbett, other demons carry the '*Political Register*', 'Paine's Treason', 'Revolution' and the 'Plague'. In the distance, standing on his island exile of St Helena, Napoleon is singing '*Ah! Ça ira*', the anthem of republican France, while in America, Quakers are shown dancing on the shore in celebration of the fact that 'the Evil Spirit has departed from us'. In England, a group of radicals – notably Henry Hunt and Thomas Wooler, depicted as a black dwarf, the title of his radical newspaper – have gathered to welcome home their fellow 'scribe'.[38] As recent historians have shown, cartoons were powerful political weapons: H.T. Dickinson has estimated that between 50,000 and 200,000 individual copies of a popular political print could be in circulation at any one time. As V.C. Gatrell has argued, the exhibition of the latest humorous print often caused a sensation on the streets of London.[39]

Even Lord Byron, radical sympathiser and *enfant terrible* though he was, could not resist a pointed jibe at Cobbett's expense, albeit in a private communication:[40]

In digging up your bones, Tom Paine
Will Cobbett has done well;
You'll visit him on earth again
He'll visit you in hell.

Thus Earl Grosvenor was not exaggerating in the House of Lords when he asked with a rhetorical flourish on 17 December: 'Was there ever any subject treated with more laughter, contempt, and derision, than the introduction of those miserable bones'.[41] The ferocity of these attacks are eloquent testimony to the widespread fear of Cobbett's popularity among those outside the political nation, as well as to the importance of laughter in regency politics. Cobbett had some measure of revenge in

September 1821 when it was reported that the Duke of York had ordered the remains of Major John André, who had been executed as a spy by the Americans during the War of Independence, to be disinterred and returned to England for burial in Westminster Abbey. What was the difference, Cobbett asked, between the Duke and me? 'We are both "*bone-men*", both "*grave-robbers*", both "*resurrection-men*" if either of us is … The only difference (and that, indeed, is a very great one)', he continued, 'is found in the *character and deeds* of the original owner of bones.'[42]

What then were Cobbett's motives? He gave his first face-to-face account of his actions to a public meeting in Liverpool in November. Cobbett began by offering a general justification that again attempted to strike a nationalist chord. 'If I had found the bones of any Englishman, whose talents and virtues entitled him to respect, lying neglected and dishonoured', he told the crowd, 'I would have brought over his remains and deposited them in the bosom of his country.'[43] Although this was reason enough, Cobbett continued, his was an act of atonement for the fact that he had 'most shamefully' used 'Mr Paine' in the past. This was an understatement. Cobbett's opponents never tired of reprinting the withering assaults on Paine that Cobbett himself had penned during his Tory youth. Is this the same person, asked 'A Briton' in a public letter to Cobbett published at the end of 1819, whom 'you call *poor, silly Tom Paine – infamous – degraded – worthless – base as the basest –* an *abominable hypocrite –* a *blood hound –* the *most degraded thing in nature – a poor, half-starved pretender to renown –* a *profane fool –* a *sot –* a *block head –* an *ass –* an *apostate –* an *impostor –* a *liar –* a *disturber of mankind – unnatural – malignant – treacherous – blasphemous!!! …* an ATROCIOUS, INFAMOUS MISCREANT!!!'.[44] *The Times* delighted in republishing what was perhaps Cobbett's most famous attack, the irony of which must have seemed irresistible in 1819. Paine, Cobbett had written in 1796, had 'done all the mischief he can in this world, and whether his carcass is, at last, to be suffered to rot on the earth, or to be dried in the air is of very little consequence … men will learn to express all that is base, malignant, treacherous, unnatural, and blasphemous, by the single monosyllable – PAINE!'[45]

Cobbett also sought to atone in a vicarious way for the treatment of Paine by the British people. 'The boys and girls of twenty years ago were led on by the clergy and other persons in authority', he reminded the Bishop of Llandaff in a public letter, to burn Paine in effigy. In practically every village in the Kingdom, he continued, burning 'a TOM PAINE was much more popular than to burn a GUY FAWKES'.[46] Other radicals shared Cobbett's conversion – 'Many a faggot have I gathered in my youth to burn old Tom Paine!', recalled the incorrigible ultra-radical publisher and Paine's self-appointed heir apparent, Richard Carlile[47] - but none had undergone a public transformation quite like Cobbett. Thus the popular leader acted to assuage the collective guilt of his people: to lead by example. 'Yes, my Lord', he told Lord Folkestone in another public letter, 'amongst the pleasures that I promise myself, is that of seeing the name of Paine honoured in every part of England, where base corruption caused him, when alive, to be *burnt in effigy*.'[48] 'The merits of PAINE are, as yet, but imperfectly known to the world', Cobbett wrote, but he would single-handedly set the record straight in a 'real' account of Paine's life.[49]

Thus Cobbett's act of expiation was no whim (even though he would later suggest that the idea had been Benbow's).[50] According to one account, Cobbett had been visiting the grave site in New Rochelle once or twice a month for more than a year, standing 'bareheaded and bowed in an attitude of reverence'.[51] As early as May 1819, Cobbett had toyed with an idea that, at that time, must have seemed like a mere rhetorical device. 'I yet hope to see', he had told readers of the *Register*, 'an Act of Parliament to cause [Paine's] ... bones to be conveyed to England and deposited in the stead of those of Pitt ... '.[52] Cobbett warmed to the idea of what French historians would later call *dépanthéonisation*,[53] sweeping away the official monuments of political opponents and replacing them with those devoted to favoured sons. Cobbett had long fumed about the honours conferred on Pitt – especially the practice of forming Pitt clubs[54] – but by September his ire had shifted to Dr Samuel Johnson. The contrast irked him: 'Yet, while such a fellow as pensioner JOHNSON, "that slave of state", stands in colossal marble in St. Paul's, PAINE lies in a little hole under the grass and weeds of an obscure farm in America.'[55]

Almost from the start, however, Cobbett was forced on to the defensive over his treatment of the remains themselves. Before the crowd in Liverpool he denied the 'false' reports that he intended 'to dress [the bones] ... up for the purpose of exhibiting them' as he travelled around. Paine's bones, he told them, had already been transported to London.[56] The allegation that the remains were to be used in some sort of travelling side-show dedicated to fomenting insurrection was at the heart of much of the criticism that had been directed against him. On 24 November, for example, the editors of the *Sun* regretted the need to mention Cobbett at all, except for the fact that they believed that 'the ominous return of that man strongly indicates his conviction that a REVOLUTION is near and inevitable'.[57] A few days later in the House of Commons, an hysterical Tory back-bencher, R.J. Wilmot, took up the case: Cobbett, he insisted, had 'dug up the unhallowed bones of the blasphemer, and brought them to this country for the purpose of creating a phrenzied feeling in favour of his projects'.[58]

The suggestion that Cobbett planned, in his own words, to 'carry the bones at the head of a Revolutionary army'[59] seems fanciful at this remove, but it is important to remember that he had arrived back at a time of intense political volatility. After all, when he had landed it was almost exactly three months to the day since the 'Massacre of Peterloo' when a force of Yeomanry Cavalry had charged into a peaceful crowd gathered in Manchester to call for political reform. The injuries to some of the protesters (more than 400 were slashed or trampled and 15 were killed) had no doubt healed, but the wounds to the body politic still festered: the radical leaders arrested at Peterloo, most importantly Orator Hunt, were still awaiting their trial and Parliament's motion of congratulation to the cavalry for their 'patriotic conduct' still echoed throughout the country. Moreover, in the week that Cobbett disembarked, the Prince Regent announced the government's intention to introduce a series of new restrictions on the freedom of the press and the right of public assembly. For radicals the 'Six Acts', as they became known, represented a fundamental challenge to the 'remaining liberties of Britain'.[60] More ominously for

Cobbett as a man with Paine's remains among his personal effects, in October Richard Carlile was imprisoned for publishing Paine's *Age of Reason*.[61] One metropolitan radical journal went so far as to proclaim the dawn of the 'Age of Persecution'.[62] Cobbett recognised that his timing was hardly propitious: 'To bring in the bones of PAINE', he wrote, 'amidst such a state of things was to put public opinion, and especially with regard to myself, to the severest test.'[63]

Implicit in the accusation that Cobbett was preparing to use Paine's corpse to ignite a revolution was the suggestion that the bones themselves possessed some sort of a talismanic power.[64] For the student of popular attitudes to death and commemoration this notion is worth lingering over. Although he denied he was planning to take Paine's bones on a tour, Cobbett freely admitted that he intended to exhibit them in the capital in order to gratify the 'Hundreds upon hundreds' of requests that he had received.[65] This plan to use the carcass itself as a corporal monument tapped deeply into the popular culture of the long eighteenth century. As Ruth Richardson has shown, this was a time when attitudes to death were characterised by many 'different levels of belief, sophistication and scepticism'.[66] Among Cobbett's legions of humble supporters there would have been many who shared what Richardson has described as a 'popular theology' that combined basic Christian tenets with animism, fatalism and a residual paganism.[67] In analysing this syncretic belief system, Richardson goes on to point to the importance of viewing and touching the corpse in *post mortem* rituals that reflected a 'prevailing belief in the existence of a strong tie between body and personality/soul for an undefined period of time after death'.[68]

Cobbett's opponents also undoubtedly recognised the implicit power of the bones. On the one hand, some sought to insinuate that he had not treated the remains respectfully. Far from honouring Paine, one critic pointed out that the skeleton had been rudely pulled apart and packed in a trunk with Cobbett's underwear.[69] By digging up a body, Cobbett did indeed risk violent popular antipathy: to dishonour a corpse was a dangerous business. After all, this was the era when the 'grave-robber' was a particularly loathed figure and often subject to crowd violence if apprehended; it was also a time when a dread of dissection regularly precipitated riots to prevent surgeons getting their hands on the corpses of executed criminals.[70] Radicals knew this well. For example, when the Cato Street conspirators were executed for treason in May 1820, T.J. Wooler vented his disgust at the surgeon, the '*scientific butcher*, the connoisseur of blood', who had decapitated the deceased conspirators in accordance with their ritualised punishment.[71] Cobbett took up the theme, railing against the authorities for refusing to hand over the mutilated corpses for burial (even the bodies, he lamented, 'were, it appears, objects of *precaution*'), and hinting in a public letter to his son at some nefarious purpose: 'Why not give the bodies to the wives? Ah! You must *guess*: for I dare not tell you what I *think* was the reason!'[72] Cobbett later attempted to fend off criticism about his own conduct by insisting that he had acted only after he had got wind of plans to relocate Paine's remains to a New York cemetery where they would be buried with '*strangers* and *soldiers* and other *friendless* persons'.[73]

Further evidence of the potential power of the bones in the eyes of Cobbett's opponents was the widespread (and potentially damaging) attempt to question their authenticity. 'There is a suspicion', editorialised *The Times*, 'that the whole of this is a falsehood – a trick arranged by certain people in London, who have put in requisition the aid of the resurrection-men, for the production of a body which will be decayed enough by the time COBBETT has occasion for it.' Similarly, in the *Gentleman's Magazine* one writer referred to Cobbett's 'American SHAM PAINE'.[74] Apparently without a shred of evidence, another version held that amidst the early morning winter gloom Cobbett's party had inadvertently dug up an anonymous Negro.[75] When these accusations were aired by Lord Grosvenor in the House of Lords, Cobbett became indignant. '[T]here is no one in England', he fumed, 'who does not believe *that they are the bones of Paine*.' In an attempt to prove his point Cobbett gave more ammunition to his opponents. His promise to 'exhibit' the remains 'in the *coffin* and with the *coffin plate*, which came out of the ground with them' would be difficult to fulfil given that the coffin had apparently been discarded in New York.[76] Again the André case allowed Cobbett to go on the offensive. 'These bones must have been dirt many years ago', he suggested, 'but I'll make them rattle in the ears of some people for many a long day to come.'[77] Linking the hapless André to his earlier attacks on the funerary architecture of the capital, Cobbett gave full vent to his splenetic wit: 'If André's bones are really to be buried in Saint Paul's, I hope that they will be deposited along with those of [Benedict] *Arnold* (raised for the purpose) and that both will lie near the statue of "*our greatest national moralist*", old dread-devil JOHNSON, with whose "*morality*" their deeds so very neatly squared.'[78]

Early in 1820 a cartoon by one of the best known anti-radical illustrators, George Cruikshank, anticipated the opening of a peep-show run by 'the Botley Showman', a reference to Cobbett's rural home, where, for a penny, people could gaze at the bones of Paine, but the imaginary scene never eventuated.[79] (See Figure 3.1.) Although Cobbett never fulfilled his promise to exhibit the bones, either in London or in Botley, he did commence the campaign for a monument by offering a tactile experience. Responding to Lord Grosvenor's claim that the people 'despised the act of bringing home the bones of PAINE',[80] Cobbett made a startling admission. Insisting that '[e]very hair of that head, from which first started the idea of *American Independence*, would be a treasure to the possessor', Cobbett announced that 'that hair is in my possession'.[81] A fortnight later he elaborated on his plan that was entirely in keeping with the practice of providing physical mementoes of the dead: 'I intend, in the course of the winter,' he stated, 'to have MR PAINE'S hair put into *gold rings*' to be sold 'at a guinea a piece beyond the cost of the gold and the workmanship'. For Cobbett this was nothing more than enlisting Paine to raise funds for himself: 'These guineas shall be employed ... in the erection of a monument to his memory, either at Thetford, his native town, or at Botley ... '.[82] Anticipating renewed howls of scorn, Cobbett offered a personal guarantee of authenticity: 'It is my intention when the rings are made, to have the workmen with me, to give him out the hair, and to see it put in myself, then to write in my own hand, a certificate on parchment and deliver it with every ring.'[83] This scheme opened Cobbett to the allegation that he was not only cynically attempting to capture the headlines, but also

Fig. 3.1   'The Botley Showman'.

that he was bent on profiting by Paine. 'Foiled in his expedient to transmute the *Bones* into his beloved Gold', sneered one critic, 'the Importer next tried what could done with the *Hair* – the "ugly uncombed locks", as he formerly called them … '.[84] Cobbett was alert to the dangers of attempting to mix politics and profit: as he told a London audience in December 1819 when promoting a substitute for excisable tea and coffee that bore his name, his appeal 'might smell rather of the shop'.[85] Ironically, Cobbett the Tory had levelled this allegation at Paine, as *The Times* was keen to point out.[86]

By September 1821, it was clear that Cobbett's campaign for a Paine monument had foundered; whether any gold jewellery had been made, let alone sold, is doubtful; whether any subscriptions at all had been received is unclear. Although he insisted that Paine's bones would 'be deposited in a place and in a manner that are suitable to the mind that once animated the body', he now admitted that this could only occur 'in due time'. 'There must be suitable preparation for this', he stated: what was needed was the *'healing* hand of *time'*.[87] In the interim the bones would remain 'in his care' which, in reality, meant they were packed in a box and tucked away in a corner of Cobbett's home in Guildford where they remained until 1835.

Most contemporaries (and historians, if they discuss it at all) agreed that it was Paine's hostile attitude to religion – actually a relatively mild deism – that doomed the campaign to commemorate him with a monument to failure. 'The bones fiasco', writes Ian Dyck, 'was the first and last great compromise of Cobbett's populism': 'Cobbett had gambled that the English worker was prepared to distinguish between Paine's economics and religion. There lay his great mistake … '.[88] Similarly Gregory Claeys concludes that 'Paine's post-war disciples took from the master what they deemed useful and set aside the rest'; and most of them 'would have nothing to do with Paine's theology'.[89] It is important not to underestimate this factor. 'If at the commencement of the American Revolution', wondered a Birmingham radical from his prison cell in Warwick, 'the immortal Paine had published his "AGE OF REASON" instead of "COMMON SENSE", what would have been the result? Why, instead of producing that excellent spirit of UNANIMITY which his *"Common Sense"* inspired, nothing but distrust, disunion, and perhaps even the shedding of each others blood, would have been the consequence … '.[90] Cobbett himself recognised that Paine's legacy was problematic on the matter of faith – a 'ticklish subject' he called it[91]– and he consistently sought to distance himself from the charge of irreligion. As he told a dinner at the Crown and Anchor in London shortly after his return, 'he begged distinctly to disavow having in view the propagation of any opinions [of Paine's] connected with religion.' Straining the credulity of his audience, he insisted that, in fact, he 'had never read [Paine's] theological works' (actually he had penned scathing attacks on the *Age of Reason* in the 1790s).[92] Following Cobbett onto the platform, Henry Hunt told the crowd that he had not read the 'theological works of Paine' until he appeared in Court to defend Carlile's right to publish the *Age of Reason* only weeks earlier.[93]

The different attitudes to religion were symptomatic of wider divisions in the radical movement over the Paineite tradition. Of course, Paine had his fervent admirers. For example, at a dinner in Cobbett's honour in Liverpool a few days after his return the first toast was to: 'The memory of our famous countryman, Thomas Paine, the "noble of nature", the child of the "lower orders", illustrious from his unrivalled talents, and still more illustrious from the employment of those talents in the cause of "the oppressed of all nations"'.[94] Similarly, the editor of the *Cap of Liberty* welcomed the news of Paine's repatriation: 'The time is now come', he predicted, 'when thousands are ready to acknowledge [Paine's] worth, and will (we doubt not) hail the return of his relics to his native country with the most ardent enthusiasm.'[95] A few days later at the Crown and Anchor, however, Hunt (with Cobbett's support) moved an equivocal toast that almost damned Paine with faint praise: 'That Noble of Nature, Thomas Paine; and may his admirers avoid his errors, and his calumniators imitate his virtues.'[96]

The list of 'errors' went beyond religion. First, as Ian Dyck has shown, many radicals (including Cobbett) upheld the historical basis of English claims for rights which was not entirely compatible with Paine's more ethereal conception of natural rights.[97] This point can easily be overstated as a simple binary: in fact, Paine's well-known 'historical' attacks on the 'patrician banditti' who had imposed the Norman Yoke on honest Saxons were readily incorporated into the popular interpretation of British constitutional history without any sense of contradiction. More important was the rejection of Paine's republicanism. Cobbett himself was no republican. Were he given the opportunity to 'displace Kingly Government tomorrow, and establish a Republican one in its stead' Cobbett insisted in 1819 that he would not do it.[98] Of course, this was a period when the Prince Regent was deeply unpopular (he was known to radicals as 'the Pig of Pall Mall'), but the institution of monarchy retained respect. By the second half of 1820, the unpopular Prince had become King, and he soon presented his many opponents with fresh grounds to attack him when he sought to divorce and depose his Queen, Caroline of Brunswick. Cobbett, along with many other prominent radicals, spent much of the next 18 months as defenders of Queen Caroline, a cause that, in many cases, drew on a reservoir of support for a popular monarchy.[99] There was even a campaign to commemorate the 'injured Queen' with a public monument following her sudden death in August 1821.[100] This was stillborn. Effectively, Caroline disappeared over the horizon of history not long after the ship that carried her coffin on its way home to Brunswick. The important point is that in the case of both Paine and Caroline the idea of a monument failed to strike a public chord.

Given Cobbett's objections to Paine's ideas in key areas, it is hard to avoid the conclusion that the bones ended up in the wrong hands, or rather in the hands of one who was not interested in 're-engaging Paine' (to borrow James Epstein's expression) into mainstream radical discourse.[101] Nevertheless, there can be no doubt about Paine's pervasive influence among the rank and file of post-war radicalism. As Edward Royle has put it, Paine spoke out 'in plain English … beyond the educated few to the semi-literate, and even illiterate, many'.[102] As early as 1793 it is estimated that parts one and two of *The Rights of Man* had together sold about 200,000 copies,[103] and by the time Cobbett made his return, it had gone through numerous editions. Accordingly, we must consider other factors when attempting to explain the collapse of Cobbett's campaign.

First, in purely practical terms a subscription campaign was inevitably going to struggle at a time when the meagre financial resources of the radical movement were already under severe strain. As Royle has shown, during the early 1820s funds were being raised around the clock to pay thousands of pounds in fines: between 1819 and 1825, over £1400 was subscribed to help Richard Carlile alone.[104] The magnitude of the effort is an eloquent testimony to the tenacity of radical culture. During one quarter in 1822, for example, radicals in Nottingham collected £18-1-6½d for the 'friends of reform' undergoing imprisonment; between October 1821 and October 1822, the Birmingham Patriots' Friend Society remitted £44-10-6d 'for the objects of ministerial and Magisterial vengeance'.[105] The list goes on. It is not difficult to appreciate why these demands took precedence over a campaign to honour Paine (or Caroline for that matter) in marble.

Perhaps the most important reason for the failure of Cobbett's campaign, however, was the rationalism of Paine's British admirers. 'Memory', writes Pat Jalland, 'was and still is a vital component in the dynamics of grief – important to both Christians and unbelievers, but more central for the latter.'[106] As indicated in a previous chapter, in making a case for the commemoration of truly 'great and excellent' men, the noted English rationalist, William Godwin, had earlier insisted that nothing but good could come from monuments that honoured those who had laboured to benefit mankind. The time had come, Godwin believed, to 'mark the spot, whenever it can be ascertained, hallowed by the reception of all that was mortal of those glorious beings; let us erect a shrine to their memory; let us visit their tombs ... '.[107] Nevertheless, Paine's most ardent disciples were apparently indifferent to the fate of his corpse. For Joseph Lawton, a member of the Salford Zetetic Society, for example, celebrating the birthdays of public characters and 'preserving and almost idolising portraits, statues, and relics' was nothing more than 'a species of idolatry'.[108] Carlile agreed. Despite the fact that visitors to his shop in the 1820s could see a statue of Paine (and buy miniatures of the same), and despite the fact that he had named his son Thomas Paine Carlile, he was unconcerned about Paine's bones. In a preface to his *Life of Thomas Paine*, published a year after Cobbett landed at Liverpool, Carlile welcomed the fact that Cobbett had apologised 'for his former abuse of Paine' by bringing his remains back to England: 'It is a volume of retraction, more ample and more convincing than his energetic pen could have produced.'[109] Having said that, Carlile left his readers in no doubt that all that mattered to him was the survival of Paine's ideas: 'whilst we have his writings, I should have felt indifferent as to what became of his bones ... '.[110] Moreover, it is clear that from a strategic standpoint few popular radicals (no matter what stripe) were alert to the oppositional potential of public monuments. The pattern that we have seen in relation to Paine and Caroline was repeated in 1824 following the death of the veteran reformer and popular leader of the Hampden clubs, Major John Cartwright. Despite the fact that his ideas most closely approximated to those of the venerable major, Thomas Wooler was the only popular radical on the committee that was established to commemorate Cartwright.[111] Thus the monument that was erected in 1831 was the work of Whigs and moderate reformers, including some of Cartwright's political enemies.[112] For popular radicals it was an opportunity lost. By seeking to bring a monument of Paine to battle with the memory of Pitt and others, Cobbett was ahead of his time.

Finally, Cobbett's campaign may also have been a casualty of bad timing in a broader sense. As outlined in a previous chapter, an important study of the collective memory of political events edited by James W. Pennebaker, Dario Paez and Bernard Rimé has recently explored the factors that impinge upon the chronology of commemoration.[113] As indicated, by calculating the date of the erection of every public monument in the United States in the hundred years prior to their study, the authors conclude that monuments 'were erected either immediately after an event, or in 20 to 30 year cycles thereafter'.[114] Ostensibly, this finding appears to be directly relevant to the commemoration of Paine. As noted, Cobbett himself came to believe that the monument would have to wait until a more appropriate time, and, it is worth noting, that he had arrived back in England in the middle of a 'memory cycle' as defined above. How much further can we press this notion into service? As we will see, in the United States a monument to Paine was first erected in 1839, exactly 30 years after his death; in Britain the late 1830s and early 1840s were also marked by a resurgence of interest in Paine. There can be no doubt about the importance of Paine to many Chartists. Take J.P. Glenister of Cheltenham for example. A blacksmith by trade, Glenister was a leader among the local Chartists. As W.E. Adams recalls, at one meeting at which Glenister presided, 'somebody spoke of Tom Paine': 'Up jumped the chairman. "I will not sit in the chair", he cried in great wrath, "and hear that great man reviled ... There is no such person as Tom Paine. Mister Thomas Paine, if you please".'[115]

Adams himself recalled that *The Rights of Man* and 'other political works of Thomas Paine', had 'seduced me from my bed at five o'clock for many mornings in succession'.[116] W.J. Linton was another Paineite; his interest was so great that he wrote a biography of Paine in the early 1840s.[117] Perhaps the best example is Henry Vincent. At the age of 17, Henry Vincent was elected vice-president of a discussion group in his native Hull which had been formed too disseminate the principles of *The Rights of Man*.[118] According to R.G. Gammage, Vincent used to 'appropriate and weave' passages from Paine so skilfully into his speeches 'that it was almost impossible to feel that it was other than his own'.[119] 'Paine is evidently a great favourite with him', said Bronterre O'Brien in 1837, 'for not only does he delight in recommending that writer, but he has all his best maxims and arguments at his fingers' ends.'[120] Gammage himself numbered Paine's *Common Sense* as an essential part of his political education.[121]

Renewed interest of Chartists in Paine was also evident at a broader level. For example, the East London Democratic Association, an important organisation in the coming together of the Chartist movement, was formed on the anniversary of Paine's birthday in 1837 to disseminate 'the principles propagated by that great philosopher and redeemer of mankind, the Immortal THOMAS PAINE'.[122] Celebrations of Paine's birthday had been held since the early 1820s – and perhaps earlier[123] – but they became more common during the flourishing of Chartism.[124] In January 1843, an editorial in the *English Chartist Circular*, which often headed its columns with a quotation from Paine, could not have been clearer about the importance of the date: 'We feel it a pleasing – and would fain believe it an auspicious – coincidence, that the completion of the first yearly volume of the *English Chartist Circular* should fall contemporaneously with the anniversary of the Birth of Freedom's Great Apostle – THOMAS PAINE.'[125] Not surprisingly, the National Charter Association published a collected edition of Paine's writings to which they appended a copy of the People's Charter.[126]

By the mid-1840s there was even a revival of the idea of a Paine monument, leading briefly to the formation of a committee for that purpose. In January 1844, William Benbow emerged from obscurity – some historians have even regarded him as dead by this time – to preside over a Paine dinner in London, a position he claimed by virtue of his role in 'the exhumation of Paine's bones'.[127] By this time, however, Paine's bones had been lost. They had remained secure 'in an old trunk' at Cobbett's Normandy Farm, near Guildford, until his death in June 1835 when they had passed, along with Cobbett's other possessions, to his eldest son, William. Cobbett's heir, however, was facing bankruptcy (as a result of a failed attempt to revive his father's newspaper), and as soon as news of his inheritance became known he was pursued by his creditors, one of whom obtained a court order to prevent the dispersal of any assets in the estate. William Junior had custody of the bones long enough to inscribe the skull and the large limbs with Paine's initials, but soon they, along with Cobbett's other possessions, were handed over to a neighbouring farmer who had been appointed as receiver. In January 1836, Cobbett's modest assets were publicly sold off, but the auctioneer balked at selling the trunk of bones. '[He] had never sold any man's bones *as yet*', he is reputed to have said, 'and he would not now begin with Tom Paine's.'[128] Consequently 'the lot' was withdrawn, 'and retained in the possession of the receiver' until legal advice could be obtained. Given the sensitivity about the treatment of human remains it is not surprising that the auctioneer stayed his hammer; nor would the Lord Chancellor have anything to do with the case, refusing to make any order in relation to human remains let alone declare them to be an asset. According to one account, the receiver was thus left to dispose of the remains as he saw fit, and, although he was relieved of his office in 1839, he kept the trunk until 1844.[129]

It was at about this time that the irascible Alexander Somerville, one of the leading publicists in the service of the Anti-Corn Law League, went in search of Paine's bones. On a Cobbett-like tour of Britain, Somerville arrived at Ash in Surrey where he engaged some of the villagers in a conversation about local farming practices, including those that had been employed at Cobbett's nearby farm. A mile down the road, he was told, he could not only see what had been Cobbett's farm, but also 'Tom Paine's bones'. Somerville headed off in a state of excitement, his interest in farming now 'secondary' to a 'desire to see ... the skull of "Common Sense" and the "Rights of Man"'. He was too late. Having reached his destination, Somerville was told that about six months previously a 'gentleman came from London and got them away to bury them there.'[130]

Somerville admitted that he did not tell all he knew: 'I heard names mentioned; but as it seems some secrecy had been enjoined, I do not repeat the names.' He concluded his account by expressing a hope that Paine had finally been reburied, but this seems unlikely.[131] In 1847, the first history of Paine's bones was published by James Watson, a veteran of London's ultra-radical underworld who had cut his political teeth as a volunteer shop-man for Richard Carlile in the 1820s before going on to be one of the authors of the People's Charter in 1837.[132] According to this *Brief History of the Remains of the Late Thomas Paine*, the bones had been collected by a London bookseller and antique dealer (described elsewhere as a furniture dealer) named Tilly (who had previously been associated with Cobbett) who intended to keep them 'until a public funeral of them can be arranged'.[133] The *Brief History* also contains quotations from an address – no longer extant – issued by the Paine Monument Committee that shows clearly that they saw their task as helping to finish what Cobbett had begun: 'Cobbett was obliged ... to abandon his design, and the committee now call upon the people – whom they consider the proper parties to carry such a design into effect – to come forward and accomplish it.'[134] Whether Watson, or others in the secularist movement, were involved in the committee is unclear. What is clear is that it was ephemeral and ineffective, its appeal falling on deaf ears. In 1854, another prominent secularist publisher, Edward Truelove, reportedly traced Paine's skull and his right hand to a Unitarian Minister who subsequently 'evaded' enquiries.[135] A further ripple of interest in the bones occurred in the late 1860s, but by this time it is fair to conclude that they had been well and truly lost.[136] As one historian has put it, 'like some secular version of a medieval holy relic', Paine's bones 'crop up in a multitude of places with an ever decreasing guarantee of authenticity'.[137]

In part, the committee that operated briefly in the mid-1840s based its case on the need to emulate the success of an American effort at commemorating Paine. Despite the indifference and disdain with which Paine had been treated in his declining years, the removal of his corpse was resented by some Americans. 'We hope it is not true: we hope Mr Cobbett has not been guilty of such sacrilege', fumed one newspaper editor, ending his diatribe with a shrill note of nationalism worthy of Cobbett: 'We hope he will not bear away the bones of a patriot from a land of *freemen* to a land of SLAVES.'[138] As noted, in November 1839 a monument to Paine was erected near the grave site in New Rochelle. The driving force behind this campaign was an English émigré, Gilbert Vale, editor of a New York secularist newspaper, the *Beacon*, who headed a list of approximately two hundred subscribers.[139] The sculptured marble pillar was repaired several times during the nineteenth century (due to vandalism); in 1899 a bronze bust of Paine was added to the top of the 12-ft column; and, following a major repair and restoration, the monument was rededicated in 1905.[140] In the second half of the twentieth century, other monuments to Paine were erected in the north-east of the United States in Morristown and Bordenstown, both in New Jersey, and in Philadelphia.[141]

A subscription by American servicemen in 1943 led to the erection of the first plaque to Paine in England. (See Figure 3.2.) 'From his talented pen', reads the inscription on the plaque near Paine's birth place, 'came the voice for the democratic aspirations of the American republic.' Emphasising the fact that monuments provide an excellent guide to the concerns of those who erect them, the plaque goes on to enlist Paine to the immediate purpose of the Allies: 'this simple son of England lives on through the Ideals and Principles of the democratic world for which we fight today'.[142] It was not until the early 1960s that Paine was finally honoured with a statue in the land of his birth. Sculpted by Sir Charles Wheeler, an eminent artist who had spent more than a decade as President of the Royal Academy,[143] this statue in Thetford seemed to suggest that the '*healing* hand of *time*' had finally prevailed, but this was not so: a local Conservative Councillor had denounced the monument as 'an insult to the town' and initiated a vocal campaign against it.[144] The statue was unveiled in 1964 by Michael Foot MP, President of the Thomas Paine Society, and a future leader of the Labour Party. Writing in 1980 at the beginning of the Thatcher years, Foot could scarcely hide his alarm at the controversy that Paine's statue had

Fig. 3.2 Plaque to Thomas Paine, Thetford.

excited: 'can it be that our Establishment, meticulously ticking off those items in [Paine's] programme still unachieved, feel that no unnecessary chances can be taken?'[145]

Cobbett failed in his attempt to raise a monument to Paine that could contest public space with those dedicated to the memory of Pitt and the other 'Borough-mongers' that he detested so fervently, but with this very idea he pointed the way forward. Ironically, the next generation of radicals would honour neither Paine nor Cobbett himself with a public monument, but they would erect tributes to others, ensuring that they challenged the established order in death as in life.

Notes

1 *Sun*, 2 December 1819. Ian Dyck was originally going to write a chapter on Paine and Cobbett but withdrew due to illness. I am grateful to Glen Barclay, Alex Tyrrell and Suzanne Pickering for their comments and suggestions.

2 *Cobbett's Weekly Political Register*, 18 September 1819.

3 Chen, D.W. (2001), 'Rehabilitating Thomas Paine, Bit by Bony Bit', *New York Times*, 30 March. See also *Observer*, 14 May 2000.

4 Burgess, H. (1995), 'Thomae Venerablis Ossa or Ossae Venerabilis', unpublished paper, Wesley College, University of Sydney; Burgess, H. (2003). 'The disownment and reclamation of Thomas Paine: a reappraisal of the "philosophy" of "common sense"', unpublished PhD thesis, University of Sydney. I am grateful to Sigrid McCausland for bringing this to my attention and for providing me with a copy of the short paper abstract. The thesis is marked 'not for loan' and has not been consulted in the writing of this chapter. The description of it is based on the paper abstract. I am also grateful to Iain McCalman for providing me with additional information about the fate of the skull since it came to Sydney.

5 *New York Times*, 30 March 2001.

6 See Dyck, I. (1992), *William Cobbett and Rural Popular Culture*, Cambridge: Cambridge University Press, p. 44; Dyck, I. (1993), 'Local Attachments, National Identities and World Citizenship in the thought of Thomas Paine', *History Workshop Journal*, 35, Spring, p. 132; Sambrook, J. (1973), *William Cobbett*, London: Routledge & Kegan Paul, p. 113; Green, D. (1983), *Great Cobbett: The Noblest Agitator*, London: Hodder & Stoughton, p. 421; Cole, G.D.H. (1925) *The Life of William Cobbett*, London: W. Collins & Son, p. 235; Pemberton, W. Baring (1949) *William Cobbett*, Harmondsworth: Penguin, pp. 109–10. Leonora Nattrass, who has not bothered to get the year of his return correct, dismisses Cobbett's 'grand gesture' as a 'flop'. See Nattrass, L. (1995), *William Cobbett: The Politics of Style*, Cambridge: Cambridge University Press, pp. 4, 217n. George Spater suggests that it caused little excitement in England but later changes his view. See Spater, G. (1982), *William Cobbett: The Poor Man's Friend*, Cambridge: Cambridge University Press, vol. 2, p. 379; (1987), 'The Legacy of Thomas Paine', in Dyck, I. (ed.), *Citizen of the World: Essays on Thomas Paine*, London: Christopher Helm, p. 137.

7 Spater, *William Cobbett*, pp. 353–4.

8 For Benbow see McCalman, I. (1988), *Radical Underworld: Prophets, revolutionaries and pornographers in London, 1795–1840*, Cambridge: Cambridge University Press; Thompson, D. (1984), *The Chartists*, London: Temple Smith, p. 38. According to McCalman, Benbow was amongst the crudest of the gutter pressmen (p. 169).

9 Woodward, W.E. (1946), *Tom Paine: America's Godfather 1737–1809*, London: Secker & Warburg, pp. 338–9. See also Keane, J. (1995), *Tom Paine: A Political Life*, Boston: Little & Brown, Chap. 12.

10 *Cobbett's Weekly Political Register*, 13 November 1819; *Morning Advertiser*, 4 December 1819.

11 *Notes and Queries*, 4 January 1868, p. 16.

12 *Cobbett's Weekly Political Register*, 13 November 1819.

13 *Morning Advertiser*, 30 November 1819.
14 *Cobbett's Weekly Political Register*, 13 November 1819.
15 Woodward, *Tom Paine*, p. 340.
16 *Cobbett's Weekly Political Register*, 13 November 1819.
17 Ibid.
18 Ibid.
19 Cited in Conway, M.D. (1892), *The Life of Thomas Paine*, New York: G.P. Putnam's Sons, vol. 2, p. 428.
20 Kearl, M.C. (1989), *Endings: A Sociology of Death and Dying*, Oxford: Oxford University Press, p. 307.
21 *Morning Advertiser*, 20 November 1819.
22 *Sun*, 27 November 1819.
23 *Morning Advertiser*, 27 November 1819.
24 *Cobbett's Weekly Political Register*, 29 April 1820.
25 *The Times*, 27 November 1819; *Sun*, 27 November 1819.
26 *Morning Advertiser*, 30 November 1819.
27 Anon. (1822), *Cobbett's Gridiron: Written to Warn Farmers of their Danger and to put Landholders, Mortgagers, Lenders, Borrowers, the Labouring, and Indeed All Classes of the Country on their Guard*, London: Henry Stenman, p. 21; *Notes and Queries*, 29 February 1868, p. 202.
28 *Manchester Observer*, 4 December 1819; *Morning Advertiser*, 30 November 1819.
29 *Cobbett's Weekly Political Register*, 27 January 1820.
30 Ibid.
31 *Morning Chronicle*, 18 November 1819.
32 *The Times*, 17 November 1819.
33 *Sun*, 29 November 1819.
34 Ibid.
35 Ibid., 2 December 1819.
36 Ibid. The symbolism here has similarities to the later radical attacks on the government for its treatment of Queen Caroline. Interestingly the bones were depicted as being suspended in a green bag. Historians have suggested that this symbol gained potency when the evidence of the government's spies against Caroline was delivered to the House of Lords in one. See Laqueur, T.W. (1982), 'The Queen Caroline Affair: Politics as Art in the Reign of George IV', *Journal of Modern History*, 54, September, pp. 436, 454–5.
37 *Cobbett's Weekly Political Register*, 15 January 1820.
38 See Microfilm, *English Cartoons and Prints 1320–1832 in the British Museum*, no. 13283. See also George, M.D. (1949), *Catalogue of Political and Personal Satires Preserved in the Department of Prints and Drawings in the British Museum*, London: British Museum, vol. 9, pp. 939–40. For other prints that attacked Cobbett's use of the bones see vol. 9, p. 940 (no. 13284); p. 950 (no. 13314); p. 955 (no. 13339); vol. 10, p. 8 (no. 13522); p. 8 (no. 13525); p. 16 (13568); p. 26 (13642); p. 28 (13655); p. 33 (13677); p. 35 (no. 13683); p. 154 (n. 14034); p. 155 (no. 14041); p. 488 (no. 14806).
39 Dickinson, H.T. (1986), *Caricatures and the Constitution 1760–1832*, Cambridge: Cambridge University Press, p. 14; Gatrell, V.C., 'Laughter and Its Enemies: Visual Humour and Cultural Change in London, 1780–1840', paper presented to the Humanities Research Centre, The Australian National University, 8 March 2002. This point has benefited from conversations with Vic Gatrell.
40 Cited in Green, *Great Cobbett*, p. 421.
41 *Hansard* [House of Lords], 17 December 1819, col. 1265. Grosvenor was not unsympathetic to radicals. For example, he presented a petition on behalf of Samuel Bamford. See Bamford, S. (1984, 1st edn 1844), *Passages in the Life of A Radical*, Oxford: Oxford University Press, pp. 230–1.
42 *Cobbett's Weekly Political Register*, 8 September 1821. André's remains were transferred to Westminster Abbey and a monument erected to him in 1821.

43   *Manchester Observer*, 4 December 1819.
44   'A Briton' (1819), *A Letter to William Cobbett*, Birmingham: T. Knott, p. 3.
45   Cited in *The Times*, 26 November 1819; also reprinted in *Notes and Queries*, 29 February 1868.
46   *Cobbett's Weekly Political Register*, 27 January 1820. See also Bohstedt, J. (1983), *Riots and Community Politics in England and Wales, 1790–1810*, Cambridge, MA: Harvard University Press, p. 9.
47   Cited in Epstein, J.A. (1994), *Radical Expression: Political Language, Ritual, and Symbol in England, 1790–1850*, Oxford: Oxford University Press, p. 101. See also *Black Dwarf*, 7 July 1819, 3 April 1822. Henry Hunt also referred to having participated in burning Paine in effigy in his youth. See *Black Dwarf*, 8 December 1819.
48   *Cobbett's Weekly Political Register*, 18 September 1819.
49   Ibid., 15 January 1820; *Cap of Liberty*, 17 November 1819. Cobbett never published his life of Paine.
50   *Morning Advertiser*, 30 November 1819.
51   Conway, *Life of Paine*, vol. 2, p. 339.
52   *Cobbett's Weekly Political Register*, 1 May 1819.
53   Ben-Amos, A. (2000), *Funerals, Politics, and Memory in Modern France, 1789–1996*, Oxford: Oxford University Press.
54   See *Cobbett's Weekly Political Register*, 9 October 1819; 22 January 1819.
55   Ibid., 18 September 1819. But, there, Cobbett promised, '*he shall not lie, unnoticed, much longer*'.
56   *Manchester Observer*, 4 December 1819.
57   *Sun*, 24 November 1819.
58   *Hansard* [House of Commons], 2 December 1819, col. 651.
59   *Cobbett's Weekly Political Register*, 27 January 1820.
60   *White Hat*, 13 November 1819; 27 November 1819; *Black Dwarf*, 5 January 1820.
61   *White Hat*, 23 October 1819.
62   *Medusa: Or Penny Politician*, 20 November 1819.
63   *Cobbett's Weekly Political Register*, 27 January 1820.
64   As noted, Cobbett himself believed that they might serve as a rallying point. See also Dyck, I. (1987) 'Debts and Liabilities: William Cobbett and Thomas Paine', in *Citizen of the World*, p. 97: 'The bones, too, might serve as a talisman for warding off the magistrates and courts of England; the people would rally around Cobbett, if only to safeguard the sanctity of Paine's corpse.'
65   *Cobbett's Weekly Political Register*, 15 January 1820. See also *Manchester Observer*, 4 December 1819.
66   Richardson, R. (1987), *Death, Dissection and the Destitute*, London: Routledge & Kegan Paul, p. 4.
67   Ibid., p. 7
68   Ibid., pp. 7–8, 22–9. According to Richardson, the practise of viewing the corpse originated in the fourteenth century and touching was still done widely until the 1940s. Touching, it was held, was 'a preventative of bad dreams; it removed fear of death; otherwise the mourner would be haunted by the dead person, or dogged by ill-luck; that it was an act of sympathy with the mourners; it signified that the toucher bore the deceased no grudge' (p. 25).
69   Anon., *Cobbett's Gridiron*, p. 21.
70   Richardson, *Death*, pp. 3, 86–9; Linebaugh, P. (1977), 'The Tyburn Riot Against the Surgeons', in Hay, D. et. al., *Albion's Fatal Tree*, Harmondsworth: Penguin, pp. 65–117. Richardson estimates that as many as a thousand corpses a year were dug up.
71   *Black Dwarf*, 3 May 1820.
72   *Cobbett's Weekly Political Register*, 6 May 1820.
73   Ibid., 15 September 1821. Cobbett was still upholding this version in 1826. See Spater, *William Cobbett*, vol. 2, p. 575n.

74 *The Times*, 18 November 1819. Grosvenor made the same suggestion in the Lords.

75 See Anon., *Cobbett's Gridiron*, p. 21; Spater, *William Cobbett*, vol. 2, p. 388.

76 *Cobbett's Weekly Political Register*, 15 January 1819. William Van der Weyde suggests that the coffin passed into the possession of J. Chennell of Guildford, but this was possibly the trunk and coffin plate, unless the coffin had been shipped separately. See Van der Weyde, W.M. (1925), *The Life and Works of Thomas Paine*, New York: Thomas Paine National Historical Association, vol. 1, p. 456.

77 *Cobbett's Weekly Political Register*, 22 September 1821.

78 Ibid., 20 October 1821.

79 The print was published in a collection entitled *The Men in the moon or the 'Devil to Pay'*, published by Dean & Mundey, London, January–February 1820. See George, *Catalogue*, vol. 10, p. 26 (no. 13642).

80 Ibid., 27 January 1820.

81 Ibid., 15 January 1820.

82 Ibid., 27 January 1820. For the importance of mementoes see Jalland, P. (1996), *Death in the Victorian Family*, Oxford: Oxford University Press, p. 294.

83 *Cobbett's Weekly Political Register*, 27 January 1820.

84 Anon., *Cobbett's Gridiron*, p. 22.

85 Anon. (1819), *A Full Report of the Proceedings of a Public Meeting Held at the Crown and Anchor Tavern, Strand, on Monday, 13 December 1819, to consider of the propriety of adopting a plan for abstaining from the of Wine, Spirits, Beer, Tea, Coffee &c*, London: Thomas Dolby, pp. 14–15. For a discussion of the general issue, see Pickering, P.A. (1991), 'Chartism and the Trade of Agitation in Early Victorian Britain', *History*, 76 (247), June, pp. 221–37.

86 *The Times*, 17 November 1819.

87 *Cobbett's Weekly Political Register*, 8 September 1821.

88 Dyck, 'Debts and Liabilities', p. 97. See also Dyck's, *Cobbett and Popular Culture*, p. 44.

89 Claeys, G. (1989), *Thomas Paine: Social and political thought*, Boston: Unwin Hyman, p. 211.

90 *Black Dwarf*, 11 September 1822.

91 *Morning Advertiser*, 8 December 1819.

92 See Spater, 'Legacy', p. 146n.

93 *Black Dwarf*, 8 December 1819.

94 *Morning Advertiser*, 30 November 1819.

95 *Cap of Liberty*, 17 November 1819. The editor of the ultra-radical *Manchester Observer*, reinforced this message a few weeks later by insisting that if pressed to choose 'the last words we were doomed to utter to the British People, we should call upon them to cherish to their expiring moments, the IMMORTAL MEMORY OF THOMAS PAINE', *Manchester Observer*, 29 January 1820.

96 *Black Dwarf*, 8 December 1819. Major Cartwright also claimed that he had not read the *Age of Reason*. See Cartwright, F.D. (ed.) (1969, 1st edn 1826), *The Life and Correspondence of Major Cartwright*, New York: Augustus M. Kelley, vol. 2, p. 156.

97 See Dyck, *William Cobbett and Rural Popular Culture*, p. 42.

98 *Black Dwarf*, 8 December 1819.

99 See Tyrrell A. with Ward, Y. (2000), 'God Bless Her Little Majesty. The Popularising of Monarchy in the 1840s', *National Identities*, ii, pp. 109–25; Pickering, P.A. (2003), 'The Hearts Of The Millions: Chartism and Popular Monarchism in the 1840s', *History*, 88 (2), April, pp. 227–48.

100 See *Black Dwarf*, 22 August 1821; 29 August 1819. See also Chapter 2 above.

101 Epstein, *Radical Expression*, p. 101.

102 Royle, E. (1974), *Victorian Infidels: The Origins of the British Secularist Movement 1791-1866*, Manchester: Manchester University Press, p. 29.

103   Collins, H. (1971) 'Introduction', Paine, T., *Rights of Man* (1st edn 1791–92), Harmondsworth: Pelican, p. 36.
104   Royle, *Victorian Infidels*, p. 37.
105   *Black Dwarf*, 14 August 1822; 16 October 1822.
106   Jalland, P. (2002), *Australian Ways of Death: A Social and Cultural History*, Oxford: Oxford University Press, p. 161.
107   Godwin, W. (1809), *Essay on Sepulchres. Or, A Proposal For Erecting Some Memorial of the Illustrious Dead in All Ages, on the spot where their remains have been interred*, New York: M & M Ward, pp. 34, 44–5.
108   Quoted in Epstein, *Radical Expression*, p. 123. According to Epstein, 'Carlile was never comfortable with the ritual elements or when the boisterous and profane aspects of popular radicalism. He contrasted traditional political dining, which invited "intoxication and gluttony" and was structured around unthinking repetition of tired toasts and songs, to zetetic celebration which occasioned "a festival of sentiment – a feast for the mind ... a festival of reason".'
109   Carlile, R. (1820), *Life of Paine*, London: M.A. Carlile, pp. xxxiii–xxxiv. According to G.J. Holyoake, Carlile's statue of Paine was carved by Edwards the notorious spy. See Holyoake, G.J (1900), *Sixty Years of an Agitator's Life*, London: Fisher Unwin, vol. 2, p. 2.
110   Carlile, *Life of Paine*, p. xxxiv. As Ruth Richardson has described, the ultimate rational approach to death was adopted by Jeremy Bentham who had left instructions for his corpse to be stuffed and, together with a wax head, put on display. This 'Auto-Icon' was designed to 'save his admirers the necessity of commissioning stone sculptures of him'. It can still be seen at University College, London. Bentham also arranged for mourning rings containing his hair to be distributed to his friends. See Richardson, *Death*, pp. 159–60.
111   Cartwright (ed.) *Major Cartwright*, pp. 297–8.
112   See Osborne, J.W. (1972), *John Cartwright*, Cambridge: Cambridge University Press, p. 152. The statue was unveiled in 1831 in Burton Crescent (now Cartwright Gardens) opposite Cartwright's residence. See London County Council (1952), *Survey of London*, vol. XXIV, pt. IV, London: W.H. Godfrey, p. 89.
113   Pennebaker, J.W., Paez, D. and Rimé B. (eds), (1997), *Collective Memory of Political Events: Social Psychological Perspectives*, Mahwah, NJ: Lawrence Erlbaum Associates, p. x.
114   Ibid., p. 12
115   Adams, W.E. (1968, 1st edn 1903), *Memoirs of a Social Atom*, New York: Augustus M. Kelley, p. 169; Ashton, O.R. (1980), 'Radicalism and Chartism in Gloucestershire, 1832–1847', unpublished PhD thesis, University of Birmingham, pp. 353–5. I am grateful to Owen Ashton for this reference. See also *Manchester Times*, 29 January 1842, for a similar exchange.
116   Adams, *Memoirs*, p. 119. See also Ashton, O.R. (1991), *W.E. Adams: Chartist, Radical and Journalist*, Whitley Bay: Bewick Press, p. 35.
117   Linton, W.J. (1970, 1st edn 1894), *Memories*, New York: Augustus M. Kelley, p. 75.
118   Harrison, B. (1972), 'Henry Vincent', in Bellamy, J.M. and Saville, J. (eds), *Dictionary of Labour Biography*, London: Macmillan, vol. 1, p. 326.
119   Gammage, R.G. (1969, 1st edn 1854), *History of the Chartist Movement 1837–1854*, New York: Augustus M. Kelley, p. 38.
120   *London Mercury*, 5 March 1837. I am grateful to Brian Harrison for this reference.
121   Maehl, W.H. (ed.) (1983), *Robert Gammage: Reminiscences of a Chartist*, Manchester: Manchester Free Press, p. 38.
122   Prospectus reprinted in Thompson D. (ed.) (1971), *The Early Chartists*, London: Macmillan, p. 55. See also Bennett, J. (1982), 'The London Democratic Association 1837–41: A Study in London Radicalism', in Epstein, J.A. and Thompson, D. (eds), *The*

Chartist Experience: Studies in Working-Class Radicalism and Culture, 1830–60, London: Macmillan, pp. 87–119.

123 According to Claeys the tradition appears to have been initiated by Wooler in 1818 although there is some evidence of it commencing in 1810. See *Thomas Paine*, p. 211. The tradition remained strong well into the nineteenth century. See Royle, E. (1980), *Radicals, Secularists and Republicans: Popular Freethought in Britain, 1866–1915*, Manchester: Manchester University Press, pp. 140, 185.

124 See for example, *Charter*, 10 February 1839; *Operative*, 13 January 1839; 10 February 1839; *Northern Star*, 26 January 1839; 14 November 1840; 6 February 1847; 5 February 1848.

125 *English Chartist Circular*, no. 52, p. 207. For epigrams see nos. 21, 22, 23, 27, 34, 48, 53, 66 and 67.

126 See Harris, 'Introduction' to *Rights of Man*, p. 45.

127 *Movement And Anti-Persecution Gazette*, no. 7, p. 56 [January 1844]. For Benbow's demise see Dickinson, W. Calvin (1979), 'Benbow, William (1784–1841)', in Baylen, J.O. and Gossman, N.J., *Biographical Dictionary of Modern British Radicals*, Sussex: Harvester, vol. 1: 1770–1830, pp. 35–6.

128 Somerville, A. (1989, 1st edn 1852), *The Whistler at the Plough*, London: Merlin, 1989, p. 305.

129 The detail in the preceding paragraph is drawn from Anon., (1847), *A Brief History of the Remains of the Late Thomas Paine, from the time of their disinterment in 1819 by the late William Cobbett, MP. Down to the year 1846*, London: J. Watson, pp. 2–8; and the letter by William Bates in *Notes and Queries*, 29 February 1868. For the legal status of remains see Harte, J.D.C. (1994), 'Law after Death, or "Whose Body Is It?" The Legal Framework for the Disposal and Remembrance of the Dead', in Davies, J. (ed.), *Ritual and Remembrance: Responses to Death in Human Societies*, Sheffield: Sheffield Academic Press, pp. 200–237.

130 Somerville, *Whistler*, p. 306.

131 Ibid., p. 306. In 1854, another former Leaguer, Absalom Watkin, who was friendly with Cobbett and his sons, stated that he believed that Cobbett had given the bones to the care of a younger son, John Paul. See Goffin, M. (ed.) (1993), *The Diaries of Absalom Watkin: A Manchester Man 1787–1861*, Stroud: Alan Sutton, p. 354.

132 For Watson see Vincent, D. (ed.) (1977), *Testaments of Radicalism: Memoirs of Working Class Politicians 1790–1885*, London: Europa, pp. 103–9. When Watson retired from the publishing business in 1854, his role in publishing the works of Paine was acknowledged.

133 Anon., *History of the Remains*, pp. 5, 7; Woodward, *Tom Paine*, p. 340.

134 Anon., *History of the Remains*, p. 3.

135 Conway, *Life of Thomas Paine*, vol. 2, p. 427. For Edward Truelove see Royle, *Victorian Infidels*, p. 316. According to John Whitbourn, a surgeon from the Royal College later opined that the hand belonged to a young woman. See Whitbourn, J. (1989), 'A Revolutionary Lays Down His Bones in Ash?', *Surrey Advertiser*, 22 September, repr. <http://www.john-whitbourn.co.uk>

136 *Notes and Queries*, 4 January 1868; 29 February 1868.

137 Whitbourn, 'A Revolutionary Lays Down His Bones'.

138 Cited in *Cap of Liberty*, 17 November 1819. See also Spater, *William Cobbett*, vol. 2, p. 575n.

139 Van der Weyde, *Life and Works of Paine*, vol. 1, p. 457. Vale published a biography of Paine in 1841.

140 Thomas Paine National Historical Association (n.d.), *A Brief History of the Thomas Paine Monument*, <http://www.Thomaspaine.org/mon.html>; Van der Weyde, *Life and Works of Paine*, vol. 1, p. 458.

141 Another monument has been erected in Paris. Paine has also been recently remembered

in the lyrics of a song by the American rock-rap band, Rage Against the Machine. I am grateful to Daniel Pickering for bringing this to my attention.

142 Plaque in Thetford reprinted in Frow, E. and R. (1994), *Radical and Red Poets and Poetry*, Salford: Working Class Movement Library, p. 91. The airmen also named their Flying Fortress 'Thomas Paine'.

143 For Wheeler see his autobiography, (1968), *High Relief. The Autobiography of Sir Charles Wheeler, Sculptor*, Fletham: Country Life Books. He does not mention the Paine sculpture.

144 Quoted in Foot, M. (1980), *Debts of Honour*, London: Picador, p. 159.

145 Ibid.

Chapter 4

Radical Banners as Sites of Memory: The National Banner Survey

Nicholas Mansfield

Banners and flags were widely used in community celebrations as well as in political protests to mark the working-class presence on the streets of early nineteenth-century Britain. At a time when radicals and others outside the formal political nation had limited access to the public sphere where permanent monuments were erected, banners provided an important means, not only of ideological declamation, but also of commemoration and memorial. They were frequently reused, and some of them have survived into the present day as honoured relics of a heroic past. Thus, although banners do not come within the conventional definition of monuments or memorials, they will be discussed here as examples of what Pierre Nora has called '*lieux de mémoire*'. For Nora and historians who have been influenced by his notion of public memory, '*lieux de mémoire*' are sites of memory that satisfy very broad criteria. In Nora's own words they include 'any significant entity, whether material or non-material in nature, which by dint of human will or the work of time has become a symbolic element of the memorial heritage of any community'.[1] They include banners and flags such as the ones that are discussed below. This chapter examines historians' use of banners in their accounts of popular politics by analysing written and visual sources. It studies the history and design of surviving examples recorded in the National Banner Survey of all United Kingdom museum collections and relates this evidence to changes in their iconography, usage and production. The rise of professionally-made banners is related to the puzzle of why there are no surviving Chartist banners. Many contemporary accounts of radical movements, particularly from the Peterloo Massacre (1819) onwards, make reference to banners. Newspapers described banners, and in 1842 Flora Tristan recorded a list of Chartist banner slogans, but in most cases the descriptions are usually tantalisingly brief. The lack of detailed description is also reflected in the many accounts in the contemporary press of the use and even 'unveiling' of banners.

This lack of clarity has not prevented later historians briefly mentioning banners, if only to add local colour to their accounts.[2] Until recently, the prevailing historiography of the early nineteenth century saw independent working-class action going 'underground' during the French wars and only painfully emerging after 1815 through a series of political conflicts with the political authorities or in struggles with the new industrial employers. This analysis was emphasised by Edward Thompson in his magisterial account of the period, *The Making of the English*

Working Class (1963). With the growth in cultural history over the last few decades sometimes challenging this view, a more focused interest in banners on the part of historians of radical movements has emerged. The pioneer of this has been Paul Pickering. The words he wrote 15 years ago are still appropriate: 'A fruitful line of enquiry into a form of communication that directly reflected the views of the rank and file of the movement is into the inscriptions and pictorial representations on the flags and banners carried in Chartist parades.' In his account of Chartism in the north-west of England, Pickering provided an analysis of the messages and meanings used on local banners derived from newspaper descriptions as well as a brief discussion of their production and use.[3]

Other recent historians have used banners in their analyses of the development of popular politics. Frank O'Gorman has mentioned how banners fitted into the election processes of the Hanoverian state. Whilst tending to follow Thompson's path, the work of John Belchem and James Epstein emphasises the importance of banners to the 'Platform' of post-1815 political protest. According to Epstein, the symbolism of the Cap of Liberty was a particularly virulent provocation to those opposing reform and was a key component in the circumstances that produced the violence used against the crowd during the Peterloo Massacre. James Vernon and other cultural historians have made some use of nineteenth-century banners in their descriptions of political processes. They were interested in how banners, as a form of expression, could inform their accounts of popular mobilisation within the 'pressure from without' which became a prominent feature of British political life during the first half of the nineteenth century. Vernon, who has discussed the use and manufacture of banners in elections both before and after 1832, has argued that popular participation through such activities became more formalised and disciplined after the Reform Act.[4]

The use of banners by more elite groups in a slightly earlier period is also mentioned in work by Peter Borsay and George A. Tressider. As will be discussed later, this older civic and non-threatening tradition was slow to decline, especially in smaller provincial towns and often involved artisan groups which are commonly thought of as forming the 'shock troops' of radicalism.[5] Although these historians mainly used written sources, visual sources exist in some contemporary drawings, paintings and cartoons. These must be treated with some care, since artists may not have been eyewitnesses of processions but were merely depicting their idea of what banners looked like or how they were carried. Many artists were also hostile or at least patronising to radical movements. Nonetheless, sufficient apparently authentic images survive which confirm the changes in banner design and usage. Whilst cartoons of the Peterloo period show flags exclusively, the first small horizontal pole banners are detailed in prints of the Birmingham New Hall Reform meeting and of the Bristol election of 1832. Though only flags are in evidence in the Chartist print commemorating the procession accompanying the 1842 petition, both flags and banners with two vertical poles are shown being used together in an *Illustrated London News* engraving of the celebrations of the incorporation of North Shields in 1849. James Parry's painting of Blackfriars Bridge, Salford during Queen Victoria's visit in 1851 similarly shows flags and banners being carried in procession. A lithograph of the Peace Festival at Salisbury in 1856 (following the Crimean War), shows that flags had generally been demoted to decorating buildings, with the main procession being of large professionally produced painted banners of the type popularised by George Tutill, Britain's foremost banner manufacturer.[6]

Tutill commenced work in 1837. Aged only 20, he was already experienced in fairground art. His adaptations of the gaudy fairground fascia board anticipated and moulded working-class tastes in processional regalia for several generations. It is probable that Chartists were many of his customers when his business prospered and that the profits he made from them and other radicals helped to provide the capital that went into the purpose-built banner factory he created in 1859. Here, protected by patents, he applied mass production techniques by installing the largest Jacquard loom in the world and introducing a strict division of labour in an early assembly line. Tutill's efficient marketing used mail order, insurance and railway transport, to establish his company as the most significant banner manufacturer in Britain. He even exported its products worldwide throughout the 'White Empire'. Home-made and semi-professionally manufactured banners continued to be made, but all makers were influenced by the layouts and production techniques that Tutill devised so successfully to meet the popular taste.[7]

Although many banners are located in museum collections, historians in Britain have been relatively slow to use them as sources. Likewise social history museums have often been woefully ignorant about their collections and unaware of their potential significance for scholars. To some extent this was because information about surviving banners was difficult to access. There was no national record of surviving specimens, and very few have been on display. Their fragility and size made them difficult to handle and even store safely. Often museums have scanty historical information about the banners they hold and how they came to be deposited. To make matters worse, banners are notoriously difficult to date from internal evidence.

The People's History Museum in Manchester has developed an expertise in the conservation and interpretation of banners. Its collection of 360 trade union and other banners (including a few rare trade society banners from the early nineteenth century) is the largest of its kind anywhere. In 1997, with the support of the Heritage Lottery Fund which provided money to undertake a National Banner Survey, the People's History Museum circularised every museum in mainland Britain. Based on a 98 per cent response rate, the Survey recorded details of over 2,500 banners (excluding military examples) on a computerised database, along with images and other historical data where these were available. These banners were carried by a wide variety of organisations, although, as might be expected, trade unions, friendly societies, political parties, church groups and women's organisations were the most represented categories.[8]

As a source, banners present many problems for the historian – their very survival may be due to accident or a self-conscious decision by a pressure group to preserve something of themselves for posterity. The latter point is linked to the way in which groups have sometimes used banners to give themselves respectable and well-established historical antecedents. It should be emphasised that the survivors are only a small percentage of the thousands of banners which contemporary sources indicate were being made and used throughout the nineteenth century. Although most banners were of more recent origin, 150 nineteenth-century trade and reform banners, hitherto unidentified or unknown for the most part, offer a useful case study as to how the survey might be used. The banners were arranged in an initial typology of three groups. The largest, consisting of those belonging to trades societies, guilds and Scottish incorporations, is around sixty-five; the second, political banners – overwhelmingly from reform movements of various sorts – account for fifty, and the third contains about thirty banners from community or civic groups. There are more examples from the early nineteenth century than from any other era. These tail off in the 1840s, when there is an almost total absence of Chartist banners, but there is a resurgence in the last decade of the century with the mass-produced banners of well-established trade unions and friendly societies.

Whilst the majority of surviving banners were for outdoor processional use, there are several small examples which seem likely to have been used as backdrops or aprons in secret indoor ritual. Edward Thompson and others have suggested that the underground nature of the trades in the early nineteenth century, compounded by persecution, resulted in radical, if not revolutionary, tendencies. Unsurprisingly perhaps, surviving regalia does not illustrate these ideologies. Instead pieces from the United Female Friendly Society and the Loyal United Free Mechanics combine Old Testament scenes with magical and possibly Masonic imagery. However, a Mechanics' apron already displays the linked hands of friendship and unity as befits one of the components of the future Amalgamated Society of Engineers. The Mechanics' apron is block printed on linen, and, as in the case of other surviving examples in museums from Preston to Oxfordshire, this suggests that it was mass produced rather than made by members or local signwriters. Another small shoemakers' hanging (displaying King Crispin's crown and a half-moon knife) is associated with a Shoemakers' Reform banner of 1832 from Duns in Berwickshire. (See Figure 4.1.) The latter expresses its sentiments in the punning doggerel typical of radical and trades banners: 'We are all true to the last' and 'The Battle's won, Britannia's sons are free and Despots tremble at the Victory'. It is also likely that an 1832 Plumbers' Reform banner (probably from Cumberland) started life as a small wall hanging before being sewn onto a larger sheet with the addition of a painted slogan for the Reform Act celebrations.[9]

These small textiles share the characteristics and purpose of a small number of painted early nineteenth-century emblems, which hung in the 'houses of call' of trade societies. A Norwich Plumbers' emblem almost certainly dates from the Grand National Consolidated Trade Union of 1834, and typically includes the tools of the trade and supporters in anachronistic dress, framing a mock coat of arms copied (without permission) from those of the City Livery Company. A Wigan Miners' emblem is of a similar style, with the addition of one supporter being dressed in working gear and the other in processional ceremonial costume holding a long stave. It also includes an underground scene of work in a bell pit. This scene, together with the invented coat of arms and the two supporters (although these are in contemporary rather than antique dress), is reproduced on the banner of the White

Fig. 4.1   Shoemakers' Reform banner of 1832 from Duns in Berwickshire.

Lion Friendly Society, Ashover, Derbyshire (c. 1830). Adorned with the slogan 'Success to Miners', it is the oldest surviving miners' banner. Thus at some point during the early century, the symbolism of miners transferred literally from a private underground world of pit and pub to the open expression of values through public procession, although it is unknown whether this banner, unlike those referred to above, was used to support radical reform. This transfer of symbolism from private to more public consumption is traceable too from the trade societies' iconography on jugs, plates and mugs used by members in public house meetings. In the first decades of the century, they used crude slipware with commissioned slogans and pewter or brass metal vessels with homemade, often secret, inscriptions. These were gradually supplemented by mass-produced ceramics with transfer-printed iconography for which there seems to have been a market. The appearance around 1830 of the first printed membership emblems and certificates for trade unions and friendly societies is probably also part of this process.[10]

As already mentioned, an older parallel trades' banner tradition already existed. In contrast to the London Livery companies, provincial town guilds were active in their various trades despite successive waves of anti-trade union legislation. Several dozen of their banners survive, some from the early eighteenth century, in several towns including Carlisle, Chester, Coventry, Ludlow and many Scottish burghs. Accounts exist of their manufacture and use which indicate that guild artisans also took part in ceremonial occasions as an integral and respected part of the civil community. Moreover, alongside the usual representations of tools and icons of the trade, their surviving slogans sometimes betray radical sympathies. Thus a weavers' banner from Cupar, Fife – a notoriously radical area – contains a rhyme indicative of a pride of trade that could also be associated with radical sympathies: 'The weaver trade it is most fine, and is renowned so: That there is neither poor, nor rich, yet doth without it go'.[11]

Although banners were used by popular reform groups from the 1790s, none were recorded by the Survey, a product no doubt of efficient repression during the French wars. Equally unsurprisingly, the *ad hoc* banners associated with violent episodes in the post-war period – where they were used as symbols of leadership or to 'bind' reluctant rioters – and those known to have been carried by revolutionary ultra-radical groups, are missing.

Only half a dozen reform banners have survived from the 1815–20 period, indicating perhaps the continued effectiveness of government action, and upholding the view that these banners could be potentially dangerous evidence which could be used in law against their holders. Radicals knew well that in the fine print of the repressive measures introduced in 1819 that would come to be known as the 'Six Acts' Lord Liverpool's government made 'bearing banners at public meetings' an offence 'liable to fine and imprisonment, for any period not exceeding two years'.[12] None of the surviving banners have a connection with the trades, and most display basic graphic imagery rather than elaborate iconography. The only surviving banner used at Peterloo itself, and reasonably well documented because of its association with Samuel Bamford, is the Middleton 'Unity and Strength' banner (still hanging in the local public library). From the post-Peterloo protests there exist a Carlisle 'Death or Liberty' banner and a Skelmanthorpe banner, the latter of which is particularly informative because it has survived along with a written narrative detailing its use in successive reform campaigns and civic celebrations. The Galston (Political) Union banner of 1819 from Scotland also dates from this era. It includes a crude Union Jack in the top pole-side canton, with a harp, thistles and roses on a red field, and the slogans 'Universal Sufferage' (*sic*) and 'The People's Charter'. Additions were sometimes made to old banners, and this one may date from 1838. A fine banner dating from the protest movement of 1820 relating to George IV's attempt to divorce Queen Caroline also exists from Trowbridge, Wiltshire. It is the only survival from this movement, and its painted silk design, together with surviving accounts of its use, suggest that it is a creation of the liberal gentry, similar in style to the election banners which this group used at that time.[13]

Surviving radical banners from the Peterloo period do not display the Cap of Liberty, with the possible exception of a Cap of Liberty made of turned wood, painted red, which is said to have been carried as a banner finial at Peterloo. This is in the Rochdale Museum collection. Only one radical banner studied, that of the 1832 Kirkintilloch weavers, shows the Cap of Liberty, although there was a revival of its use in late Victorian socialist and trade union banners, particularly those that drew on the designs of Walter Crane. As an artist best known for his illustrations in children's books and as a designer of Wedgwood ceramics, Crane had begun his career as an apprentice to the well-known Chartist and Republican engraver, W.J. Linton. Historians have also discussed the subversive nature of tricolour flags in this period, but none were recorded in the survey.[14]

One of the largest groups of banners located in the survey consists of 24 associated with the Reform Crisis of 1829–32. The extensive use of banners in the reform campaigns of these years is reasonably well documented, and banners are prominently featured in the print of the New Hall Hill meeting of the Birmingham Political Union in 1832. The print shows – amongst other designs – 'Union Jack'-type banners being flown that day. It has been impossible to establish any connection between Political Unions and Union Jacks, with only three political 'Union Jack' banners surviving from this period.[15] All but six of the 'Reform Crisis' banners are Scottish, and eight were carried by groups of tradesmen. They divide roughly evenly between banners used in the campaigns leading up to the 1832 Act and those made for its celebration. They are very varied in design, with an emphasis in the celebration banners on the heroes of the day – Russell, Grey, Brougham and William IV. The last named also survives as an icon of the people in much of the print and ceramic iconography of the crisis. Additional unofficial royal sanction for radicalism is also claimed in other reform banners. For example, the West Fife Museum's collection has a version with the royal coat of arms in the top left-hand canton, with Scottish thistle decoration in the remaining three. The surviving Carlisle Rickergate reform banner along with the Leith reform banner both contain images of Britannia. The pre-Reform banners often express trenchant views. The Kirkintilloch Weavers' banner is particularly striking; it is an extraordinary combination of a Cap of Liberty, crossed pikes and a Union Jack. Both the campaigning and celebration styles of banner used rhymes and puns to emphasise slogans. 'If United We will be, A Reform we will see', the Galston reform banner proclaims, while an Edinburgh survival admonishes that 'Rulers may Order & Kings command, But the Power of the People who can Withstand'. Several banners consist solely of slogans – probably made, like more modern examples, for specific demonstrations. The 1830–32 crisis also saw the first appearance of humorous cartoons on banners. Some, like the 'Rulers may Order' banner referred to above, were clearly copied from complex radical prints which have now been lost. Another example surviving from the Edinburgh Plumbers shows one of their products, a water pump, being operated by a plumber in working clothes to drench a Tory adversary, John Wilson of *Blackwood's Magazine*, identified here under his pseudonym, 'Christopher North'. In common with many Edinburgh examples this banner was carried in reform demonstrations later in the century with the addition of the proud 'battle honour' inscription: 'Carried in 1832'.[16]

As well as adopting specifically Scottish icons, such as thistles or the St Andrew's saltire, several Scottish Reform Crisis banners refer back to a noble heroic past and claim it for popular radicalism. Thus the Lamington banner commemorates William Wallace's connection with Lanarkshire, while the Edinburgh carpenters celebrated the example of a covenanting 'blue bonnet soldier'. The discovery of a covenanting flag from Cumnock, Ayrshire, may conceal forgery in the cause of Reform. Said to have been carried against Claverhouse (Bonnie Dundee) at the battle of Drumclog in 1679, it was conveniently rediscovered in the attic of a radical doctor around 1830: 'Its value and interest were at once recognised. In the public processions held at the time of the Reform Bill, it was frequently borne, as if to proclaim the kinship of the Covenanters of the 17th Century with the Reformers of 1832.'[17] It is possible to read an anachronistic sense of nationalism into the Scottish iconography that appears on the banners; the use of roses, thistles and shamrocks, demonstrating the unity of the United Kingdom, was widespread on banners on both sides of the border. The *Scotsman's* account of the 1832 Jubilee procession indicates that the Leith Incorporation of Wrights and Masons was even prepared to march under a banner emblazoned with the 'Lion of Old England'.[18]

The survival of banners from the early 1830s is in marked contrast to the Chartist years. The total absence of Chartist banners was a key factor that shaped the National Survey project. There are very few banners of any sort from the late 1830s and 1840s. Halifax has a remarkable, but simple, slogan banner from Richard Oastler's Ten Hours Bill agitation, and there are three survivals from the Anti-Corn Law League, of which two are probably Reform Bill celebration banners that were reused in 1846. The League used banners mainly as backdrops for indoor meetings, and its rapid success may explain why so few were preserved in public collections. It is likely that thousands of Chartist banners were made and used. Scores of contemporary accounts, both hostile and friendly, make reference to them. Chartist political rhetoric and Chartist poetry are full of imagery related to banners. It is possible to catch glimpses of them in surviving prints and (tantalisingly) blowing in the wind in the famous photographs of the 1848 Kennington Common meeting. As noted, academics have analysed Chartist banner slogans and described their production as part of the 'Trade of Agitation'. Although a few of the radical banners already discussed were used in Chartist demonstrations, not a single Chartist banner has survived.[19]

Three banners survive from demonstrations during the 1866–67 Reform Act, all carried by tradesmen in Edinburgh. All are of a small size and are clearly part of the locally made, sign-writing tradition, rather than the larger, commercially made productions to which working-class organisations were now aspiring. Firmly Liberal, this group includes two slogan banners and the suitably updated 1832 Plumbers' banner referred to above. The cartoon shows Robert Lowe MP, an opponent of the franchise extension, receiving a ducking with the new technology of shower and bath being operated by a working plumber. 'Quench the Lowe' is the advice of a *Frenchified* pun. The tradition of parading banners inherited from previous reform campaigns – also found elsewhere – continued, with many of these earlier Edinburgh banners being carried in the 1884 franchise demonstration. The United Brushmakers sewed their 1832 banner on one side of a new creation made for the latter event. Contemporary accounts of the Nine Hours Movement indicate that banners were used extensively during the demonstrations or celebrations that welcomed its adoption in 1871–72, but only three of these banners have survived – two from Sunderland and one from Edinburgh. These are fairly elaborate local constructions, though made in the larger modern style pioneered by Tutill. The Sunderland Employers' banner has probably the first depiction of the sort of reconciliation scene between capitalist and worker which was to become typical of British trade union banners.[20]

The last group of political banners relates to the 1884 franchise agitation in Scotland. It consists of ten banners from Edinburgh, Elgin, Hawick and Perth together with a related group of three others from North Lanarkshire. One trade union banner – commissioned for the occasion by the Hawick Tailors – was locally produced in the grander 'Tutill' style, which was now *à la mode* for trade union and friendly society banners. Four banners which were also locally made for the workpeople of particular factories feature images of William Ewart Gladstone and/or John Bright. Three banners are from trade incorporations and still include the adopted coats of arms and tools of the trade, typical of much earlier iconography. In the case of the Elgin Squarewrights, a new banner was made for the 1884 demonstration, an exact replica of a much older design, which includes a 'Union Jack' in the top left-hand canton, as well as the tools of the trade. Thus organisations which saw themselves as progressive could deliberately choose symbolism with backward-looking references.[21]

In contrast to the plentiful reform banners, the National Banner Survey located surprisingly few election banners – only twenty-eight examples are known to have been carried for particular candidates. Eight of these were used by Gladstone when he stood as a Tory in the 1832 election in Newark. Moreover, only a handful of Liberal or Conservative *party* banners survive, though with more from ancillary organisations like the Primrose League or from particular campaigns. One likely explanation for this poor rate of survival is that most election banners were elaborate constructions using candidates' coats of arms and costly metallic paint, which is particularly harsh to textiles.[22]

It is also worth pointing out that radical banners form only a small minority of those surviving in museums. Friendly Society banners like that of the Goosnargh Amicable Society, already discussed, contained iconography – Cap of Liberty and clasped hands - which could be evidence of radicalism. Other banners were undoubtedly used to convey loyalist messages. Friendly Society banners form one of the largest categories within the Survey, and many of the earlier surviving examples display explicitly royalist iconography such as crowns, royal arms, ciphers, Britannias and oak trees – the latter connected with the cult of Oak Apple Day, a popular celebration in the West Country and the Welsh Marches. Other Friendly Society banners lionise Lord Nelson, with some displaying his famous Trafalgar signal: 'This Day England Expects Every Man to do his Duty'. The National Maritime Museum has an early nineteenth-century banner with a naive representation of the 'Hero of the Nile', which may well be the sole survivor of the banners which were specifically made to greet his triumphant tours of the country. Even trades banners might well have been used for loyalist purposes. One of the earliest, a Dunstable Shoemakers' banner dated 1810, is said to have been made to commemorate George III's Jubilee.[23]

The Union Jack was a symbol which could be used by radicals and their opponents. Whilst the use of the Union Jack on trade society banners was known before the National Banner Survey – on, for example, the Liverpool Tinplate

Workers' banner of 1821 (See Figure 4.2) and the later Edinburgh Tobacconists' banner – the project has uncovered many more examples. The Union Jack is also used in a similar way in many other surviving banners, ranging from reform groups through friendly societies to an ex-service association. The widespread use of a potentially loyalist symbol during the anti-democratic repression of the early nineteenth century may question Thompson's 'heroic' interpretation and give support to more revisionist or diverse interpretations of the period, including recent ones which stress 'radical constitutionalism'.[24]

The Union Jack seems to have been used from the very beginning of popular banner making. What is considered the oldest extant trades society banner – that of the Hawick Hosiers – displays the pre-1801 Union Jack in the top left-hand canton. The blue field is decorated with crude representations of the tools of the trade and emblematic Scottish thistles. If, as seems likely, the painted date of 1797 is accurate, then surely at the height of the wars with revolutionary France the intended message was loyalist.

The form of design in these Union Jack banners had already been used since the early eighteenth century in the regimental colours of regiments of the British Army. The copying of this style *may* have come about after widespread working-class military service in the Revolutionary and Napoleonic Wars. The work of Clive Emsley and Linda Colley has indicated the prevalence of military service and the relative success of the British state in mobilising popular support for the war effort and for the monarchy. Some Union Jack banners may be demonstrating this. On the other hand, historians have emphasised the role of ex-soldiers in post-war radicalism. It may be that ex-service tradesmen adapted well-known military

Fig. 4.2   Liverpool Tinplate Workers' banner of 1821.

symbols for their own organisations in the hope that trade societies would achieve an honoured national role and significance.[25]

In this way Union Jacks may represent a bid for inclusion as part of the nation by organisations opposed to the current political status quo. Dorothy Thompson sees them as icons of contested loyalty in a fluid political discourse where radicals were laying claim to symbols and iconography, which they believed had been appropriated by their enemies. John Belchem regards them as evidence of a sophisticated attempt of the trades and reformers to relate to the geo-political agenda of the newly created United Kingdom and to the participation of their members in a free labour market. James Vernon, who has posited that the 'union jacks may not simply denote loyalism, but that they may denote a radical constitutionalism', has warned that the 'only way you can interpret them is by looking locally at how and when they were used'.[26] Unfortunately, press reports from the early nineteenth century have only brief descriptions of banners and their use; often doing no more than identifying the main slogan, they make a deeper analysis difficult. This was confirmed by an attempt to ascribe correct dates to the surviving Liverpool Tinplate Workers' banners of 1821 and 1838 through reports in the local press. Tantalisingly, although tinplate workers' banners were mentioned in press reports of coronation celebration processions in 1821, 1831 and 1838, as well as in political reform marches, no descriptions were published. Likewise archive sources of trade societies from the early nineteenth century are extremely rare, and where they do exist, like the brushmakers and tinplate workers, references to banners are generally not revealing about design and iconography.[27]

The Survey has identified that a number of trade society banners – including Union Jack types – were made especially for the coronation processions of Queen Victoria and George IV, and in Scotland for the latter's pivotal visit in 1822. It is difficult to conclude that the use of the Union Jack in this way was anything other than a symbolic demonstration of an organisation's loyalty to the monarch and state. Admittedly, by the time of the Reform crisis it is known that the same Union Jack banners in Liverpool and Edinburgh were used by the trades in the radical cause. Possibly because of the temporary alliance with middle-class reformers, the Union Jack then became the symbol of a nation united in a new political cause. Likewise, several surviving pieces of transfer-printed pottery commemorating the Reform Act, along with a more primitive Ewenny pottery slipware piece from South Wales, are decorated with flags which have the Union Jack in the upper left canton.[28]

The continuing uncertainties over the political significance of the Union Jack on banners can be illustrated by drawing on several Scottish examples. The two recently discovered banners in Galston, Ayrshire, have the crude Union Jack form with colours and design not conforming to the correct heraldry of the union flag, perhaps indicating an ironic or opposite intention. In addition, the Survey has recorded over a dozen trade society banners with the St. Andrew's saltire in the upper canton, and similar examples were used in the 'Common Riding' ceremonies of the Scottish Lowlands. Several of these were reused in reform demonstrations. What are we to make of the Wanlockhead Lead Miners' banner which displays *both* the Union Jack and the St. Andrew's saltire, or the Stirling Incorporation of

Shoemakers banner which includes the St. George's cross, a device that appears nowhere in surviving *English* trades banners? Perhaps the safest conclusion is that they represent what Colley terms 'a classic case of multiple identities'.[29]

The design of banners is directly related to how they were used. Virtually all banners from the early nineteenth century and before were technically flags which were carried on one pole and waved. It was these flags which were used in the existing banner tradition, as the remains of the guilds took part in civic and national ceremonial occasions as an integral part of their community. Many English guild and Scottish incorporation banners are long and thin flags with tapering ends, often forked or swallow tailed. They were used in the urban ritual described by Borsay and others. Some towns had small groups of semi-professional ceremonial workers, whose display rituals were probably similar to those of military colours, as they took part in a regular round of elections, royal birthdays, coming-of-age celebrations, feasts, mayor-making, and more occasional coronations and jubilees. In an era of public reform and economic change, such practices looked increasingly archaic, and they sharply declined. So the 'streamers' of the Ludlow Guilds were flourished for the last time in 1824 and Norwich corporation's 'Snap', 'Whiffler' and 'Speech Boys' were pensioned off after the Municipal Reform Act in 1835.

Using evidence from surviving examples, contemporary accounts and illustrations of banner carrying, it is clear that during the second quarter of the nineteenth century, there was a major change in design and usage. Banners began to be attached to a horizontal top-pole and/or two vertical poles, with the fabric held rigidly by two or more people. Consequently, the iconography and the slogans were easier to read, and the banner's message was more powerful. These changes may be related to the more formalised and disciplined political and civic participation identified by Vernon and others. They are probably also related both to the declining ability of viewers to understand the iconography of the older banner rituals and to the more direct messages which reformers or trades unions could now transmit.

More research on early banner makers could usefully be done, but indications are that whilst large towns seem to have had professional regalia manufacturers, most plebeian reform or trades banners were the products of local signwriters or even of talented members. There is clear evidence that banner making became more professionalised in the 1830s as entrepreneurs identified a gap in the market. The rise of professionalism in banner making coincided with the widespread adoption of the new carrying system and is probably linked with the demand from the Chartist movement for banners as 'mobile monuments'. Major firms like Henry Slingsby of London and Henry Whaite of Manchester, started banner making in the early 1840s. Above all, John Gorman's researches have underlined the importance of George Tutill.

An additional explanation for these cultural changes may lie in the increasing part that consumer goods played in the lives of Victorians. Older traditions of production and consumption of locally made items were gradually replaced by mass-produced objects, readily available through dynamic changes in transport, retailing, and marketing. The Great Exhibition of 1851 and other similar industrial design projects accelerated this whole process. Historians of such diverse subjects as the black letter press and quilts have noted the tendency of older home-made forms to be undervalued and potentially discarded in the mid-Victorian period in favour of shop-bought replacements.[30]

Both homemade and manufactured banner traditions went on side by side in the late nineteenth century, although the richer and more metropolitan trade union branches aspired to fashionable products ordered from Tutill's catalogue. Later, for less wealthy customers, the firm introduced cheaper lines available via hire purchase. Tutill's materials – oil painting on silk – were a throwback to more aristocratic election banners. This caused them to be inherently fragile, especially given any rough usage in the open air and probably explains why so few of his early products survive, although many more homely and less sophisticated examples exist in public collections. Whilst it is impossible to be definitive, because the evidence was lost when Tutill's voluminous correspondence was destroyed in the London Blitz during the Second World War, it was likely that the growth of Chartism, alongside that of the affiliated friendly societies and trade unions, fuelled initial demand for his products and led to the firm's dominance of the trade.

The extraordinary absence of extant Chartist banners has given rise to something like a quest by the present author. The quest has involved international enquiries, following up (unfounded) rumours from old members of the Communist Party of Great Britain that British Chartist banners had been presented in the inter-war period to the Museum of the Revolution in Moscow or to mining museums deep within the former USSR. A photograph of a banner from an unknown book illustration in the John Gorman papers typifies the problems associated with this search. It is of a 'banner used in the Chartist riots' with a plain slogan 'Westminster District' and was said to be 'in the possession of the Police Authorities, New Scotland Yard'. Sadly the Metropolitan Police Museum can find no trace of it and there is a strong possibility that it was used *by* the police to muster special constables, since it bears a strong resemblance to a surviving near-contemporary special constables' banner in the Greater Manchester Police Museum.

It is worth outlining some theories for the absence of Chartist banners. During periods of government prosecution, banners were clearly targeted by the police during demonstrations and raids. For example, in his account of his radical family in 1842, Andrew Carnegie describes being 'deeply impressed with the great danger overhanging us because a lawless flag was secreted in the garret'. Dorothy Thompson is of the opinion that banners could have been destroyed by their owners, because their slogans could have been used as evidence of seditious intent. It is also possible that, as many ex-Chartists became Gladstonian Liberals, Disraelian Conservative or stalwarts of the local Co-operative Society, they may have wished to play down the confrontational activities of their youth. This may have involved disposing of Chartist regalia and banners which – unlike the Reform period banners – did not yet have the patina of antiquarian respectability required for preservation in a local museum.[31] It was also important that working–class people had small homes, with little storage space. Chartism also had no direct successor in organisational terms and a 'no politics rule' was often enforced in tangential organisations like friendly societies, co-operatives and trade unions, which would make them less inclined to give space to Chartist banners.

These arguments may be taken too far. When Prince Albert visited Liverpool in 1846, workers joined the celebratory procession carrying banners that hailed their trade union and Chartist affiliations. Among their companions that day were banner-waving Tory sympathisers of Pitt the Younger and the Duke of Wellington. As the *Liverpool Chronicle* put it, all 'the clubs and public bodies, who pride themselves on their banners, flags, and emblems have either had the old ones "touched up" or new ones painted' for the occasion.[32] Much later there is even a surviving photograph of Chartist pikes proudly being displayed outside the Failsworth Liberal Club in 1911.[33]

Surviving descriptions of Chartist banners make it clear that the banners soon adopted the large-scale oil painting on silk style, which Tutill was to make his own. Often these banners were impressive representations of Feargus O'Connor, or dead heroes of the previous generation of heroic radicalism, like Henry Hunt. Portrayal of these figures gave an immediate tradition to Chartist banners and enabled them to be used as 'mobile monuments' to past and present campaigns in processions and on other public occasions. The funding of Chartist banners – through penny subscriptions from working-class Chartists – also encouraged a sense of ownership for these 'mobile monuments'. This was a process that went too far for Bronterre O'Brien, who lamented the 'thousands of pounds of hard earned money squandered upon flags and banners and coaches and triumphal cars – and such like trumpery'. Ironically, in their determination to secure the 'best' banners for their protest, the Chartists were perhaps ensuring that none of their proud symbols of protest were preserved for posterity. Impressive though Tutill's designs were, they were fragile, and it was difficult to manoeuvre such monstrous objects in the British climate and streets.[34]

As repositories of antiquated design, banners are notoriously difficult to date. Although textile conservators are skilled at identifying clues in construction – particularly materials and stitching – gut feeling and long experience have played a major part in establishing provenance for the National Banner Survey. The problem of accurate dating is compounded by the almost total lack of archival sources from makers and carriers of banners. Almost all custodians of banners think that their treasures are older than they actually are. The old-fashioned style of many trade union banners causes romantic myths to be adopted of a similar nature to those that suffuse military colours. This attitude also affects 'professional' custodians of banners, and the survey was told by more than one curator that a banner was carried at a historic event which was clearly impossible given its actual age. Given inherent fragility and large size, banners prior to the nineteenth century are very rare, and earlier survivals are much altered and repaired.

In his work on eighteenth-century urban ritual, Borsay refers to the way that ceremonial regalia became 'magically imbued'. The way in which banners were used to seek out the power of past campaigns to aid present ones may be related to this concept. The tendency for historical banners to be honoured as 'holy relics' or battle honours has already been mentioned, but there are more self-conscious references to the past in a number of examples. In the Scottish Lowlands, fascinating groups of 'Common Riding' banners commemorate the ancient custom of riding burgh boundaries and common lands in an important statement of local identity. The Common Riding banners in Hawick, for example, include some made and used for the 1832 Reform Act Jubilee that were later reused in the 1884 franchise reform demonstrations. Arguably Common Ridings were dying out in the late Victorian period – when the banners were deposited in local museums – and were revived as an 'invented tradition' related to the issue of Scottish nationhood. In a similar way other trades banners – like those of the Liverpool Tinplate Workers or the Plumbers' Reform banner – were preserved as half understood 'holy relics' of a heroic past by their successors in modern trades unions such as the sheet metal workers' section of the MSF trade union and the plumbers' trade group of Amicus.[35]

Also in Scotland, the survey uncovered covenanting banners, the authenticity of which must be questioned, given the rareness of large textiles from the seventeenth century. As previously mentioned, the covenanting flag from Cumnock may well be an 1830s forgery, and, if substantiated, the claim that a glovers' banner from Perth was carried by members of that trade in battle against the Duke of Montrose in 1644 would make it the only banner to survive today from the Civil Wars. As the author discovered when he visited Middleton parish church, north of Manchester, and identified a banner as a nineteenth-century replacement rather than an original carried by local men at the battle of Flodden, it is sometimes better to leave custodians with their myths![36]

Most of the museums in northern England were coincidentally formed during the heroic period of radical agitation. Started by literary or philosophical societies, mainly middle class, but from the earliest days with a substantial contribution from working-class collectors, they were largely absorbed by local municipalities in the late Victorian period. Many society members were themselves involved in reform. The Sheffield society had no doubt as to the cause of its own lack of progress: [37]

> The political events which have rendered the year 1832 for ever memorable in the annals of history so strongly and universally arrested attention, as scarcely to admit the intrusion of literary pursuits ... Agitated, however, and intently occupied as the minds of the people were, your Council did not consider the time favourable to their exertions.

The material culture of reform was often thought worth preserving by middle-class community leaders as important icons of the glorious and complete settlement of 1832, and for the next hundred years radical banners which had been kept as family mementoes were thought worthy of deposit in local museums as symbols of local support for universal progress. The process of collecting went on for longer still. The Duns Shoemakers' reform banner was handed down thorough the family of a reformer until donated to the People's History Museum in 1996, and the Elgin incorporations' collection was still paraded around the burgh in the Common Ridings until 1994, when it was deposited in the local museum.

A survey of the material culture of early nineteenth-century radicalism undertaken by the People's History Museum in 1992 found that the vast majority of objects in museum collections were connected with the Reform Crisis period, and that only a few were connected with Chartism. This finding was confirmed by the National

Banner Survey. Museums were not interested in trade union material until very recent times, and where union banners did arrive in museum collections it was because they related to current events that seemed likely to retain 'historic' importance. An example of this is the Dunfermline Bakers' banner of 1881. It was made locally for a visit of the town's most famous son, Andrew Carnegie, himself a concealer of radical banners in early life.

As Antony Taylor points out, there was an interest in Chartists and their material culture amongst late Victorian socialists, but little of this seems to have survived either with individuals or institutions. Although as early as 1931, G.D.H. Cole organised an exhibition of Labour history, it was not until after the Second World War that concerned individuals including James Klugman, Ruth and Eddie Frow and the members of the TULC group made systematic collections of working-class objects. By then the rich material culture of Chartism had all but disappeared.[38]

Banners are symbolically indicative of changes and continuities in British society. The study of surviving examples now available through the National Banner Survey can be used to contribute an additional layer of meaning to the teasing out of popular ideologies. It is possible to find evidence for working-class demands for radical, perhaps revolutionary, change in some of the symbolism and language displayed on banners. On the other hand, the widespread use of Union Jacks and crowns may support the revisionist historians who have emphasised the overarching loyalties of all social groups in the Hanoverian and early Victorian state. In the political fluidity of the early nineteenth century, when class had yet to develop as an all-defining concept, it is small wonder that interchangeable notions like nationhood, loyalty, radicalism and patriotism were contested and iconographically represented by adaptable symbols like the Cap of Liberty and Union Jack.

Legend has it that in 1877, when Manchester Corporation was about to open its new Town Hall, designed by Alfred Waterhouse, it privately approached Queen Victoria to perform the opening ceremony. The Queen, through her advisors, made it known that she would not feel comfortable shaking hands with the Lord Mayor who had once been a felon. Alderman Abel Heywood, before becoming a respectable Liberal, had indeed been imprisoned for selling unstamped newspapers and was later active in Chartism. With the full co-operation of Manchester's employers, the Corporation therefore decided to open the Town Hall at a ceremony that included a monster procession of trades and friendly societies. Some radical symbols were carried on the march, including Reform banners from 1832 which were proudly displayed by the trades that still treasured them. One of the principal themes that day was the harmony between capital and labour. As the banners filed out of the west side of Albert Square to the accompaniment of the Duke of Lancaster's Yeomanry band, their carriers were seemingly unaware that on that very spot in 1819 bloody conflict involving workers and the unreformed state had taken place. Victorian capitalism's *rapprochement* with its radical workforce had, by now, even extended to the manipulation of working–class tastes in symbolism. But no one seemed to notice.

A contemporary watercolour of the occasion survives in the Manchester Art Gallery collection. The unknown artist almost certainly observed the event and included some intimate details. A group of carriers, consisting of two men on each vertical pole and four guide rope handlers, can be seen unsuccessfully struggling with their sail-like banner, almost certainly one of George Tutill's fashionable creations. In the windy conditions the fabric had split in two.[39] The scene bore testimony to two of the themes of this chapter: the importance of banners for the radical working class, and the fragility of the banners themselves.

Notes

1 Nora, P. (1996), *Realms of Memory. Rethinking the French Past*, New York: Columbia University Press, vol. 1, p. xvii.
2 Hawkes, J. (1987), *The London Journal of Flora Tristan 1842*, London: Virago, p. 36. For examples and a fuller discussion of the arguments made in this chapter see Mansfield, N. (2000), 'Radical rhymes and union jacks: a search for evidence of ideologies in the symbolism of nineteenth century banners', *Working Paper in Economic and Social History*, 45, University of Manchester. Available on <www.man.ac.uk/history/research>.
3 Pickering, P.A. (1986), 'Class without words: Symbolic Communication in the Chartist Movement', *Past and Present*, 112, August, p. 153; Pickering, P.A. (1995), *Chartism and the Chartists in Manchester and Salford*, Basingstoke: Macmillan, pp. 160–5 and Appendix C. The material culture of the movement is covered in his (1991), 'Chartism and the 'Trade of Agitation' in Early Victorian Britain', *History*, 76 (247), June, pp. 221–34.
4 O'Gorman, F. (1992), 'Campaign Rituals and Ceremonies: The Social Meaning of Elections in England 1780–1860', *Past and Present*, 135; Belchem, J. (1981), 'Republicanism, popular constitutionalism and the radical platform in early nineteenth century England', *Social History*, January; Belchem, J. (1988), 'Radical Language and Ideology in early 19th c. England: The Challenge of Platform', *Albion*, Summer; Epstein, J.A. (1994), *Radical Expression: Political Language, Ritual and Symbol in England 1790-1850*, Oxford: Oxford University Press, especially Chap. 3; Vernon, J. (1993), *Politics and the People – A Study in English Political Culture c.1815–c.1867*, Cambridge: Cambridge University Press.
5 Borsay, P. (1984), 'All the town's a stage': urban ritual and ceremony 1660–1800', in Clarke, P. (ed.), *The Transformation of English Provincial Towns, 1600–1800*, London: Hutchinson; Tressider, G.A. (1992), 'Coronation Day Celebrations in English Towns, 1685–1821: Elite Hegemony and Local Relations on a Ceremonial Occasion', *British Journal for Eighteenth Century Studies*, 15 (1), Spring. There is also some discussion of early trade society banners in Gorman, J. (1986), *Banner Bright – An Illustrated History of Trade Union Banners*, London: Scorpion.
6 For examples, see Mansfield, 'Radical Rhymes', p. 30
7 Gorman, *Banner Bright*, pp. 48–50; Mansfield, 'Radical Rhymes', p. 18.
8 Mansfield, 'Radical Rhymes', p. 30. The National Banner Survey report is available, price £10, from The People's History Museum, 103 Princess St., Manchester, M1 6DD, United Kingdom. The Survey is available on-line at <www.peopleshistorymuseum.org.uk>.
9 The United Female Friendly Society example is in the collection of the Rural History Centre, Reading, and the others are at the People's History Museum.
10 For the Plumbers emblem (in the Norfolk Museums Service collection) see Mansfield, N. (1987), 'The Norwich Plumbers Emblem', *Social History Curators Journal*, 14. The Miners emblem is in the Wigan Museums Service collection, with the Ashover banner and the ceramic collections referred to at the People's History Museum.

11   See Borsay, 'All the town's a stage'; Tressider, 'Coronation Day'; and Simpson, F.
      (1914), 'The City Gilds (sic) of Chester: The Smiths, Cutlers and Plumbers Company',
      Journal of Chester Archaeology Society, 20. The Cupar banner is in the Fife Folk
      Museum. For the town as a centre of the revolutionary United Scotsmen in which the
      trades were active, see Wells, R (1983), *Insurrection – the British Experience
      1795–1803*, Gloucester: Sutton, pp. 51, 74 and 124.
12   See *Black Dwarf*, 5 January 1819.
13   For the Carlisle banner, see Barnes, J.C.F. (1984), 'Liberty or Death', *Cumberland and
      Westmoreland Antiquarian and Archaeology Society Transactions*, LXXXIV. For the
      Skelmanthorpe example, see Lawton, F. (1926), 'Skelmanthorpe's Flag of Freedom',
      Hirst Buckley's Annual. See also Vernon, *Politics and the People*, p. 109. The
      presentation of the Trowbridge banner to Queen Caroline herself and its subsequent
      return in triumph to the town is covered in the broadside *Trowbridge Address to Her
      Majesty* in Trowbridge Museum.
14   The Goosnargh banner still hangs in the parish church near Preston. For accounts of
      tricolours, see Mansfield, 'Radical Rhymes', p. 15; for Walter Crane's banner designs see
      Gorman, *Banner Bright*, p. 89.
15   For Political Unions see LoPatin, N.D. (1999), *Political Unions, Popular Politics and
      the Great Reform Act of 1832*, Basingstoke: Macmillan. Many trades banners were also
      at the New Hall Meeting. See (1904), *A Short History of the Birmingham Branch of the
      Brushmakers*, MS in William Kiddier Collection, Working Class Movement Library,
      Salford.
16   The Rickergate banner is in the Tullie House collection and the Kirkintilloch in the East
      Dunbartonshire Museums Collection. For the Edinburgh material see Clark, H. (2001),
      Raise the Banners High – The City of Edinburgh's Banner Collection, Edinburgh: City
      of Edinburgh Museums and Galleries, pp. 57, 58, 60–4 and 77.
17   See (1925) *The Covenanting Flag of Cumnock*, published by the Baird Institute, where
      the banner is still housed.
18   For the nineteenth-century William Wallace cult, see Kidd, C. (1997), 'Sentiment, race
      and revival – Scottish identities in the aftermath of Enlightenment', in Brockliss, L. and
      Eastwood, D. (eds), *A Union of Multiple Identities*, Manchester: Manchester University
      Press; Clark, *Raise the Banners*, pp. 57, 242.
19   The two Anti-Corn Law League/Reform Bill banners are from the Scottish Lowlands,
      with an elaborate 'No Corn Law' banner at Wednesbury Museum in the Black Country.
      I am grateful for the advice of Paul Pickering about Anti-Corn Law banners. The best-
      documented radical banners used in Chartism are from Carlisle and Skelmanthorpe, see
      note 10 above p. 5.
20   See Clark, *Raise the Banners*, pp. 81–7; Mansfield, 'Radical Rhymes', pp. 19–20.
21   Mansfield, 'Radical Rhymes', p. 20.
22   Ibid., p. 11. The construction of election banners is discussed in Vernon, *Politics and the
      People*, p. 113–14.
23   Mansfield, 'Radical Rhymes', pp. 22–4. For Oak Apple Day, see Mansfield, N. (2001),
      English Farmworkers and Local Patriotism, 1900–1930, Aldershot: Ashgate, pp. 17–18.
24   The Union Jack issue is discussed at length in Mansfield, 'Radical Rhymes', pp. 7–10.
      Thompson and his critics are summarised in Tilly, C. (1995), *Popular Contention in
      Great Britain, 1758–1834*, Cambridge, MA.: Harvard University Press, Chap. 1.
25   Colley, L. (1992), *Britons. Forging the Nation, 1707–1837*, New Haven: Yale University
      Press, pp. 284–7; Emsley, C. (1979), *British Society and the French Wars, 1793–1815*,
      Basingstoke: Macmillan, pp. 169 and 176–7.
26   These summaries are from personal communications and meetings with these historians
      at various times from the autumn of 1999 to the spring of 2000.
27   The Brushmakers material, assembled by William Kiddier, is at the Working Class
      Movement Library and the Tinplate Workers collections are at The Modern Records
      Centre, Warwick University (archives) and the People's History Museum (material

culture). The tinplate collections were assembled by Ted Brake, for his history of the sheet metal workers. See Brake, T. (1985), *Men of Good Character*, London: Lawrence and Wishart.

28 Mansfield, 'Radical Rhymes', pp. 18–19. Ceramics from the People's History Museum collection displaying Union Jacks are 1995.91.4, a Peterloo Jug, and 1998.24, a Reform Union Jug. The Ewenny example is in Cytharthfa Castle Museum, Merthyr Tydfil.
29 Mansfield, 'Radical Rhymes', pp. 24–5. Letter from Linda Colley, 6 April 2000.
30 Briggs, A. (1999), *Victorian Things*, London: Penguin.
31 Carnegie, A. (1920), *Autobiography*, London: Constable, p. 8.
32 Tyrrell, A. with Ward, Y. (2000), "" God Bless Her Little Majesty." The Popularising of Monarchy in the 1840s', *National Identities,* 2 (2), July, p. 120.
33 Mansfield, 'Radical Rhymes', p. 17. For the use of Chartist material culture, see Pickering, 'Trade of Agitation', and for its use in subsequent decades see Taylor, A. (1999), 'Commemoration, Memorialisation and Political Memory in post Chartist Radicalism: The 1885 Halifax Reunion in Context', in Ashton, O., Fyson, R. and Roberts, S., *The Chartist Legacy*, Rendlesham: Merlin. The pike photograph is reproduced in Frow, E. and R. (1980), *Chartism in Manchester*, Salford: Working Class Movement Library.
34 Mansfield, 'Radical Rhymes', pp. 20–1. O'Brien's opinion is from *National Reformer*, 22 March 1847, quoted in Thompson, D. (1984), *The Chartists – Popular Politics in the Industrial Age*, London: Temple Smith, p. 129.
35 Borsay, 'All the town's a stage', p. 246; Mansfield, 'Radical Rhymes', p. 25.
36 Mansfield, 'Radical Rhymes', p. 21.
37 Brears, P. (1984), 'Temple of the Muses: The Yorkshire Philosophical Museums 1820–50', *Museums Journal*, 84 (1), p. 5.
38 Taylor, 'Commemoration'.
39 A full account of the procession, with details of the banners is in booklet published by Heywood himself. See Axon, W.E.A. (1878), *An Architectural and General Description of the Town Hall, Manchester*, Manchester: Heywood.

Chapter 5

The Chartist Rites of Passage:
Commemorating Feargus O'Connor

Paul A. Pickering

When Francis White and Company's *History, Gazetteer and Directory* of
Nottingham was published in 1864, it included a detailed description of what in
many ways had become the best-known feature of the overcrowded midlands city:
its Arboretum. Established in 1852 at a cost of £6554, the Nottingham Arboretum
was a testimony to the growth of civic pride and the mid-nineteenth-century march
of mind.[1] 'Beautifully situated on the rise of two long and somewhat irregular hills'
to the north of the city the 17-acre park provided a point of convergence for many
of the fashionable ideas of the day: from a belief in the efficacy of fresh air in
combating the deleteriousness of modern urban living to the widespread
commitment to rational recreation and the passion for natural science that made up
a considerable part of the mentality of consumers of popular education. Here was an
open air Mechanics' Institute where citizens could nurture mind and body.

By 1864, some of these lofty aspirations had already begun to seem out of touch
with working-class realities: one correspondent, for example, complained that the
populace had been using the park merely for fun in violation of its educational
goals.[2] Nevertheless, there was no disagreement about the Arboretum's abiding
beauty. Entering the park through the main gate comprising six 'massive Gothic
stone pillars' from Waverley Street at the south-west corner brought the visitor into
'the most lovely and favourable spot for such a purpose that can well be conceived'.[3]
'Proceeding a little further on the left, and ascending the hill as the path begins to
wind' were commodious refreshment rooms. Designed by the Nottingham
Corporation's own surveyor – a detail undoubtedly included because it represented
a particular source of local pride – these rooms were constructed 'in the Tudor style'
that was very fashionable in early Victorian Britain.[4] In this part of the park was also
an 'ornamental piece of water' containing two islands on which had been planted a
'large variety of trees, shrubs, evergreens, and flowers' under the supervision of
an 'eminent horticulturist'. Running through the Arboretum the principal walk was
15 feet wide with numerous branch paths – each about 10 feet wide – extending in
various directions. Along the main path rows of cedars provided a demarcation from
the clusters – scientifically determined – of a huge variety of trees, plants and shrubs
each marked with 'an imperishable porcelain label'.[5] At a time when the creation of
botanical gardens reflected deeply held religious and cultural aspirations to recreate
a garden of Eden,[6] here was a cornucopia of over a thousand species.

Numbers on the trees along the principal path indicating which member of the local Corporation had planted them provided, if obliquely, the first evidence of a political presence amid the blooms. A much more direct attempt to claim political ownership of the park was to be found on a building near the main gate known as the principal gardener's lodge. Built in the favoured 'Tudor' architectural style, the lodge doubled as a gate-keeper's house which reflected the fact that, originally, unlimited access to the Arboretum had only been permitted three days a week, with the remaining days set aside for subscribers.[7] Over its windows 'brass tablets' paid tribute to the local council and, in particular, to the committee that had overseen the enclosure of the land in 1845 and introduced this restrictive regime. By 1864, however, the brass plates had been surmounted by a new inscription: 'open free to the public daily'. This had become a people's park.

The Arboretum also contained evidence of a particular sense of nation and Empire.[8] In 1863, a tower was erected at a cost of £700 to house a 'Chinese Bell' that had been captured by the county regiment during the Canton War of 1856–58. The bell was a reminder of the patriotic fervour which had given Palmerston's government a crushing electoral victory in 1857. Around the bell tower were four cannons captured at Sebastopol in the Crimea: the spoils of one war guarding the trophy of another.[9] For all the detail of its description, however, White's *Gazetteer* omitted any reference to what was among the most prominent and undoubtedly the most controversial features of the Arboretum: the statue of Feargus O'Connor that had been erected in 1859.

The death of the man who had formerly been the most popular leader of Chartism at the end of August 1855, had briefly returned the democratic movement to the centre of national political stage. The funeral procession through the streets of London drew a crowd of mourners and onlookers estimated at not less than 50,000. 'Perhaps no ceremonial of this description', mused G.W.M Reynolds in his eponymous radical newspaper, 'saving the burial of Nelson, Queen Caroline and the Duke of Wellington – has attracted during the present century such vast crowds to witness it.'[10] Even before O'Connor's remains had been placed in the cold ground of west London there were calls for him to be honoured by the erection of a monument. On this point Reynolds undoubtedly caught the public mood: 'if ever there was a man who deserved a monument at public expense', he editorialised, 'Mr Feargus O'Connor is that man.'[11] Ignoring the forest of statues to Sir Robert Peel that had been erected in the years since his death in 1850,[12] the Tory London *Standard* was thankful that 'the national taste does not run' to 'statues and memorials to individuals ... or we should, no doubt, before this have had a statue or monument raised to Mr Feargus O'Connor.'[13] Within a month of O'Connor's death, plans had been conceived for several monuments: at the grave site in London's Kensal Green Cemetery, along a 'principal London thoroughfare', in Nottingham, in Manchester, in Scotland, and on one of the Chartist Land Company farms at O'Connorville in Hertfordshire.[14] This is a striking example of the radicalisation of what was called the 'Monument Mania' that gripped Britain in 1850.[15]

By 1860, two monuments had been erected: at the grave site in London and in the

Nottingham Arboretum. Just as Francis White and Company effectively erased the statue from the townscape of Nottingham, so too have both monuments been virtually lost to the history of Chartism. Commenced with such enthusiasm, they have all but vanished into oblivion. With an air of casual indifference, O'Connor's biographers, for example, note in their penultimate chapter that the London monument was 'probably' erected in 1857.[16] The neglect of the O'Connor monuments is symptomatic of a general lack of attention to the cultural artefacts of Britain's first predominantly working-class movement. This chapter aims to return these monuments to their rightful place in local and national history and, by treating them as 'sacro-secular political sites',[17] to highlight the value of a more sensitive approach to the study of the culture of popular radicalism. One historian has written that we 'cannot separate' a 'monument from its public life',[18] and thus our task must be to understand the O'Connor monuments in context by recapturing the different story that each had to tell. Our discussion will commence with the national monument in London before returning to the Nottingham Arboretum. Together, these stories not only shed important light on the final years of the movement – about which relatively little has been written – but also on the politics of Victorian cities, where the erection of Chartist monuments was part and parcel of the Chartists' assertion of their rights as citizens. Moreover, a comparison of the commemorations of O'Connor with previous Chartist monuments provides an important insight into popular politics during the early years of what has been called the mid-Victorian consensus.

The London monument to O'Connor was nearly a casualty of the wider malaise that affected metropolitan Chartism in the 1850s. Numerous commentators agreed that most of the problems confronting the democratic movement in this period arose from the 'destructive game' of 'follow my leader'.[19] According to W.E. Adams the divisions among the later Chartists were 'almost endless': 'at least as endless as the men who set up as leaders, for every little leader had his little following, while the bigger leaders had bigger followings. It was these divisions which robbed the movement of the power it would have otherwise have wielded.'[20]

By the time of O'Connor's death, the sharpest rivalry in the movement, both in the capital and in the nation at large, was between Ernest Jones and G.W.M. Reynolds. A barrister by training, Ernest Jones was an artist by inclination. In 1855, he was busily engaged attempting to re-establish a national democratic organisation, and in promoting his last important newspaper venture, the *People's Paper*, which was enjoying moderate success with a quarterly circulation of 43,000.[21] George Reynolds had cut his teeth as an agitator in the 1840s in the temperance movement (he also dabbled with the Anti-Corn Law League) before embarking on a successful career as a writer of popular fiction. His novels made him a 'household name' in the 1840s, long before he returned to journalism.[22] Towards the end of the decade Reynolds sought to establish a career as a radical leader, throwing his considerable energy into reviving the flagging fortunes of London Chartism and, early in the 1850s, commencing a radical journal, *Reynolds's Newspaper*, which attracted an ever-increasing audience. When Jones boasted of the circulation of the *People's Paper* in comparison with its rivals, it is notable that he did not include *Reynolds's*

News in the list. By 1855, Reynolds was selling approximately 150,000 copies of his newspaper a week.[23]

Almost inevitably, O'Connor's death and its commemoration became a pawn in this leadership struggle between Jones and Reynolds. Controversy was touched off when the *Morning Advertiser*, a moderate liberal journal, reported (undoubtedly with malicious intent) that O'Connor had been interred in a 'mean, unbricked grave, in one of the obscurest corners of the cemetery'.[24] The article provoked the undertaker, Giles Lovett,[25] himself a radical sympathiser, into a detailed defence of the arrangements he had overseen. According to Lovett, four days after O'Connor's death he had been called on for professional advice. Some members of the Working Men's Literary and Scientific Institution in Friar Street, one of the few surviving Chartist organisations in London, were also contacted, although it was unclear whether O'Connor's family or officers of the Coroner's Court had taken this action. On arriving, so Lovett told readers of the *People's Paper*, he was 'astonished to see that the great leader of the working classes was without a coffin or any preparation'. The problem, he continued, was that at the time of his death O'Connor 'did not possess a shilling'.[26] Lovett claimed that he offered to pay for the funeral himself on the understanding that a subscription would be commenced to recompense him. He also met with John Arnott, a senior member of the staff of *Reynolds's News* and a leading metropolitan radical, together with George's brother, Edward. According to Lovett, at this meeting Edward gave him a 'blank cheque' on his brother's behalf but this was later withdrawn.[27]

This revelation gave Jones an irresistible opportunity to smite his political rival, even if it required a promethean ability to uphold both sides of the argument. On the one hand, Jones was harshly critical of Reynolds's apparent *volte-face*, or perhaps rather vault farce, as evidence of insincerity and parsimony, and, with a note of indignant pomposity, he personally took charge of the debt. 'Parties desirous of seeing a suitable tribute of respect erected over the grave of O'Connor, and his funeral expenses honourably paid,' he wrote, 'can send their contributions to me, when I will undertake – 1. That the monies received shall be paid DIRECT BY ME, for the purpose subscribed. 2. That I will personally see to the erection of a suitable monument.'[28] The upshot of this was that Jones published a weekly list of subscriptions alongside, but separate from, those collected by other Chartists. On the other hand, he took a principled stand against patronage that was clearly designed to touch a deep chord among the rank and file: 'We can only say that the dignity of the Chartist body and the working classes should spurn charity for burying their champion', he contended,'Let the people bury the people's leader.'[29] For his part Reynolds had stumbled into an invidious position. When he learned that a working men's committee had been formed he had hastily withdrawn the 'blank cheque' – making a donation of £5 instead – in deference to the very principle that Jones was now using to attack him. In this way, Jones and Reynolds ensured that any monument would again raise the question that had dogged O'Connor's leadership: how was a gentleman by birth to lead a predominantly working-class movement?[30]

By October 1855, the campaign to commemorate O'Connor must have seemed hopeless. All parties agreed that there were debts of between £60 and £70 for the funeral and associated activities that had to be cleared before a monument could be contemplated, but Jones and Reynolds, and two separate commemoration committees – one headed by Jones's ally, William Jones (no relation) and the other by Reynolds himself – traded insults in the press. Reynolds's committee numbered several leading Chartists, including T.M. Wheeler, a former director of the Chartist Land Company, and W.P. Roberts, a radical lawyer who was known as the 'miners' attorney general', as well as O'Connor's nephew, Roger, among its members, but Jones was not impressed. This committee, he fumed, consisted of the 'pettiest revilers, persecutors and enemies of O'Connor',[31] while his lieutenant insisted that theirs was the only genuine committee in operation.[32] Jones also began to muse over the possibility not only of alternative sites, but also of other forms of commemoration. 'A suggestion has occurred to me', he wrote, 'whether it would be most appropriate to erect a monument at Kensall [*sic*] Green, or one at O'Connorville, the first estate of the Land Movement.'[33] One correspondent agreed. O'Connorville was O'Connor's 'first love', his 'London', wrote Henry D. Griffiths,[34] but generally the suggestion was not well received. Determined not to let the matter rest, Jones continued to canvass alternatives: 'could not a few square feet of land be purchased by the side of some leading thoroughfare in London, there to erect a suitable monument?'[35] Moreover, when one Chartist group wrote to suggest that funds be devoted to the erection of a hall, for example, Jones endorsed the idea as 'excellent'. In the end, however, the case for a monument proved compelling. 'It will be a disgrace', he warned, 'if Democracy cannot raise a statue to its hero, when the Peels, and Pitts and Wellingtons of the aristocracy have their effigies all around us.'[36] This was one of the few occasions when Jones recognised that a monument had a role to play in the 'statumania' that had become an integral part of the mainstream of British political discourse; for the most part, he appears to have regarded the contest over the provenance of the monument as part of an internal struggle to control the movement. Feargus's gaze must be to the future, but in a direction determined by Jones.

Elsewhere the effect of the rancour in the capital was equally insidious. At Bilston in Staffordshire, for example, the Chartists resolved to hold on to their subscriptions until 'one competent committee is formed.'[37] From several places came expressions of regret and reproach as well as calls for amalgamation of the two central committees which Jones 'emphatically' dismissed as an 'indecorous and disgraceful' notion.[38] Division and suspicion proved to be infectious. A meeting of delegates from various Chartist groups in South Lancashire, for example, resolved to shelve plans for their own monument in Manchester and to throw their weight behind the campaign in the capital, but, at the same time, they placed severe restrictions on the Treasurer, making it extremely difficult to comply with the resolution itself.[39]

By the end of 1855, the situation appeared to have reached its nadir when Jones began to have a change of heart. During December he quarrelled with some members of the Friar Street committee, including William Jones, who resigned as Secretary to be replaced by Edwin Harman. Jones also came into conflict with Lovett the undertaker. In both cases, he was concerned by reports that monument funds were being used for frivolous expenses such as 'taxi cabs' and 'omnibuses'. 'I do not intend any offence to the Friar-street Committee', he opined, 'there are some excellent democrats in it ... but there are also others who have not been as careful as they should have been of the administration of the sums entrusted to their care.'[40] At a time when the leisured gentleman still provided an important model for public life and 'independence' remained a powerful political virtue, there were many radicals who were quick to believe that their comrades were, to use the words of Samuel Bamford, 'guzzling, fattening and replenishing themselves, at the expense of the simple and credulous multitude'.[41] Despite the fact that the Charter called for payment of MPs as a fundamental condition of independent working-class activity, as late as 1852 the Chartists were still debating whether or not to pay their officials, with many arguing that it would be better for the movement to function without a national executive 'than have traffickers in office'.[42] Having assailed his own supporters in a way that he must have known would touch a raw nerve, Jones then issued a call for unity. 'Let me now ask you this question', he wrote, 'shall O'Connor have a monument worthy of his name? If so, then unite, subscribe, organise! ... let him not slumber unmarked and unrecorded among the proud tombs of aristocrats and usurers, without a monument!'[43] Described as the 'first great metropolitan cemetery in Britain', Kensal Green had provided a resting place for many aristocrats, including members of the royal family (two of George III's children were buried there in the 1840s), since its consecration in 1833.[44]

In the wake of Jones's call for unity, however, the situation improved quickly. By mid-February 1856, a total of £66-15-6d in debts for the funeral and associated activities had been cleared, and the two warring committees had been merged into a central body with Arnott and Wheeler acting as joint Secretaries. Despite having burned his fingers at the outset, Reynolds was happy to let amalgamation occur: indeed, he retained the chairmanship of the united committee (a fact that Jones managed to avoid mentioning, either then or subsequently, in the columns of the *People's Paper*).[45] Within months, firm plans for a monument at Kensal Green were announced. A design had been submitted by W.H. Lovett junior of Roxburgh Terrace, Notting Hill.[46] This was 'highly approved of' by the Central Committee and Jones concurred, declaring it to be 'most appropriate, chaste and elegant'. According to Arnott, the Committee was determined that O'Connor's monument would be 'most splendid'. '[V]ery few' of the monuments in the cemetery, he boasted, would 'equal' it; none would 'surpass' it.[47]

At this stage the committee estimated that the proposed monument, comprising approximately 14 tons (14.2 tonnes) of 'good Sicilian marble', together with the extra land and associated work, would cost about £200. Consequently, a new program of fundraising was commenced. Despite the prevailing atmosphere of division and decline, these activities are a testimony to the tenacity of late Chartist culture. The campaign included a door-to-door appeal – at which the Chartists were so adept – undertaken by a small army of canvassers, as well as through subscription boxes located at a range of radical haunts, such as bookshops, newsagents, pubs and clubs. The published subscription lists show that the Chartists were active in most parts of the metropolis from Bermondsey to Bethnal Green, from Chiswick to

Chelsea, from Poplar to Pimlico, and from Shoreditch to St John's Wood. In Marylebone funds were raised at the Cork Tavern; in Bethnal Green it was at the Whittington and Cat, the Suffolk Arms and among workers at Sun Brewery.[48] Like most Chartist activities, both in the capital and in the national at large, the lists show that the cause was supported by a range of people: the anonymous as well as the famous, the rich as well as the poor, women as well as men, and the young as well as the old. Scattered through the list, for example, were some household names belonging to hardened veterans such as Philip McGrath, George Julian Harney and S.M. Kydd, as well as those known only by a pseudonym or abbreviation such as 'A republican', 'C.D., Old Street' and an 'Old Guard'. G.J. Holyoake's subscription list included Mrs A. Holyoake (presumably a relative); another list identifies Mary Ann Heath as both contributor and collector. The lists contain numerous groups of labourers and tradesmen as well as supporters of radicalism from the business world such as Joseph Cowen junior and Robert Le Blond.[49] One of the many elderly contributors was Richard Moore, a veteran of post-war radicalism in London; one of the youngest was Louisa Feargus O'Connor Boucher, bearer of another Chartist rite of passage, the practice of naming children after popular radical leaders.[50] On the whole, however, it is clear that the typical subscription was small, coming from a pocket that was not deep. From Wakefield, a 'poor, divided' town in the West Riding of Yorkshire, for example, the total contribution of £10 to the monument came from 361 subscribers (an average of just over 6d each).[51]

A systematic examination of the subscription lists also provides a valuable index of late Chartist activity across the nation. Several conclusions can be drawn. First, from a negative point of view, the lists highlight the relative weakness of later Chartism on the Celtic fringe. Over the twenty months during which subscriptions were collected, there were contributions from less than two dozen places in Wales, Ireland and Scotland (approximately 6 per cent of the total). The handful of subscriptions from Wales came, not surprisingly, from the industrial valleys of Monmouthshire and towns in Mid-Wales where a rich tradition of religious dissent and a bitter campaign against the implementation of the New Poor Law Amendment Act of 1834 had provided fertile ground for early Chartism.[52] According to David Williams, the Chartist movement was, by contrast, feeble in Wales during the 1840s – O'Connor's Land Plan excited little or no interest there – and ended in defeat in 1848.[53] This conclusion is supported by the evidence examined here.

O'Connor had devoted relatively little effort to promoting the cause in Wales, but the same is not true of Ireland. Despite the fact that Daniel O'Connell was nominally one of the authors of the People's Charter, his relationship with the Whig government and his support for some of its unpopular policies, as well as his long-standing feud with O'Connor, had soured Chartist relations with a significant section of the immigrant Irish in many British cities and drastically restricted the progress of the movement in Ireland. Nevertheless, O'Connor had headed successive attempts to set Chartism on foot in his native land, the most sustained (and successful) of which had taken place in 1849–50 when he had helped to promote the establishment of the Irish Democratic Association. Based in Dublin, the Association also had 'branches' in Cork, Limerick, Kilkenny, Drogheda, Dundalk, Carlow and

Belfast.[54] After just four months' operation, boasted the editor of the Association's newspaper, the *Irishman*, an 'army of Democrats' had been recruited that had assured the Democratic Association 'a broad and recognised existence in the hearts and history of this country'.[55] Even allowing for a degree of understandable exaggeration, it is surprising that there was no echo of this organisation during the campaign to commemorate its patron a few years later.[56]

More still might have been expected from Scotland. Shortly after O'Connor's death some Chartists at Edinburgh had formed a committee with a view to erecting a monument to his memory in Scotland. Regretting that 'that great and good man' had 'found a resting place in a pauper's grave' (a reference to O'Connor's penury rather than Kensal Green), the committee believed that a monument is 'all we can offer in return for a life sacrificed in our cause'.[57] They had every reason to be confident of success. According to the foremost historian of Scottish Chartism, Alexander Wilson, one of the 'most remarkable' features of late Chartism in Scotland 'was the confidence and warm affection with which Feargus O'Connor continued to be regarded by his large following'.[58] Moreover, in 1850, the Ayrshire Chartists had successfully raised a monument in Ayr to Dr John Taylor, a local veteran of the French revolution of 1830 and a militant leader of the Scottish Chartists who had died in 1842.[59] Nevertheless, the Edinburgh appeal to 'every city, town, village, and workshop, every family, and every individual member of a family' excited no response, and Edinburgh itself failed to contribute to the national monument in London.

It is not surprising that the majority of the Scottish contributions that did come in emanated from the west of the country. Glasgow and Paisley had been key centres for Chartist activity in the west of Scotland from the inception of the movement – in 1839, the two cities had together contributed nearly 100,000 signatures to the first National Petition. Unlike in other parts of Scotland, Chartists in these places remained loyal to O'Connor. Three years later, for example, when the second National Petition was opposed by many Scottish Chartists, partly because of O'Connor's role in introducing repeal of the Irish Union into its demands, Glasgow and Lanarkshire provided a notable exception, contributing 78,062 signatures. Glasgow was the first Scottish 'locality' to embrace O'Connor's Land Plan and both places were active in 1848.[60] Glasgow and Paisley were also at the forefront of efforts north of the border to promote political reform in the 1860s. For example, both places were represented at National Reform Conference in London in May 1865, over a year before the formation of the Scottish National Reform League.[61] In this way the O'Connor subscription lists provide a glimpse into the future by emphasising the link between late Chartism and subsequent campaigns for political reform. By contrast, the subscriptions to the monument from Port Glasgow were accompanied by a note pointing out that the town had never before had a Chartist organisation,[62] but, as will be seen, this was the exception rather than the rule.

At first glance, the subscription lists for England suggest that the movement continued to enjoy a national presence – from Walsoken in Norfolk and Banbury in Oxfordshire to Torquay in Devon and Bristol in Gloucestershire – but this is misleading. The first point that must be made is that, as with Scotland, the localities where funds were raised had, almost without exception, been the sites of earlier Chartist activity, in most cases stretching right back to the early years of the movement.[63] Chartism had shrunk back to a hard core. Moreover, nearly 70 per cent of contributions came from three English regions: London, the industrial north (Lancashire, Cheshire and Yorkshire), and the North East. Again, as with the Scottish contributions, this pattern allows the historian to look into the future. In contrast to earlier periods of relative weakness, historians have identified London as an important radical centre during the 1860s.[64] Similarly, on Tyneside the Northern Reform Union (formed in 1857) and, subsequently, the Northern Reform League, advocated a program of militant democracy which ensured that, in the words of George Julian Harney, 'Chartist principles did not die with the organisation.'[65] By contrast, historians have emphasised the absorption of Lancashire Chartism into advanced liberalism.[66] The commemoration of Feargus O'Connor suggests that well into the 1850s independent radicalism had not disappeared from the political landscape of the industrial North.

Given that the monument was to be located in London, it is not surprising that the largest number of contributions was raised in the capital, but even in a period of decline the needs of a national movement were never lost sight of. An important element of the national campaign was an engraving of Lovett's design for the monument which was sold to Chartists for 6d (7d with post). As well as raising much-needed funds, this engraving served as a link throughout the movement. 'Every Democrat ought to be possessed of a copy of the engraving', recommended Ernest Jones, and soon 'many' orders for the engraving had been received from around the country.[67] From Coventry, the local Chartist secretary, Thomas Pickard, explained the importance of the lithograph at a time when, despite the rapid spread of inexpensive railway travel, many provincial Chartists were unlikely to visit the capital: 'We want the plate sent by return of post if possible, so that we may show what is really being done in London in respect to the monument.'[68]

The use of an engraving as a surrogate for the experience of seeing the monument itself is also significant from a methodological point of view as it provides an important insight into the way the Chartists themselves regarded monuments. Historians of radicalism have been long been aware of the importance of the visual element in print culture that developed through the eighteenth and into the nineteenth century. Chartism came on the heels of the golden age of 'radical squibs' when the public display – in a shop window – of a new satirical cartoon could draw a crowd of spectators.[69] Some Chartists were veterans of this culture of radicalism, and others were its heirs. Studies of the tremendous impact of the leading Chartist newspaper, the *Northern Star*, for example, have pointed to the importance of the prints that were given away with the paper at regular intervals beginning in January 1838.[70] According to the *Star*'s own estimation, the 'Portrait Gallery of the People's Friends' excited tremendous interest and boosted sales, although the editor received as many brickbats as bouquets over the selection of subjects, and the quality and timeliness of the prints.[71]

The level of passion was an index of importance. Like personal adornments –

Chartist hats, scarves, medals and ribbons – portraits were used as a form of social or cultural shorthand to display allegiance at the individual or family level and to demarcate limited personal space.[72] William Farish, for example, remembered that the houses of ardent politicians in his native Carlisle 'honoured many of their champions by making their portraits do duty as ornaments above the doors'.[73] Similarly, in his grandmother's cottage in Cheltenham the young W.E. Adams fondly remembered seeing a china statuette of George Washington and a portrait of John Frost, the leader of the Newport Chartists who was tried for treason in the winter of 1839.[74] Secondly, the portraits acted as marks of differentiation or expressions of group solidarity in the public sphere. Accounts of Chartist meetings often recorded how portraits were employed as decorations – a broader, albeit temporary, means of contesting public space.[75] Although equally provisional, Chartist banners and emblematic flags were also employed as decorations for local association rooms and meeting halls.[76] During parades they acted almost as moveable monuments, serving to catch the eye of a journalist, to impress other groups or their opponents, to advertise a local presence, or as a public expression of a collective identity. Typically, newspaper reports referred to 'district associations' 'preceded by bands of music, [and] flags, explanatory of their name, locality and objects'.[77] After the parade, flags and banners were often arrayed around the perimeter of the meeting again serving as a temporary demarcation of the radical ground. Monuments of stone made a bolder and more permanent claim on public space, but the cultural vocabulary was the same: tacking up a 7d engraving of O'Connor's monument over a hearth on Tyneside was, in important respects, the same as putting up the monument itself in Kensal Green. Both served as what sociologists have called 'mnemotechnic aids':[78] according to the central committee the monument would stand as a reminder of O'Connor's 'distinguished eminence in the political service of the people'.[79] Importantly, moreover, each was also a declaration of faith in a better future.

Sales of the engraving boosted the coffers of the metropolitan committee. By September 1856, the campaign had sufficient momentum for Jones to feel confident enough to hand over the money that had been sent to him creating, for the first time, a unitary fund.[80] At the eleventh hour, however, dissension returned. Many readers of the *People's Paper* of Saturday, 11 April 1857 would have been bemused to learn that the O'Connor Monument had been erected on Kensal Green 'in a private surreptitious sort of way, the Monument Committee not even knowing anything about it'. Jones did not try to hide his outrage: 'By this secret proceeding a public ovation to Feargus O'Connor has been scandalously burked.'[81] Contrary to Jones's claim, however, at least some members of the Central Committee were certainly aware of what had occurred, but they offered no explanation of their conduct. The directors of the cemetery may have interceded to prevent a public unveiling, but the very fact that such an intervention was not reported in the radical press makes it unlikely.[82] It is more likely that some committee members deemed the implied internal victory of a calculated act of proprietorship to be more important than a symbolic public display of Chartist power. In this way the monument fulfilled its worst potential; standing as a symbol of disunity that made it clear to anyone who cared to look that by 1857 Chartism had become a movement that had turned in on itself.

Moreover, the unseemly dispute over the clandestine erection of the monument encouraged further recrimination. According to some correspondents, the completed monument was unworthy of O'Connor. Joseph Pacey, a mason from Paddington, for example, suggested that 'the design is completely spoilt by the execution of the Portland stone': 'It is a disgrace to the position it stands in, and to those who executed it.'[83] Others complained, tellingly, that the monument was nothing like the engraving that had been widely circulated, threatening to break the symbolic link that allowed far-flung comrades to participate in the London experience. As no copy of the engraving is extant, this question is impossible to resolve. The monument – as it is today – was both smaller and less expensive than had been envisaged. (See Plate 5.1.) Nevertheless, at over twenty feet in height and weighing more than seven tons (7.1 tonnes) it was an imposing structure.[84] Built from Yorkshire and Portland stone with a marble front panel (costing in total £140), the monument comprises a hexagonal spire in the 'pointed gothic' style that had become *de rigueur* in mid-Victorian funerary architecture, surmounted by a 'gilded star', and standing on a hexagonal base.[85]

On the base is carved the O'Connor family coat of arms together with their motto, 'Fair and Easy goes Far'.[86] On the front panel of the spire are the dates of O'Connor's birth and death which, together with a record of his parliamentary service, form part of a lengthy inscription:[87]

TO THE MEMORY OF
FEARGUS O'CONNOR ...
WHOSE PUBLIC FUNERAL WAS DEFRAYED,
AND THIS MONUMENT ERECTED, BY
A SUBSCRIPTION CHIEFLY FROM
THE WORKING CLASSES.

—

READER, PAUSE!
THOU TREADEST ON THE GRAVE OF A
PATRIOT. WHILE PHILANTHROPY IS A
VIRTUE, AND PATRIOTISM NOT
A CRIME, WILL THE
NAME OF
O'CONNOR
BE ADMIRED, AND THIS MONUMENT RESPECTED.

The inscription is worth lingering over. First, it highlights the ambiguity at the heart of O'Connor's Chartist career and the unresolved questions that emanated from the mixed social composition of the movement. Note the uneasy juxtaposition of O'Connor's aristocratic background – the family crest and motto – and the celebration of his philanthropy, a traditional attribute of a 'gentleman leader', with the pointed reference to the independence of those working people who 'chiefly' paid for his funeral and his monument. Was this a monument to the leader or the led? At the same time, the monument underscores Chartism's unambiguous claim to represent a purer form of patriotism which, in turn, emphasises the constitutional nature of their challenge. Monument making was not the act of revolutionaries, especially those who saw themselves as patriots.

Fig. 5.1   Monument to Feargus O'Connor, Kensal Green Cemetery, London.

This panel was the only aspect of the O'Connor monument that escaped controversy and the reason is not difficult to find. Both by procedure and content the inscription was a testimony to one of Chartism's most important achievements: practical democracy. Historians have noted the Chartists' ingenuity in giving practical application to their principles both within their organisational structures and in their performance as elected public officials.[88] Although he did not invent the practice, O'Connor provided the best-known example of how to effect a practical implementation of Chartism by giving his Nottingham constituents – not merely the electors – the opportunity to vote on his conduct as their MP (and offering to resign his seat in the House of Commons if a majority disapproved) on an annual basis. Here were universal suffrage and annual parliaments despite the indifference and hostility of the political elite. So famous was O'Connor's annual gesture that it attracted comment and imitation at the far end of the British world in New South Wales.[89] The inscription on the O'Connor Monument provided another example of practical democracy. When, as early as 1838, the *Northern Star* received numerous complaints about the selection of individuals being honoured in the 'Gallery of People's Friends', the editor, William Hill, invited readers 'in future to meet and select a perfect man, and they shall have him'.[90] Although Hill had his tongue in his cheek, it was a suggestion that was later embraced by the Central Monument Committee. In March 1856, one of the first acts of the unified committee was to call on 'friends and admirers of Mr O'Connor to forward their ideas as to what shall be the inscription on the monument'.[91] Like the 7d engraving, this inclusive process offered all Chartists a sense of ownership over the monument.

The invitation, however, was not open-ended. Although Kensal Green was explicitly modelled on the Père Lachaise in Paris where the public 'was at liberty to erect whatever sort of monuments they wished', the directors of the cemetery, so the monument committee advised the Chartist public, would not allow 'extreme political matter'.[92] They were not being overly cautious: the London Chartists already knew exactly how far they could go. When Joseph Williams, Alexander Sharpe and Henry Hanshard died in custody in 1849, their comrades in several London localities determined to commemorate them by erecting a monument at their collective grave site in Victoria Park Cemetery, in Bethnal Green. The campaign to commemorate the 'London martyrs', as they were known, bore many similarities to the later O'Connor commemoration: it produced its own engraving, the Portland stone tribute was manufactured by the same mason, and its promoters conducted a similar consultative process to determine an appropriate inscription.[93] The Committee's subsequent decision to inscribe 'Victims of the Whigs' on the 9-ft monument led to an angry stand-off with the private cemetery company that controlled Victoria Park until 1853. Not only did the company directors refuse to allow the monument to be erected with this inscription, but they exacerbated the dispute by billing the Chartists for damage caused by the crowds of up to 30,000 mourners who had attended the public funerals.

The commemoration remained unresolved for 16 months until February 1851 when the monument was erected bearing the names of the deceased and no inscription, but on each of the corners was a 'bundle of sticks' – a Roman *fasces* –

'emblematical of union' and, pre-eminently, the monument was surmounted by a Cap of Liberty.[94] As James Epstein has shown, the 'visual etymology' of Cap of Liberty (also known as the Phrygian Cap or *bonnet rouge*) was 'complex', with many historical resonances, Classical and English as well as French, and the Chartists themselves felt that it spoke for Sharpe, Williams and Hanshard with a 'mute eloquence',[95] but the subtlety was entirely lost on at least some of the cause's many enemies. Within a few months of its erection the memorial was seriously vandalised and the Cap entirely removed.[96] The 'desecration' of the monument quickly became front-page news in the democratic press. The nature of the Chartists' response is significant here: not only did they seek to bring the pressure of public opinion to bear on the directors of the cemetery company and the police for failing to protect the 'people's property', but they also engaged a lawyer to seek recourse through the courts.[97] Had not they paid for flowers trampled by 30,000 mourners, reasoned one Chartist; 'on the same principle the Directors should pay for the damage done to property entrusted to their keeping.'[98] Unfortunately, as the records of the cemetery company are no longer extant,[99] it is unclear whether the directors responded to public pressure or the threat of legal action, but by July 1851 they agreed to pay to restore the monument and replace the Cap of Liberty that they had found so distasteful.[100] Ironically, by asserting their rights as citizens in a legalistic way, the London Chartists were emphasising the limits of their challenge. For all that these Chartist monuments vigorously contested public space and the laws governing it, the language they used was invariably constitutional. Although they taunted and threatened the existing political elite, in Geertz's terms their monuments were ultimately symbols of the 'inherent sacredness of central authority'.[101]

Asserting the rights of citizenship was at the heart of the most successful campaign to commemorate Feargus O'Connor in Nottingham. The Nottingham region had a well-established reputation for radicalism – one in four of the total population signed the 1839 Chartist petition, a higher percentage than Newcastle, Manchester, or London.[102] The local Chartists remained active during the 1840s, and, in 1847, they captured the national headlines when they successfully campaigned to have O'Connor elected as one of their MPs.[103] Nottingham Chartism remained vigorous into the 1850s, including a strong contribution to the national campaign to commemorate O'Connor in London. The latter achievement is all the more impressive given that during the same period they were also continuously fundraising to erect their own monument to their former MP.[104]

The Nottingham Monument Committee was formed in September 1855 and during the next two months a pattern of meeting every Sunday evening was established that would be sustained over the next four years.[105] The leading members of the committee were William Welbond, its secretary, and William Vardy, its chairman, who was the publican of the Wellington Inn where the committee held its weekly meetings. At this time, Ernest Jones, who was undoubtedly already musing over the possibility of contesting the borough in an attempt to replicate O'Connor's success, visited the town and praised the determination of the local Chartists to raise a 'splendid' monument that would 'show the people's gratitude' to 'their great champion'.[106] The campaign in Nottingham was boosted by the efforts of the

Chartists in nearby Sutton-in-Ashfield. What these comrades lacked in numbers – the town took only twelve Chartist membership cards in 1856 compared with three hundred in 1842[107] – they made up for in enthusiasm. The town was divided into districts with two persons assigned to each, and over Christmas the entire population of over six thousand was canvassed.[108]

By May 1856, the Nottingham Committee had raised £20 which they regarded as a 'most cheering' outcome.[109] In July, Jones contested a by-election in Nottingham caused by the resignation of one of the local MPs, and Vardy was drafted in to head his campaign committee.[110] The following month a further £20 was raised by a theatre night at the Theatre Royal. The success of this event bore testimony to ongoing community support for Chartism as the various performers donated their time.[111] On the night the 'house was crammed to suffocation in all parts, and hundreds who presented themselves for admission' had to be turned away; those fortunate enough to gain entry were treated to performances of two relatively recent plays, Bulwer Lytton's *Eugene Aram* and Douglas Jerrold's *The Rent Day* (which gave 'particular satisfaction'), as well as several 'excellent pieces of music and recitations'.[112] The monument was the product of a cultural system.

Jones again unsuccessfully contested the borough at the general election in March 1857, which put further strain on local resources, and, by August 1857, the coffers of the monument appeal stood at only £41. At this stage the Committee was aware that its monument would cost at least £100, but they were undeterred. In September 1857 another theatre night raised a further £24,[113] and the committee began to consider the final form and location of the monument. During 1858, the committee engaged J.B. Robinson of Derby to execute a life-size statue of O'Connor to stand on a pedestal of approximately eight feet. The monument, as it stands today, is thus about 14 feet high and depicts Feargus, his dress formal, including a full-length flowing cape, in the act of giving a speech. O'Connor's right foot is forward, his left hand on his breast inserted Napoleon-like in his jacket, and his right hand clutching a roll of papers – the People's Charter. This was O'Connor as he appeared for most of his public life: the gentleman leader. Recording his first impression of O'Connor in 1836, a Barnsley radical described his appearance as 'decidedly aristocratic. He wore a blue frock coat and a buff waist coat and had rings on the fingers of each hand.'[114] The inscription is uncontroversial, although as with the London monument, it is as much about the led as the leader:

FEARGUS O'CONNOR ESQ MP
THIS STATUE WAS ERECTED BY HIS ADMIRERS
1859

Later the Committee estimated, with understandable exaggeration, that their campaign had benefited from the support of 'thousands of subscribers' over the years.[115] One member went further: the subscriptions had come from 'the working classes who could only give their pence'.[116] The message was clear: O'Connor's 'admirers' were working people.

Nor did the inscription need to court controversy: the location of the statue in the Arboretum was controversial enough. To understand why the Chartists selected this as the home for their statue (and why it was a contentious choice), we must return to the Arboretum to linger over the brass plates on the gatehouse. As indicated at the outset, the intention of the park's founders was to restrict the entry of the general public to three days a week with the other days set aside for the exclusive use of 'subscribers'. An unexceptional practice followed in many places, this decision touched a raw nerve in Nottingham. The historical context was crucial. When Daniel Defoe visited the town in the 1720s he was struck by the 'excellent ALE' and the beauty of the surrounding countryside.[117] Surrounding the town, the lands that caught Defoe's eye were private estates and common lands endowed with rights stemming back before the Norman Conquest. By the 1840s, Nottingham was affected by severe overcrowding due to the fact that there was no room for expansion. Enclosure was no easy solution. The attachment of the local populace to the common lands was emotional rather than practical: it was estimated in 1843 that less than two hundred burgesses actually took advantage of the right to graze animals there twice a year.[118] Nevertheless, the creation of the Arboretum (and other public open space) was, in part, an attempt to mollify the widespread opposition to enclosure that drew on powerful notions of traditional rights. By implementing a policy of restricted entry to the Arboretum the Council, therefore, seemed to be giving with one hand and taking with the other.

Although White's *Gazetteer* did not make it clear, during the decade following the opening of the park the Whig council's vision had been systematically subverted. According to one historian, 'constant pressure' from the people led to the abandonment of restricted entry after five years in 1857.[119] The seemingly innocuous inscription – 'open free to the public daily' – was thus the legacy of a bitter struggle for equal access for all citizens that bore eloquent testimony to the increasing democratisation of public space in Victorian Britain. The O'Connor Monument was the next, and in many ways, the final, episode in this struggle. Shortly after the triumph in the matter of restricted entry, the Chartists approached the Council with a request for a site for their monument in the Arboretum. During the 1840s, the Whig control of local politics (parliamentary and municipal) had been severely challenged by the Tories and by the Chartists themselves, culminating in the stunning defeat of both sitting Whig MPs (including a Cabinet Minister, John Cam Hobhouse) in 1847 by O'Connor and a prominent Tory, John Walter.[120] O'Connor's foremost local supporter and the leading 'Chartist' on Council was James Sweet, a sometime hairdresser, newsagent and toy seller in Goose Gate. A veteran of early Chartism, Sweet was first elected to the local council in 1854 as an 'ultra-Liberal', and he remained active in local politics until the 1870s.[121]

In February 1859, Nottingham Council was finally called on to approve a site in the Arboretum. The discussion lasted less than half an hour and only two of those present voted against it. How had it happened? There is no detailed record of the debate, but one particularly vitriolic critic, Giles Overreach, was in no doubt about what had taken place: both 'liberals and conservatives' had become caught up in a simple contest for 'mob popularity'.[122] Historians have estimated that in 1865 as much as 39 per cent of the Nottingham electorate was 'working class' in social composition (much higher than Birmingham, Leeds, Manchester or Newcastle).[123]

Thus it is possible that the spectre of democratic accountability – combined with the lingering memory of O'Connor's victory in 1847 – had a persuasive impact on the Council. The Chartists had put a good case based on their putative political power; as one later wrote: 'the Arboretum is the property of the people ... the admirers of O'Connor are largely in the majority, therefore they have a right to erect a monument in their own grounds ... '.[124]

The brevity of the initial Council debate, however, was not an indication of unanimity. The decision was bitterly opposed by what was later called a 'formidable phalanx' comprising 26 clergymen and magistrates, 62 professional men, 201 merchants and manufacturers, 553 shopkeepers and 13 members of the 50-strong Council.[125] In his public letter Overreach made two points which illustrate how much monuments had become part of the *lingua franca* of politics. First, he argued that the statue would convey the wrong impression. 'What would a stranger think and say on seeing such a statue in a public pleasure ground?', he asked, '"Nottingham is proud of Feargus O'Connor", would be his reflection. So much for Nottingham!' Secondly, Overreach believed that it would devalue other memorials: 'If statues are raised to the Feargus O'Connors of England', he argued, 'what "honour" does a similar tribute confer on a Pitt, a Wellington, or a Newton?'[126] After suggesting that the 'mobocracy' find 'some secluded spot trod only by themselves' for their statue, Overreach ended his diatribe with an ominous warning: 'Many thousands of the inhabitants of Nottingham are so averse to the scheme, that I would not insure the entirety of the statue for twelve hours after its erection ... '.[127] The threat drew an immediate response. 'How does he know that the monument will stand a good chance of being destroyed in a short time,' responded one Chartist in a series of rhetorical questions that grew increasingly shrill: 'Does he and the clique to whom he belonged intend to hire some ruffian or other for that purpose? ... Does he not know that the Arboretum belongs to the people, and that they have a full right to place any statue or other work of art, not offensive to public morals, in any part thereof, without asking the permission of any clique whatever?'[128]

The monument was unveiled without incident on 22 August 1859 before a crowd of about five hundred. The ceremony was deliberately understated, the Council insisting, perhaps as a belated gesture to the opposition, that no political speeches were given.[129] It was the calm before the storm. Within a few days, the statue had been seriously defaced with printer's ink. Not unexpectedly some emotions ran high. The editor of the radical-liberal *Nottingham Telegraph*, for example, condemned the 'dastardly outrage' as an insult to the dead and to 'the whole body of working men who subscribed to the fund', suggesting that 'some strong arm', possessing a whip, be delegated to 'to cut the meaning of the O'Connor statue into the hide' of the perpetrator.[130] By contrast, the response of the monument committee was measured, taking the legal and moral high ground, as well as the opportunity to restore the statue quickly with the aid of about £50 in new donations.[131] At the opening of the park seven years earlier, the Mayor had suggested the only political presence that was worth invoking was Robin Hood, and that, had he been alive, he would undoubtedly be a supporter of the Constitution.[132] By the end of the decade, not only had the gates of the 'people's park' been thrown open, but the right of equal access to public space was now watched over by the statue of the man who had helped to set 'the people' on the road to democracy.

For all their differences the two monuments to Feargus O'Connor both looked forward: the London monument was part of the struggle for control of the movement; the Nottingham statue was part of the contest for equal access to public space in the mid-Victorian city. As such, they were markedly different from the best known of the previous Chartist efforts at commemoration: the monument to 'Orator' Henry Hunt, the leader of the post-war radicals, that was erected in Manchester during the early 1840s. The tremendous significance of this memorial in the Chartist mentality had been evident in April 1841 when the laying of the foundation stone was celebrated in grand style. On this occasion, thousands of spectators had crowded Every Street in the heart of the working-class suburb of Ancoats, to catch a glimpse of O'Connor, the man reputed to be 'Hunt's Successor', as he performed the 'sacred duty' of placing a collection of memorials in the lead-lined time capsule on which the monument was subsequently built. Throughout this ritual, a sense of continuity between Chartism and the struggles of Hunt's generation was repeatedly emphasised: from the selection of memorials which included an account of Peterloo, a copy of Hunt's memoirs and a likeness of O'Connor, to the presence of several witnesses to the 'never-to-be forgotten' massacre in 1819 who provided a flesh-and-blood link between the struggles of past and present.[133] This monument was about ownership of the past.

Historians have recognised the pervasive Chartist interest in history, and in depicting their struggle as part of a universal tradition that embraced 'the illustrious dead of every nation who, by their actions or their writings, have contributed to the cause of freedom',[134] but for popular radicals the Hunt monument represented an important new departure. As noted in a previous chapter, radical calls for monuments to Tom Paine, Queen Caroline and Major Cartwright in the 1820s, had either fallen on deaf ears or, in the case of the venerable Major, been usurped by Whigs and moderate reformers, including some of Cartwright's political enemies.[135] In March 1835, shortly after Hunt's death, a meeting of the 'Radical Reformers of Manchester' decided to erect a monument to his memory.[136] This committee, which saw its work to completion in the Chartist years, was made up principally of working men and included no Whigs or moderate reformers. The memory of Orator Hunt was not negotiable.

On the one hand, this highlights the point that is often made by historians about the transformation of popular politics from the post-war years – a time when 'gentlemen' (Cartwright, Cobbett and Hunt) had led the people in a movement founded on the critique of 'Old Corruption' – to the development of an exclusively working-class radicalism during the 1830s.[137] By the time of O'Connor's death, the Chartists were less concerned about securing their place in history than they were with the struggles of the future. The O'Connor monuments are a record of the Chartists' determination to assert their rights as citizens that reflected an even sharper sense of self-awareness and independence. In this way they tell us more about the led than the leader. The opponents of the Chartists recognised this, but if politically charged monuments could not be prevented or destroyed what was to be done with them? One commentator wrote to the *Nottingham Telegraph* to dispute working-class ownership of O'Connor's legacy: not only workers, but also 'several manufacturers and tradesmen' had contributed to the construction of the monument he insisted.[138] The point was not taken up: there was no room in the mid-Victorian consensus for Feargus O'Connor. As it transpired, the most effective response to the O'Connor monuments was simply to ignore them. The failure of White to admit O'Connor to his gazetteer set a pattern that has prevailed until very recently.[139] The monument did remain a 'sacro-secular' site for ageing activists such as old Ben Wilson of Halifax who took a day trip to Nottingham in the summer of 1883 to finally see the monument with his own eyes,[140] but this was the exception rather than the rule. In the 1980s, it seemed that O'Connor might benefit from the boom in the British 'memory industry', and, in particular, from the growing interest in 'labour heritage' that seemed apposite during the harsh reality of Thatcherism.[141] '[S]triving for democracy', wrote the then leader of the Labour Party, Neil Kinnock, at the height of the Thatcher years, 'was not long ago and far away.'[142] After years of neglect, a tourist guide published by the Nottingham council in 1983 noted that the Arboretum contained a statue of 'Feargus O'Conner [*sic*] ... a leader of the radical Chartist movement'.[143] O'Connor's rehabilitation did not last long: the reference to the statue was deleted from the next edition published in 1986.[144] A recent visit by the present author to the sadly neglected grave of O'Connor in Kensal Green reinforced what seemed to be the inescapable conclusion: monuments have done little to give this champion of the people a secure place in public memory.

Notes

1 F. White & Co. (1864), *Nottinghamshire. History, Gazetteer, and Directory of the County and of the Town of Nottingham*, Sheffield: Samuel Harrison, pp. 167–8. The present description has been embellished with detail from *Nottingham Review*'s report of the opening. See 14 May 1852. See also Beckett, J. (ed.) (1997), *A Centenary History of Nottingham*, Manchester: Manchester University Press, p. 404.

2 Cited in Beckett, *History*, p. 404.

3 White, *Nottinghamshire*, p. 167.

4 See Pickering, P.A. and Tyrrell, A. (2000), *The People's Bread: A History of the Anti-Corn Law League*, London: Leicester University Press, p. 204.

5 *Nottingham Review*, 14 May 1852.

6 See Prest, J. (1981), *The Garden of Eden: The Botanic Garden and the Recreation of Paradise*, New Haven, CT: Yale University Press; McCracken, D.P. (1997), *Gardens of Empire: Botanical Institutions of the Victorian British Empire*, London: Leicester University Press, Chap. 1. I am grateful to Helen Tiffin for bringing these references to my attention.

7 *Nottingham Review*, 14 May 1852; Beckett, *History*, p. 404.

8 William Cobbett admired 'fair Nottingham with its public-spirited people, willing to carry on the noble struggle'. Cited in Thomis, M. (1968), *Old Nottingham*, New York: Augustus M. Kelley, p. 22. See also Wyncoll, P. (1966), *Nottingham Chartism*, Nottingham: Butler & Co.; Chambers, J.D. (1959), 'Victorian Nottingham', *Transactions of the Thoroton Society of Nottinghamshire*, LXII, p. 6.

9 White, *Nottinghamshire*, p. 167. See also Conway, H. (1991), *Peoples' Parks: The Design and Development of Victorian Parks in Britain*, Cambridge: Cambridge University Press,

pp. 159–60. According to Conway, the bell was captured by the Nottingham regiment in 1857.

10 *Reynolds's Newspaper*, 16 September 1855. See also Tinsley, W. (1900), *Random Recollections of An Old Publisher*, London: Simpkin, Marshall, Hamilton, Kent & Co., vol. 1, p. 45.

11 *Reynolds's Newspaper*, 9 September 1855.

12 See Read, D. (1987), *Peel and the Victorians*, London: Basil Blackwell, pp. 287–312. Read identifies 'Alfred' (Samuel Kydd) as one of the leading promoters of the Peel monuments, although he incorrectly suggests that Kydd, a tailor, was a barrister.

13 *Standard*, 1 September 1855.

14 See *Reynolds's Newspaper*, 9 September 1855; *People's Paper*, 29 September 1855; 13 October 1855.

15 See *The Times*, 12 August 1850. I am grateful to Alex Tyrrell for this reference.

16 Read, D. and Glasgow, E. (1961), *Feargus O'Connor: Irishman and Chartist*, London: Edward Arnold, p. 144.

17 Lacquer, T. (2001), 'In and Out of the Panthéon', *London Review of Books*, 20 September, p. 6. Two important, but little-known exceptions, among the historians of British radicalism are Salveson, P. (1987), *The People's Monuments: A Guide to Sites and Memorials in North West England*, Manchester: Workers' Educational Association; Kahan, A. and Bowyer, H. (1993), 'The Ernest Jones Memorial', *Working Class Movement Library Bulletin*, 3, pp. 28–36. I am grateful to Owen Ashton for this reference.

18 James Young cited in Dabakis, M. (1999), *Visualising Labor in American Sculpture: Monuments, Manliness, and the Work Ethic, 1880–1935*, Cambridge: Cambridge University Press, p. 5.

19 *Star of Freedom*, 20 November 1852.

20 Adams, W.E. (1968, 1st edn 1903), *Memoirs of a Social Atom*, New York: Augustus M. Kelley, p. 174. See also *Northern Star*, 13 April 1850; *Red Republican*, 22 June 1850; *Friend of the People*, 12 April 1851; Stevens, W. (1986, 1st edn 1862), *A Memoir of Thomas Martin Wheeler*, New York: Garland Publishing, p. 61; Leno, J.B. (1876), *The Aftermath: with Autobiography of the Author*, London: Reeves & Turner, p. 54; F. Engels to K. Marx, 18 March 1852, in (1982), *Collected Works*, London: Lawrence & Wishart, vol. 39, p. 67; Slosson, P.W. (1916), *The Decline of the Chartist Movement*, New York: Columbia University Press, p. 149.

21 *People's Paper*, 3 March 1855. This compared favourably with the *Leader* (30,000) and the *Nonconformist* (38,000).

22 McWilliam, R. (1996), 'The Mysteries of G.W.M. Reynolds: radicalism and melodrama in Victorian Britain', in Chase, M. and Dyck, I. (eds), *Living and Learning: Essay in Honour of J.F.C. Harrison*, Aldershot: Scholar Press, pp. 185–8.

23 See Berridge, V. (1978), 'Popular Sunday papers and mid-Victorian society', in Boyce, G., Curran, J. and Wingate, P., *Newspaper History: from the 17th century to the present day*, London: Sage Constable, p. 263. By 1872 the weekly circulation had grown to over 350,000 copies. See also James, L. and Saville, J. (1976), 'Reynolds. G.W.M.', *Dictionary of Labour Biography*, London: Macmillan, vol. 3, pp. 146–51; Pickering and Tyrrell, *People's Bread*, p. 170.

24 *Morning Advertiser*, 11 September 1855.

25 Not to be confused with O'Connor's bitter enemy, William Lovett, a fundamental mistake made by Read and Glasgow. See *O'Connor*, p. 144.

26 *People's Paper*, 15 September 1855.

27 Ibid., 15 September 1855. Lovett also implied that Reynolds had leaked the details of the burial to the *Advertiser*. See *Reynolds's Newspaper*, 23 September 1855.

28 *People's Paper*, 22 September 1855.

29 Ibid., 15 September 1885.

30 For a fuller discussion of this issue see Pickering, P.A. (1986), 'Class without words: Symbolic Communication in the Chartist movement', *Past and Present*, 112, August, pp. 144–62.
31 *People's Paper*, 13 October, 1855.
32 Ibid., 29 September 1855.
33 Ibid.
34 Ibid.
35 Ibid., 13 October 1855.
36 Ibid., 13 October 1855; 27 October 1855.
37 Ibid., 6 October 1855. From a detailed examination of the subscription lists it appears that the Bilston Chartists did subsequently send their donations. See Ibid., 1 March 1856.
38 Ibid., 29 September 1855; 13 October 1855; 29 March 1856; *Democrat and Labour Advocate*, 3 November 1855.
39 *People's Paper*, 1 March 1856.
40 Ibid., 22 December 1855.
41 Bamford, S. (1984, 1st edn 1844), *Passages in the Life of A Radical*, Oxford: Oxford University Press, pp. 35–6. See also Ross, D. (1842), *The State of the Country*, Manchester: Abel Heywood, p. 6.
42 *People's Paper*, 22 May 1852. Monument making itself became the object of the 'trade of agitation'. In July 1856, C. Pollard, sculptor and monumental mason of Padiham in Lancashire, placed an advertisement in the *People's Paper* offering to supply 'Brother Democrats' with 'quality articles' and pointing to the statue of Peel standing in Blackburn as evidence of his skill. See *People's Paper*, 19 July 1856. For a full discussion of this issue see Pickering, P.A. (1991), 'Chartism and the "Trade of Agitation" in Early Victorian Britain', *History*, 76 (247), June, pp. 221–37.
43 *People's Paper*, 22 December 1855.
44 Curl, J.S. (1972), *The Victorian Celebration of Death*, Newton Abbot: David & Charles, pp. 54, 68, 69–70.
45 *People's Paper*, 23 February 1856, 1 March 1856; *Reynolds's Newspaper*, 24 February 1856.
46 Whether he was related to the undertaker, Giles Lovett, is unclear, but he was not connected in any way with William Lovett who had one child, a daughter.
47 *People's Paper*, 22 March 1856.
48 Compiled from various weekly lists in the *People's Paper* and *Reynolds's Newspaper* between September 1855 and August 1857.
49 For Le Blond, see Royle, E. (1974), *Victorian Infidels: The Origins of the British Secularist Movement, 1791-1866*, Manchester: Manchester University Press, p. 177; for Cowen, see Todd, N. (1991), *The Militant Democracy: Joseph Cowen and Victorian Radicalism*, Tyne and Wear: Bewick Press.
50 For a discussion of radical naming, see Pickering, P.A. (1995), *Chartism and the Chartists in Manchester and Salford*, Basingstoke: Macmillan, pp. 40–42.
51 *Reynolds's Newspaper*, 14 October 1855, 27 January 1856. The collector, Abraham Lockwood, described himself as a 'hobbling, broken-down old coachman going on two sticks' and regretted that he had been unable to raise more. According to Dorothy Thompson the town contributed 2962 signatures to the 1839 petition from a population of 29,992. See Thompson, D. (1984), *The Chartists*, London: Temple Smith, p. 367.
52 Only one subscription from North Wales (from Brecon) was received.
53 Williams, D. (1959), 'Chartism in Wales', in Briggs, A. (ed.), *Chartist Studies*, London: Macmillan, p. 222; Williams, D. (1939), *John Frost: A Study in Chartism*, Cardiff: Evelyn, Adams & Mackay, pp. 337, 340. Williams argues that the 'movement's supreme misfortune', was the leadership of Feargus O'Connor. See *Frost*, p. 341.
54 *Irishman*, 31 November (*sic*) 1849, 29 December 1849, 19 January 1850, 16 February 1850, 23 February 1850, 9 March 1850.

55   Ibid., 9 March 1850. See Pickering, P.A. (1999), '"Repeal and the Suffrage": Feargus O'Connor's Irish "Mission", 1849–50', in Ashton, O., Fyson, R. and Roberts, S. (eds), *The Chartist Legacy*, Rendlesham: Merlin, pp. 119–46.

56   Only Belfast contributed to the monument.

57   *People's Paper*, 29 September 1855. The only familiar name among the committee was Robert Hamilton, a veteran of 1848. See Wilson, A. (1970), *The Chartist Movement in Scotland*, Manchester: Manchester University Press, pp. 224, 232 and 238.

58   Wilson, *Chartist Movement in Scotland*, p. 243.

59   See Gammage, R.G. (1969, 1st edn 1854), *History of the Chartist Movement*, New York: Augustus M. Kelley, pp. 28–9; Wright, L. (1953), *Scottish Chartism*, Edinburgh: Oliver & Boyd, pp. 219–21; Wilson, *Chartist Movement in Scotland*, p. viii, facing p. 51. Ironically, after returning from France in 1830 Taylor had first become involved in Ayr politics in opposition to a 3d charge to see the Burns monument in Auld. See Troon and District Family History Society (1996), *Monumental Inscriptions: Wallacetown Cemetery, Ayr*, Troon, pp. 41–2. I am grateful to the Ayr Library for bringing this booklet to my attention.

60   *Hansard* [House of Commons], 2 May 1842, col. 1373; *Northern Star*, 27 November 1841; Thompson, *The Chartists*, pp. 350, 362; Wilson, *Chartist Movement in Scotland*, pp. 204, 213–14.

61   Wilson, *Chartist Movement in Scotland*, p. 264.

62   *People's Paper*, 5 April 1856.

63   This point is based on a comparison between the subscription lists in the *People's Paper* and the comprehensive table of Chartist activity complied by Dorothy Thompson. See *The Chartists*, pp. 341–68.

64   See Breuilly, J., Niedhart, G. and Taylor, A. (1995), *The Era of the Reform League: English Labour and Radical Politics 1857–1872*, Mannheim: J and J Verlag, p. 6; Cannadine, D. (1983), 'London's Recent Past', *History*, 83, pp. 429–31; Prothero, I. (1997), *Radical Artisans in England and France 1830–1870*, Cambridge: Cambridge University Press, p. 114.

65   *Northern Tribune*, 1 (2), January–May 1854; Ashton, O.R. and Pickering, P.A. (2002), *Friends of the People: Uneasy Radicals in the Age of the Chartists*, Rendlesham: Merlin, pp. 132–7.

66   Taylor, A.D. (1992), 'Modes of Political Expression and Working-class Radicalism 1848–1874: The London and Manchester Examples', unpublished PhD thesis, University of Manchester; Pickering, *Chartism and the Chartists*, Chap. 10. See also Kirk, N. (1998), *Change, Continuity and Class: Labour in British Society*, Manchester: Manchester University Press, pp. 79–84.

67   *People's Paper*, 29 March 1856, 12 April 1856; *Reynolds's Newspaper*, 20 April 1856.

68   *People's Paper*, 12 April 1856.

69   This point has been helped by a discussion with Vic Gatrell. See also James, L. (1976), *Print and the People*, London: Peregrine Books.

70   *Northern Star*, 6 January 1838. The portrait series was emulated by others radicals such as T.P. Carlile in his *Regenerator and Chartist Circular* (1839–40) and G.W.M. Reynolds in his *Political Instructor* (1849–50). In 1843, the Anti-Corn Law League commenced its own 'Gallery of the League, or Portraits of the Leaguers' which were still appearing at the end of 1845. See *Manchester Times*, 21 January 1843, 29 November 1845.

71   See Epstein, J.A. (1976), 'Feargus O'Connor and the Northern Star', *International Review of Social History*, 21 (1), pp. 51–97; *Northern Star*, 4 August 1838, 25 May 1839.

72   See Pickering, 'Class Without Words', p. 155f. This point has been developed in Korff, G. (1993), 'History of Symbols as Social History? Ten Preliminary Notes on the Language and Sign Systems of Social Movements in Germany', *International Review of Social History*, 38 (supplement 1), p. 108.

73   *The Autobiography of William Farish: The Struggles of a Hand Loom Weaver, with some of his writings*, (1889), n.p: printed for private circulation only, p. 23.

74 Adams, *Memoirs of a Social Atom*, p. 164.
75 For example see *Northern Star*, 20 June 1840.
76 See for examples *Manchester and Salford Advertiser*, 10 April 1839, 27 April 1839, 22 August 1840; *Northern Star*, 29 May 1841, 4 September 1841, 28 May 1842.
77 *Manchester and Salford Advertiser*, 1 June 1839. See also 27 April 1839, 27 July 1839; Gorman, J. (1973), *Banners Bright: An Illustrated History of the Banners of the British Trade Union Movement*, London: Allan Lane, p. 45.
78 Berger, P.L. and Luckmann, T. (1973), *The Social Construction of Reality*, London: Penguin, p. 83. See also Sennett, R. (1974), *The Fall of Public Man*, Cambridge: Cambridge University Press, pp. 65–6, 87.
79 *People's Paper*, 14 June 1856.
80 Ibid., 6 September 1856.
81 Ibid., 11 April 1857.
82 The archives of the General Cemetery Company are not open to the public, but according to the current Clerk and Registrar of the Company, Mr D. J. Burkett, they contain no information in relation to O'Connor other than that which relates to the original purchase of the plot by Lovett and T.M. Wheeler. I am grateful to Mr Burkett for providing me with a copy of the extract. It indicates no caveat or condition attached to the plot. I am also grateful to Henry Vivian-Neal, Secretary of the Friends of Kensal Green, for helping me to contact the Company. Earlier the press had reported that the Company had 'approved' the inscription, but this must have been done verbally. See *Reynolds's Newspaper*, 10 August 1856.
83 *People's Paper*, 30 May 1857.
84 The monument is now in a dilapidated condition.
85 *People's Paper*, 16 May 1857, 30 May 1857; Curl, *Victorian Celebration of Death*, pp. 22–6. The Chartists offered no explanation of why they chose this style in particular.
86 The reports in the *People's Paper* and *Reynolds's Newspaper* indicated that the inscription also contained the words '*Meen Secker Reague*'. I have been unable to identify this language. On the monument itself, the relevant section has long since eroded away so it is impossible to check the spelling in the press. It is possible that the words were actually the Gaelic '*Meas Sether Riogh*' meaning respected good/strong leader. It is also true that O'Connor's father, Roger, referred to himself as '*Cier-Rige*', or chief of the people of Eri, which is phonetically similar to the words reported in the press. See Shaw, W. (1780), *Gaelic and English Dictionary Containing all the words in the Scotch and Irish dialects of the Celtic that could be collected from the Voice, and Old Books and Mss*, London: W & A. Strahan; O'Connor, R. (1822), *Chronicles of Eri; Being the History of Gael Sciot Iber: or, the Irish People*, London: Sir Richard Phillips & Co., vol. 1, frontispiece.
87 *People's Paper*, 16 May 1857. The O'Connor Coat of Arms is not in the standard works of heraldry.
88 See Yeo, E. (1982), 'Some Practices and Problems of Chartist Democracy', in Epstein, J. and Thompson, D. (eds), *The Chartist Experience: Studies in Working Class Radicalism and Culture 1830–1860*, London: Macmillan, pp. 345–80; Pickering, *Chartism and the Chartists*, Chaps 2 and 4; Pickering and Ashton, *Friends of the People*, pp. 67–8, 116–17.
89 See *People's Advocate*, 5 January 1850, 15 March 1851. The former Birmingham Chartist and future Premier of New South Wales, Henry Parkes, emulated the practice following his election to the Legislative Assembly in 1854. See *People's Advocate*, 6 May 1854, 16 December 1854, 23 December 1854.
90 *Northern Star*, 4 August 1838.
91 *People's Paper*, 15 March 1856. According to his nineteenth-century biographer, T.M. Wheeler, O'Connor's long-standing friend and ally, composed the inscription, but this is almost certainly incorrect. See Stephens, *Wheeler*, p. 63. The inscription was approved

by General Cemetery Company in July–August 1856. See *People's Paper*, 9 August 1856.

92   Curl, *Victorian Celebration of Death*, p. 58; *People's Paper*, 15 March 1856.

93   *Northern Star*, 22 September 1849, 29 September 1849, 10 November 1849.

94   *Reynolds's Newspaper*, 16 February 1851.

95   Epstein, J. (1994), *Radical Expression, Political Language, Ritual, and Symbol in England, 1790–1850*, Oxford: Oxford University Press, pp. 75–77; *Northern Star*, 21 June 1851.

96   *Northern Star*, 17 May 1851, 7 June 1851.

97   Ibid., 17 May 1851, 7 June 1851, 14 June 1851.

98   Ibid., 7 June 1851.

99   The cemetery passed into public control in 1853 and the records, held at the Public Record Office, commence at that date. The website of the East of London Family History Society incorrectly states that burials commenced in 1853. See <http://eolfhs.rootsweb.com/eolcem03.htm>.

100 Many Chartists felt that public opinion had provided them with their triumph. See *Northern Star*, 1 July 1851.

101 Geertz, C. (1977), 'Centres, Kings, and Charisma: Reflections on the Symbolics of Power', in Ben-David, J. and Clark, T.N. (eds), *Culture and Its Creators*, Chicago, IL: University of Chicago Press, p. 171.

102 Calculation based on figures in Thompson, *The Chartists*, pp. 342–68.

103 See Wood, A.C. (1955), 'Nottingham 1835–1865', *Transactions of the Thoroton Society of Nottinghamshire*, LIX, pp. 77–81; Zegger, R.E. (1973), *John Cam Hobhouse: A Political Life 1819–1852*, Columbia: University of Missouri Press, pp. 237–9; Wyncoll, *Nottingham Chartism*, p. 44.

104 See *People's Paper*, 22 September 1855, 13 October 1855, 9 August 1856. In addition to the monuments, not only did the Nottingham Chartists support Jones's election campaigns, but they also ran a national campaign to provide financial relief to the family of the late Chartist leader, Dr Peter McDouall. See *People's Paper*, 30 August 1856, 20 December 1856, 11 April 1857.

105 Ibid., 29 September 1855, 17 November 1855.

106 Ibid., 1 December 1855 quoting a report from *The Times*.

107 Ibid., 26 January 1856; Thompson, *The Chartists*, p. 361.

108 *People's Paper*, 15 December 1855.

109 Ibid., 3 May 1856.

110 Ibid., 16 August 1856. Jones won the nomination but did not go to the poll. See McCalmont, F.H. (1880), *The Parliamentary Poll Book of All Elections From the Passing of the First Reform Act in 1832 to July 1880*, London: E. Stanford, p. 209. Neither John Saville nor G.D.H. Cole mention this election. See Saville, J. (1952), *Ernest Jones: Chartist*, London: Lawrence & Wishart, p. 62; Cole, G.D.H. (1941), *Chartist Portraits*, London: Macmillan, pp. 351–2.

111 The success of this night, as well as the campaign itself, supports James Epstein's conclusion that Nottingham Chartism 'retained substantial working-class allegiance into the 1850s'. See Epstein, J. (1982), 'Some Organisational and Cultural Aspects of the Chartist Movement in Nottingham', in Esptein and Thompson, *The Chartist Experience*, p. 261. Epstein does not mention the monument.

112 *People's Paper*, 6 September 1856. The story of neither play – both published in 1832 – was particularly political. The London Chartists had also held very successful theatre nights to raise funds for the national monument. See *People's Paper*, 22 March 1856, 5 April 1856.

113 Ibid., 12 September 1857.

114 Cited in Epstein, J.A. (1982), *The Lion of Freedom: Feargus O'Connor and the Chartist Movement 1832–1842*, London: Croom Helm, p. 34. According to *The Times* O'Connor appears as a barrister, and has a brief in his right hand. See 23 August 1859.

As Donald Read notes, the 'temptation to dress Victorian gentlemen in Roman togas was strong', but most of the statues of Peel depicted him in modern 'non-classical' dress. See *Peel and the Victorians*, pp. 295–6.

115 *Nottingham Telegraph*, 12 February 1859.
116 Ibid., 17 September 1859.
117 Defoe, D. (1971, 1st edn 1724–6), *A Tour Through the Whole Island of Great Britain*, Harmondsworth: Penguin, pp. 451–6.
118 Wood, 'Nottingham', p. 6.
119 Beckett, *Nottingham*, p. 404.
120 Wood, 'Nottingham', p. 73n; Zegger, *Hobhouse*, pp. 237–9.The threat subsided in municipal terms after 1844.
121 Wood, 'Nottingham', p. 51; *Dictionary of Labour Biography*, vol. 4, pp. 171–3. Sweet had quarrelled with some local Chartists in 1853 but remained loyal to the cause throughout the remainder of his life. He co-ordinated donations for the London monument to O'Connor and nominated Jones in 1856. See *People's Paper*, 22 September 1855, 2 August 1856, 9 August 1856.
122 *Nottingham Telegraph*, 12 February 1859.
123 Fraser, D. (1979), *Urban Politics in Victorian England: The Structure of Politics in Victorian Cities*, London: Macmillan, p. 223.
124 *Nottingham Telegraph*, 26 February 1859. As Jones demonstrated in three successive elections, the Chartists believed that they could repeat Feargus's triumph. See Wood, 'Nottingham', p. 81.
125 *Nottingham Telegraph*, 17 September 1859. The decision was reaffirmed in May but on this occasion the discussion was described as 'protracted and warm'. See *The Times*, 14 May 1859.
126 *Nottingham Telegraph*, 12 February 1859. The controversy has been noted by Darke, J. (1991), *The Monument Guide to England and Wales*, London: Macdonald Illustrated, p. 175. The O'Connor Monument is the earliest listed in Darke's selection.
127 *Nottingham Telegraph*, 12 February 1859.
128 Ibid., 19 February 1859.
129 Ibid., 27 August 1859. This supports Epstein's point that there was a 'subtle interplay between control and accommodation' by local authorities. See 'Some Organisational and Cultural Aspects', p. 260.
130 *Nottingham Telegraph*, 17 September 1859.
131 Ibid.
132 *Nottingham Review*, 14 May 1852.
133 *Manchester Times*, 26 March 1842; *Northern Star*, 2 April 1842.
134 *Manchester and Salford Advertiser*, 9 June 1838.
135 See Osborne, J.W. (1972), *John Cartwright*, Cambridge: Cambridge University Press, p. 152. See also Chapter 3 above.
136 Manchester Public Library, Local History Collection, Handbill: 'A Monument to the Memory of H. Hunt Esq.', 1835; *Poor Man's Guardian*, 26 September 1835; *Manchester Times*, 11 April 1835.
137 See Hollis, P. (1970), *The Pauper Press: A Study in Working Class Radicalism of the 1830s*, Oxford: Oxford University Press, pp. 220–59; Hollis, P. (ed.) (1973), *Class and Conflict in Nineteenth Century England*, London: Routledge & Kegan Paul, p. xxi.
138 *Nottingham Telegraph*, 24 September 1859.
139 A guide-book published in 1894, for example, also omitted O'Connor from its description of the Arboretum. See White, W. (1894), *History, Gazetteer and Directory of Nottinghamshire*, Sheffield: William White Ltd. The same is true of Wylie, W.H. and Briscoe, J.P. (1893), *A Popular History of Nottingham*, Nottingham: Frank Murray. By 1959, Wood described the statue as 'forlorn'. Recently, attention has been drawn to the monument as a result of a fine colour photograph of it appearing on the cover of an

important collection of Chartist essays. See Wood, 'Nottingham', p. 81; Ashton, Fyson and Roberts, *The Chartist Legacy*.

140 Wilson, B. (1887) 'Struggles of an Old Chartist', repr. in Vincent, D. (ed.) (1977), *Testaments of Radicalism: Memoirs of Working Class Politicians 1790–1885*, London: Europa, p. 222. The London monument fared better, at least in the short term. See W.J. (1861), *Illustrated Guide to Kensal Green Cemetery*, London: Petter & Galpin, pp. 13–14; Croft, H.J. (1867), *Guide to Kensal Green Cemetery*, London: C. & E. Layton, p. 19.

141 See Hewison, R. (1987), *The Heritage Industry: Britain in a Climate of Decline*, London: Methuen; Williams, C. (1992), 'History, Heritage and Commemoration: Newport 1839–1989, *Llafur: Journal of Welsh Labour History*, 6 (1).

142 Kinnock, N. (1989), 'The value of hard-won freedom', *South Wales Argus*, 15 August, p. 12. In this article Kinnock compared the march on Newport in 1839 with the events that had recently taken place in Tiananmen Square.

143 City of Nottingham (1983), *Nottingham*, Public Relations Office, p. 75.

144 City of Nottingham (1986), *Nottingham*, Public Relations Office. Another local publication entitled 'Nottingham Heritage Trail' does not include the statue.

Chapter 6

Preserving the Glory for Preston:
The Campo Santo of the
Preston Teetotalers

Alex Tyrrell

Fig. 6.1   Preston teetotallers' burial ground.

> ... this splendid monument (and it was a splendid one) would preserve the glory
> for Preston when they were dead and gone.
>
> John Catterall, teetotaller.[1]

Constructed as a decorated pinnacle in Victorian Gothic style, the Preston Teetotal
Monument stands in the obscurity of the Preston General Cemetery; any claim that
it ever had to splendour lay in the eyes of its long-dead creators. It has not been
noticed in modern histories of the temperance movement or in writings concerned
with Victorian rituals of death.[2] This would have surprised and disappointed those
who participated in the inaugural ceremony on 22 April 1859. Watched by crowds

of their fellow townspeople, the local teetotalers gathered at their Temperance Hall, formed 'a most respectable procession' and marched through the streets led by a band. Having arrived at the cemetery, two miles from the town centre, the marchers listened to speeches that told them a great deal about public monuments, not only as memorials of great men and great deeds but also as the silently eloquent prophets of a better world to come. Speakers compared this monument with famous examples from the remote past of Egypt, Greece and Rome. They also noted the phenomenon that historians would describe as the 'statumania' of the Victorian era.[3] Their tone was one of pride. Britain was being 'overspread with monuments', but this one would be very different from the usual commemorations of warriors, politicians, artists and scientists. It would create a vision of the transforming power of teetotalism 'to save life, to raise men from their degradation, and deliver them from the bondage of intoxicating drinks'.

Two of the speakers welcomed the recent erection of a monument to Sir Robert Peel, but they insisted that even his great achievement in repealing the Corn Laws had not done one-tenth of the good for Preston that the teetotalers were doing. Cheap bread could not save a town where four hundred drink outlets threatened to overwhelm the work of thirty churches and chapels. Standing in the midst of 'a field of graves', their monument would speak to passers-by through a symbolism that would be evident to all. It would rise above the surrounding tombstones to proclaim, not only the Christian belief in the resurrection of the dead, but also the resurrection of those multitudes of the living that had risen from the death of intemperance. It would be like the altar before which Hannibal had stood to proclaim eternal vengeance against the Romans: 'at their monument [teetotalers would] swear eternal vengeance against intoxicating drink.' John Catterall, the organiser of the Teetotal Monument Fund, envisaged visitors deferring to Preston's pre-eminence in the history of this reform movement. They would only have to read the words on the monument: 'Erected by public subscription, A.D. 1859, to commemorate the origin in Preston of total abstinence from all intoxicating liquors'.[4]

The Preston teetotalers were correct to describe this as an unusual memorial, and over the years they made it the centrepiece of an even more unusual phenomenon. It was designed to stand in a section of the cemetery that the Teetotal Society had purchased for the burial of some of its poorer members.[5] The implication was clear; as their ultimate counter-cultural statement these teetotalers, in death as in life, would distance themselves from their unredeemed fellow citizens and rally under their own standard to proclaim the values of a better world.[6] By the end of the century, the Monument stood in the midst of the headstones of some of the town's teetotal pioneers, a few paces distant from the ornate tomb of Joseph Livesey, their well-known leader.[7] Constructing what was virtually a cemetery within the cemetery, the Preston teetotalers made the area round the Monument a *campo santo* for the burial and veneration of those who had taken the pledge when this was a novel and hazardous commitment.[8] Doubtless, friendships forged from shared experiences over many years influenced those who chose this as their final resting place, but these teetotalers were looking beyond the present. Like others of this era who appreciated the pedagogic importance of monuments and public spaces, the Preston teetotalers were taking command of the historical record with an eye to the future; the epitaphs on their tombstones would rise up before the passer-by as so many citations on a roll of honour.

Thus it is as didactic artefacts of proselytism and hagiography that these funerary monuments have value as historical sources. They express the values that the teetotalers held most dear and link the life stories of their pioneers to a metanarrative of reform in which teetotalism appeared, not as a mere anti-drink creed, but as part of a wide-ranging radical ideology that was destined to overthrow the tradition-bound elites who controlled most aspects of British public life. This metanarrative was summarised as an illustration in one of Joseph Livesey's best-known periodicals, *The Struggle,* which was published in the 1840s to support the campaign against the Corn Laws. Under the title 'Storming the Castle of Monopoly', it offers an interpretation of nineteenth-century British history as a story of reform – past, present and to come. Its centrepiece is the great Castle of Monopoly, a visual

Fig. 6.2   Storming the Castle of Monopoly.

metaphor that inevitably must have turned minds to that most grim of literary fortresses – the Doubting Castle in *Pilgrim's Progress* that barred Christian's way to the Celestial City.[9]

The Castle of Monopoly was Livesey's metaphor for the domination of Britain in his day by a ruling establishment consisting of reactionary Tories, corrupt politicians, greedy landowners, the Church of England hierarchy, the armed forces, slave owners and other time-worn agencies of darkness and oppression. Not the least of these was the drink trade and its ancillaries. Unlike John Bunyan who was content to allow Christian to escape from Doubting Castle, Livesey envisaged full-scale assault and destruction. His woodcut shows the castle fortifications being overthrown and occupied by successive storming parties from the army of reform. Their standards flutter over the captured outworks – the standards of tariff reform, Catholic Emancipation and the Reform Act of 1832. The battering-ram of the Anti-Corn Law League is shattering the fortified gatehouse, and the Chartists are pressing forward to attack. In the background, massing in mighty numbers on the hillsides, is the army that will deliver the *coup de grace* – the teetotalers who will smash the last remnants of the castle and raise a new society on its ruins.[10] The *campo santo* in the Preston General Cemetery reinforced this metanarrative of reform. It was intended to be a place of funerary pilgrimage where the radical teetotallers of Preston and other parts of Britain could celebrate their vision of a better world.[11]

The Preston Teetotal Monument took its place in a long series of attempts by the local teetotalers to claim public spaces in an unredeemed town and hold out the promise of a time when their combative worldview would reign supreme. Challenging the contemporary popular culture of the public house and the drinking customs that were entwined around nearly every aspect of life, teetotalers came together during the 1830s in meetings that often resembled religious revival gatherings. Not surprisingly, they experienced the wrath of hostile crowds that were often actively patronised or tacitly encouraged by publicans and magistrates,[12] but they quickly learned how to assert their right to use the public spaces of their towns. Banner-waving processions such as the one that preceded the inauguration of the teetotal monument became one of the features of Preston life. The teetotalers' public presentation of self rested on what was virtually a counter-culture with its own forms of consociality, icons, rituals and sacred places. They had their distinctive rites of passage with teetotal christenings, marriages and funerals. There was even a report of a teetotal flitting.[13] Often their favoured leisure pastimes took the form of rational recreation of the sort that other moral reformers of that era favoured – lectures, reading rooms, concerts, soirées and tea parties.

Much of the money that went into the building of the Preston Teetotal Monument was raised at one of these tea parties. It was a splendid occasion. On 20 January 1859, eight hundred teetotalers from Preston and its neighbourhood – women as well as men – gathered in the Exchange Rooms, consumed a 'supply of edibles' that was 'liberal in the extreme' and settled down to enjoy the entertainments of the evening. They heard songs that had been written as rallying cries – 'The Real Staunch Teetotaler', 'The Meeting of the Waters' and 'Come, come and sign the pledge' – and they heard speeches by reformed drunkards including Thomas Swindlehurst whom they had nicknamed 'The King of the teetotalers'.[14] This tea party took place in the midst of a revival of teetotalism that brought back much of the atmosphere of the movement's early days in the 1830s. A new temperance hall was built where night after night there were lectures, Band of Hope gatherings, and meetings of the Sons and Daughters of Temperance at which converts and activists gave short speeches. There were Saturday night concerts where temperance melodies were sung. There were colourful tea parties, replete with flags, banners and bands of music. Tens of thousands of tracts were distributed. Members had their own reading room and baths for free use. Success was not far distant they told each other: soon Preston would become 'a model ... sober town' that would show the way forward for Britain and the world.[15]

The Teetotal Monument was the expression in stone of this optimistic mood during the 1850s. It was meant to introduce observers to a myth of origin that had become part of the folklore of the movement – the story of how seven of their fellow townsmen had administered the first teetotal abstinence pledge to themselves, and set out to revolutionise Preston from their headquarters in a disused cockpit that they transformed into a temperance hall. The story made Preston the centre point of the map of Britain from which the pioneers of total abstinence had set out like so many missionaries to take their ideas to all parts of the country.[16] Largely because of the industry and business acumen of Joseph Livesey, Preston became an important centre of the teetotal press,[17] with the result that events and people there attained a special place of pre-eminence in the history of the movement. The early Preston teetotalers ('the Seven Men of Preston') and the Cockpit where for many years they held their meetings became household names in teetotal circles. Not surprisingly, when the Preston pioneers of the movement died, their funerals were extensively reported. They were not forgotten. Preston earned a reputation as the 'Bethlehem' or 'Jerusalem' of the teetotal movement,[18] and, true to the metaphor, it became the focal point of a nineteenth-century version of the medieval pilgrimage. There were reports of visitors arriving to follow something like a *via dolorosa* round places that had been hallowed by their association with the pioneers of the movement.[19]

A striking example of this development occurred in August 1854 when a cheap one-day railway excursion arrived in Preston from Bolton. This form of mass travel was one of the exciting innovations of the age, and there were many reports of workers, often in factory groups, making use of it. Early teetotal activists, of whom Thomas Cook is only the most famous, had been quick to realise the importance of railway excursions for their adherents who could be kept from backsliding by this form of rational recreation,[20] and Joseph Livesey started organising annual railway trips to seaside resorts in 1845,[21] but the Bolton excursion was different from others. It consisted of three railway trains, and on board were 1300 teetotalers who had come, so the *Preston Guardian* reported, in a spirit of reverence to pay their respects to Preston as the place where the doctrine of total abstinence was first enunciated and given its name. Thus they spent the day visiting the sites of interest that they had often seen reported in the press. They saw the Cockpit, and they went to St. Peter's Churchyard, where they visited the grave of Richard Turner.[22] 'Dicky' Turner's story was one of the best-known parts of teetotal folklore. So one version of the story went, this redeemed drunkard suffered from a speech impediment, and when he stood before the Preston Temperance Society to tell his tale of personal redemption he had stumbled on the word 'teetotal' by proclaiming that he was a convert, not to the anti-spirits doctrine, but to 't-t-total' abstinence from all intoxicating beverages.[23]

Over the years, the Preston teetotalers had learned how to devise funerary icons and impressive dramaturgical displays to disseminate their message and proclaim their prominence in the movement. When Richard Turner died, his funeral was a splendid affair. Headed by a Rechabite band and marching teetotalers, the hearse was followed by the singers and Sunday School children of the Primitive Methodists (a teetotal sect) as it progressed through crowded streets.[24] The place of burial had been chosen by 'a few zealous friends of the cause' to be near the spot at which Turner had signed the pledge, and a tombstone was erected to stand over it as an *architecture parlante* that would proclaim his name and zeal to future generations. To this day it remains there, offering its inscription for the edification of passers-by: 'Beneath this stone are deposited the remains of Richard Turner, author of the word Teetotal, as applied to abstinence from all intoxicating liquors, who departed this life on the 27th day of October, 1846, aged fifty-six years'.[25]

Like Turner's tomb, the Preston Teetotal Monument was a celebratory icon of death that showed how well the local teetotalers were in touch with the culture of the mid-nineteenth century. Contemporary literature was suffused with images of death; in evangelical circles there was something like a recommended way of dying that was often 'improved' in sermons for the edification of the living; funerals were frequently occasions of conspicuous display; and cemeteries were designed to be places of public resort.[26] One of the hymns chosen for the inauguration of the Monument breathed this pensive spirit of melancholy: 'While walking at the close of day among the silent dead'.[27]

References to the planning of the Teetotal Monument show that it was designed to be an even more impressively didactic site of celebratory death than Turner's grave – one that would summon up memories from the heroic past and leave the visitor in no doubt as to Preston's place of pre-eminence in teetotal history. At the fund-raising tea party in January 1859, John Catterall was very explicit in setting out what he saw as the principal purpose of the Monument: he had been appalled, he said, to discover that people in other towns were claiming the credit for inventing teetotalism. Thus the planning committee intended the monument to silence anyone who 'scribbled a bit, and tried to prove that Preston was not the cradle of the cause'; it would 'preserve the glory for Preston when they were dead and gone'.[28] Catterall's claim was misleading. As Brian Harrison has shown, 'the Preston teetotalers were the first who vigorously propagated the new cause', but several societies that were dedicated to the idea, though not the term 'teetotalism', emerged almost simultaneously during the early 1830s, the first of them in Paisley in 1832.[29] This was an era when assertions of local pride and personal claims to fame were often articulated through the medium of memorials and commemorative literature, and, as the anti-slavery movement had already demonstrated, in the disputatious world of nineteenth-century reform there were many examples of attempts to dominate the historical record in this way.[30] The dispute over historical primacy between the teetotalers of Preston and other towns in the 1850s was followed in the 1860s by a similar dispute within Preston between James Teare and Joseph Livesey.[31]

By designing their Monument as a beautiful artefact of instruction and placing it in the General Cemetery as a focal point for the burial of their members the Preston teetotalers were associating themselves with a reform movement that was attracting considerable interest in the 1850s. Prior to that time, most urban burial grounds repelled rather than attracted visitors. Between 1801 and 1851, the population of Britain doubled, and all over the country the outcome was the same – reports of overcrowding, disinterment, neglect, squalor, disease and disgust. Public concern went beyond the health issues that were involved. The cultural shift that Thomas Kselman has detected in France at this time can also be seen in Britain; it took the form of a desire to end the practice of burying the dead on top of each other in mass graves, and to create separate graves where the living could establish a direct relationship with the dead by means of funerary architecture.[32] The need for reform was unquestionable, but the proposals were contentious. They aroused the sectarian animosities of the day, for the Church of England owned most of the churchyards, and burial offerings formed part of the perquisites of the clergy. When Lord Althorp listed the grievances of the Dissenters in 1834, he included their 'complaint with regard to burial in Church-yards without the ceremonies of the Church'.[33] No matter how well intentioned any new system of public burial might be, Dissenters would condemn it if the established church retained a privileged position. In an era when *laissez-faire* ideas commanded widespread assent there were also misgivings about involving the state in such matters,[34] and there were many attempts to find a solution through the free market by means of joint-stock cemetery companies. The Glasgow Necropolis and Kensal Green Cemetery in London are well-known examples of these.[35]

The attempts by private enterprise to combine familial piety with beauty, instruction and sanitary precautions served only to proclaim the distance in death as in life between the rich and the poor. By mid-century, the need for a reform that went beyond piecemeal measures was inescapable. The joint-stock cemeteries did not touch the wider demographic and sanitary problems, and repeated outbreaks of cholera and typhus were often traced to the scandalous state of the old churchyards. Beginning in the 1840s, special Acts of Parliament enabled town councils to establish their own burial grounds, and in 1852, 1853 and 1854, Acts of Parliament gave local Burial Boards powers to establish rate-supported public cemeteries. As a consequence municipal cemeteries were created all over the country.[36]

The campaign that preceded these changes developed at two levels. In Parliament, there were debates, select committees and lobbying. In the meanwhile, local reformers kept up an agitation across the country to press for national legislation and exert an influence on its application to their towns. Two of the Preston teetotalers were in the forefront of this struggle, John Catterall and Joseph Livesey. Following a visit by a government inspector who found that some of the town's burial grounds were in an 'objectionable state',[37] Catterall wrote to Livesey's newspaper, the *Preston Guardian,* in July 1849 to spell out what this meant. He estimated that during the preceding 50 years, 40,000 bodies had been buried in the town's

17 church and chapel grounds, which, as a consequence, had become places that were 'continually reeking with animal fluids'. He and another correspondent were particularly concerned by the state of St. Paul's burial ground, where the graves of the poor were left open and coffin was piled on coffin with so little covering of soil that the stench was wafted to the houses in the district. Catterall had good reason to know this story; for more than two years he and his family had lived in St. Paul's Square where they had experienced 'repeated nauseous smells' from the overcrowded graveyard opposite their home. The situation in St. Paul's was typical of Preston, he concluded: 'there is not a church or chapel burying ground that is not pregnant with rattling skeletons and mouldering bones. Our cities are built upon corpses; the ground heaves and trembles beneath our feet, and every step we take is upon the manes of our ancestors.' Like others of his era, Catterall based his argument on the miasmatic theory of disease that attributed death-threatening effects to 'gases emanating from decaying animal matter'. It was scandalous, he insisted, that nothing had been done to act on this basic theory by taking some simple measures to ensure the means of good health for the individual and the community. The answer was obvious; the churchyards must be closed, and a public cemetery must be created away from the populated areas of the town.[38] Catterall's protest accompanied the announcement of plans for a private enterprise cemetery of twenty acres that would be adjacent to Preston but comparatively secluded. If it had been created, it would have been 'both useful and ornamental'. A brook would have run through the cemetery; there would have been 'sheets of water', and the slopes would have been planted tastefully. No less significantly, the plan was intended to accommodate the wishes of Dissenters and Catholics for their own burial areas and facilities.[39]

By 1849, the ideas that influenced this form of cemetery improvement were well known. They can be traced back to the planned and regulated cemeteries of Père Lachaise, Montmartre and Montparnasse, that were created in Paris during the opening years of the century, but it was not until the 1830s that the new ideas gained prominence in Britain.[40] As a consequence, cemetery reform began almost coincidentally with the teetotal movement. Many of the ideas that guided the designers of the new cemeteries may be seen in the writings of John Claudius Loudon. The proprietor of the *Gardener's Magazine* and the author of a stream of highly respected works on gardening, landscaping and architecture, Loudon devised reform projects that were imbued with the rationality and zeal for education that characterised the Scottish Enlightenment during his time as a student at Edinburgh University in the 1790s. His utilitarian, liberal ideas – in 1834 he referred to Jeremy Bentham as 'the greatest benefactor to mankind, in our opinion, since the commencement of the Christian era'[41] – placed him on the side of those who spoke of the need for wide-ranging reforms that would sweep across all aspects of British society. Free trade, national education and a fairer system of parliamentary representation were parts of his radical creed.[42] A similar spirit informed his book, *On the laying out, planting and managing of Cemeteries: and on the improvement of Churchyards* (1843). Carefully buried with six feet of earth over every coffin, the dead would return to the earth in ways that would be safe for the living and respectful to the feelings of the bereaved. Loudon saw cemeteries as botanic gardens, places of education, areas of recreation and breathing spaces for a rapidly increasing population of townspeople. The cemetery that he envisaged would be embellished by carefully designed tombs that would impart a knowledge of architecture, and it would be planted with trees and shrubs that might even be named for the instruction of passers-by. The outcome would be a historical record of a district and 'a school of instruction in architecture, sculpture, landscape gardening, arboriculture, botany, and in those important parts of general gardening, neatness, order, and high keeping'.[43] Reinforced by associations with familial piety, this new model cemetery would take its place alongside the other institutions of a reformed society as an instrument of moral and social uplift for an untutored population.[44] Loudon's proposals were denounced for their rationalist ethos that did not cohere well with some Christians' attitudes to death,[45] but their influence was widespread. James S. Curl writes that 'nearly all the public cemeteries formed after 1850 incorporate many of the ideas for layout and planting set out by Loudon in this remarkable book.'[46]

Similar ideas emerged in Preston as early as 1838. In that year Joseph Livesey took up the cause of cemetery reform in his *Moral Reformer* where he anticipated many of the theories in Loudon's book. Denouncing the condition of the nation's urban churchyards as 'revolting' and a threat to public health, he attacked the superstitious beliefs and vested interests that stood in the way of reform. The new cemeteries that had recently been created in Liverpool and Manchester showed what could be done in 'every town' to take account of public health and decency. Built outside towns, public cemeteries could include botanical gardens where trees, shrubs and flowers would be planted to interest visitors and assist the studies of botanists. 'These objects combined would render the place pleasing, healthy, retired and solemn', making it an 'addition to the conveniences and ornaments of a town'. It was typical of Livesey that his proposal embraced the entire community; the wealthy would be charged for plots, and the profits would be used to provide an area for the burial of the poor. The outcome would be 'another step gained towards the good order and rational arrangements of society'.[47]

The story of cemetery reform in Preston resembled developments nation-wide. The joint stock company that was mooted in 1849 would have done little to cope with the extent of the urban burial problem, and arrangements for constructing a satisfactory cemetery had to wait until 1854, the year in which a Burial Act empowered town councils to establish rate-supported burial boards. The Preston Burial Board was set up which acquired 45 acres and divided them into separate areas for the churches. According to the original proposal, the Anglicans were to receive 24.5 acres, Catholics 13.5 acres, and Dissenters 6 acres. One acre would have been set aside for buildings including separate denominational chapels.[48] The new system brought burials in the town's churchyards to an end (the last two were closed in 1855 and 1856[49], but immediately, the usual sectarian animosities broke out. There were accusations that the Burial Board had been appointed in a 'hole and corner way' that discriminated against Dissenters, and that as a consequence the apportionment of land was unfavourable to them.[50] Livesey's *Preston Guardian* insisted that Dissenters were entitled to the same amount of ground as the Anglicans, and the *Preston Chronicle* reasonably pointed out that, as the cemetery had enough land to last a hundred years, there was no need to apportion the entire area immediately.[51] The *Chronicle's* point of view won the day: the Dissenters retained their 6 acres, but the Anglicans and Catholics were scaled down to 19 and 11 acres respectively, leaving 8 acres unappropriated.[52]

A late nineteenth-century report compiled at a time when the trees in the cemetery had reached maturity shows that the Burial Board had done more than accede to sectarian feelings; it had created a cemetery that was 'beautiful – to the extent one can apply such a word to such a place'.[53] Evidently the planners had followed the principle laid down by Loudon, Livesey and other reformers that a cemetery should be a garden of remembrance and civilising influences. As one of the earliest of the funerary memorials that were erected in the cemetery, the Teetotal Monument marked the triumph of this reform movement. Its location in the Dissenters' section was one indication of this. The leadership as well as much of the rank and file of teetotalism came from Protestant Dissent,[54] and they were celebrating a victory over the Anglican confessional state that sheltered within the walls of the Castle of Monopoly. At a time when there were acres of unoccupied space, and the tree plantations were in their infancy, the 'splendid' qualities with which the teetotalers endowed their monument must also have given a much needed demonstration of support for the aesthetic principles of cemetery reform. The choice of Gothic as the most appropriate style was a boldly modern endorsement of these principles; by the mid-nineteenth century the neo-classical symbols that had previously represented death were giving way to imagery in the Gothic Revival style as an expression of Christian spirituality.[55] In the recent past, Dissenters had been hostile to this architectural form because of its association with 'Popish superstition', but their attitude had changed by the 1850s. They wished to find an appropriate English style to display their increasing power and status. 'The result', in Clyde Binfield's words, 'was Dissenting Gothic.'[56] Evidently the Dissenting teetotalers of Preston were guided by similar ideas; Livesey's *Preston Guardian* described the Teetotal Monument as a 'beautiful column' that was 'exceedingly ornamental in appearance'.[57] Like the builders of the chapels and Sunday schools described by Binfield, Catterall's Monument Committee was adopting Gothic as a style of beauty, splendour and moral uplift. It would proclaim their ideal of the cemetery as a place that would edify the mind at the same time as it ministered to the health and hygiene of the community. Thus the modern criticism that the teetotalers were consigning their Monument to obscurity by siting it in a cemetery was one that they would have refuted without difficulty; cemeteries were important places of public resort in the Victorian city, and their memorials were meant to provide object lessons for the passer-by. If they had wished, the teetotalers could readily have found an alternative site. In 1859, Joseph Livesey erected six drinking fountains in Preston, any one of which could have been devised as a focal point for a Teetotal Monument, but it was the cemetery that was chosen as the most appropriate place.[58]

With the passage of time, the surrounding tombstones of teetotal stalwarts enhanced the Monument's message of mental uplift and reforming aspiration.[59]

Sometimes the epitaphs are merely formulaic in the information that they convey – names, dates and brief invocations of familial piety – and they have to be supplemented by obituary and other notices to reveal the sort of mentality that caused people to select this as their place of burial. James Huffman is a case in point – a teetotaler whose range of radical enthusiasms went far back in time and exemplified the sort of campaigns that were caught up in Livesey's metaphor of the embattled Castle of Monopoly. With five members of his family, Huffman is commemorated on a tombstone that had space only for the most basic information about the individuals in the group, but from newspaper sources it is evident that he had come to teetotalism after participating in several of the best-known radical movements of his day. Huffman's obituary described him as 'The Veteran Reformer' (he was born in 1775) about whom it would be impossible to write without giving 'the history of every struggle for political and religious liberty that has taken place within the greater part of the present century'. Trained as a boot and shoe manufacturer in Manchester, he moved to Preston in 1795, where he soon plunged into local politics against the predominant aristocratic family, the Stanleys. He presided over the first reform meeting ever held in the town (in 1812), welcomed Orator Hunt after the massacre of Peterloo and acted as Hunt's proxy in the next parliamentary election. Although Huffman was an advocate of peaceful protest, he made his house a haven for armed radicals who were sought by the government at that bitter time. Always a man for the grand gesture, in his hatred of the window tax he blocked up the fanlight over his doorway by inserting a board showing three books entitled *Pitt's Works* under which he placed the words "Manchester Massacre, 1819' in crimson characters. At the time of George IV's coronation in 1821 he displayed a huge placard with an even more flamboyant inscription: 'May the enemies of Queen Caroline and the British Constitution be compelled to wear short shoes and long toe nails during their journey downhill to the pit of perdition.'[60] It was entirely in character for such a man to proclaim the strength of his beliefs by choosing a spot in proximity to the teetotal monument as his family's final resting place.

Several of the tombstones are more informative than Huffman's, and they can be read as historical sources in their own right. The 'lapidary inscriptions in nineteenth-century cemeteries', writes Roy Porter, 'perpetuate positive and tangible identities, established through civic chauvinism, fierce family and district loyalties, and pervasive occupational pride'; they 'also commemorate lives dedicated to civic munificence and Christian charity'.[61] In the case of some of the teetotalers who were buried near the Monument, the identity is one that explicitly shows total abstinence as a branch of a more general philanthropic and radical reforming commitment. Some of the inscriptions are anything but formulaic. They bear testimony to the qualities that the movement cherished in its leaders and point to the wide range of their reforming aspirations, especially those that identified them with the poor and disadvantaged. Thus Livesey is commemorated for his 'philanthropy and usefulness as author and worker, as the pioneer of temperance, the advocate of moral and social reform and the helpful friend and counsellor of the poor'. Edward Grubb's tombstone reiterates the message that Preston was 'the birth-place of teetotalism' and fulsomely hails him as 'the noblest Roman of them all' because of his dedication to making teetotalism a 'world-wide movement'. A 'brilliant orator' and 'philosophical teacher', he had shown an 'incorruptible integrity' that rendered him 'proof against the blandishments of wealth'. John Catterall is honoured on his tombstone by 'the friends of temperance, orphan & blind institutions'.[62]

It would be possible to say more about these commemorations of the local leaders of the teetotal movement, but here attention will focus on the tombstone of an activist who has not hitherto been noticed by historians. The epitaph reads as follows:

> Sacred To The Memory Of Mary Graham;
> Who departed this life on the 4th of February 1868,
> in the 90th year of her age.
> She was a devoted friend to the temperance cause,
> & a teetotaler 33 years.
> She refused to take either medicine, or intoxicating
> liquors, up to her death.

Tantalising and even eccentric though it seems, this is one of the most important epitaphs in the cemetery. It makes a statement about gendering in nineteenth-century Britain, and it draws attention to a reform movement that attracted considerable support from Victorian radicals – the campaign against the nineteenth-century pharmacopoeia.

By giving her a place of prominence in the *campo santo* of a reform movement, Mary Graham's tombstone stands out as a most unusual phenomenon in the Victorian era. The dominant belief that regulated the lives of women at that time was the doctrine of separate spheres according to which men and women were expected to fulfil different roles in life. Public life was seen as the masculine sphere, and home was seen as the feminine domain. The doctrine never fitted the facts of working-class life, where women had to contribute to the family income, but even there historians have detected a withdrawal of women from great reform movements such as Chartism.[63] Nonetheless, every so often a gap appeared in the wall of domesticity, and there is evidence of women playing parts in public life. The history of the teetotal movement provides several examples of women activists including Joseph Livesey's wife, Jane, who taught in his school, promoted tea meetings and managed Preston's first temperance hotel.[64]

Mary Graham went further than most women teetotalers, and she did so in her own right. Thus her epitaph, especially when it is supplemented by obituary and contextual information, is of historical significance.[65] An Irish woman, like many of her compatriots she had joined the exodus to Britain. She was a war-time bride, and the British soldier she married during the Napoleonic Wars took her to Preston when peace returned. She became a dressmaker, and, when her husband died she stayed on in Preston to make a living by sewing and dyeing ribbons and silks. She was described as 'a great politician' and newspaper reader – almost certainly an indication of radical tendencies – and it was another indication of her radical temperament that she was one of the first to declare for teetotalism and subsequently become a Rechabite. She was often referred to as 'Temperance Mary' or 'The Queen of the teetotalers'. In an era when convention frowned on women who took an active part in public meetings, she was so zealous that she embarked on a great public-speaking campaign that took her to Liverpool, Manchester, Blackburn, Bolton and other places in Lancashire. Her performances were described as being characterised by 'fluency of speech and attractive style'. Graham continued to give speeches to the Preston teetotalers until very late in life, and when she died her death notice saluted her as 'the oldest female temperance lecturer'. Appropriately, her funeral seems to have been a great public event with a procession of marching teetotalers who were joined by Joseph Livesey in his carriage.

This brief biography explains the reference on Mary Graham's tombstone to her abhorrence of drink; it does nothing to explain the strange reference to her repudiation of medicine. To understand what this meant, it is necessary to return to Joseph Livesey's image of the teetotalers as part of the army that was storming the Castle of Monopoly. As he explained, teetotalism was 'a dietetic and an hygienic question' to be taken up 'on moral, social, domestic, and national grounds'.[66] Like other reforms it would only be implemented after a struggle against the forces of darkness, for, just as there was a political and ecclesiastical establishment, so, as far as Livesey and many teetotalers were concerned, there was a medical establishment that was intent on defending its vested interests against the public good.

The critique that teetotalers directed against contemporary medicine was one that was often voiced in the early Victorian era: doctors were inflicting poisonous and addictive medicines on their patients. Some reformers such as Thomas Wakley, the founder of the *Lancet*, hoped to find a solution in a scientifically trained medical profession, but prominent teetotalers went further. They would have liked to overthrow orthodox medicine altogether. The teetotalers' relationship to the campaign for medical reform was an especially close one, because intoxicants formed an important part of the mid-nineteenth-century pharmacopoeia. There were reports of doctors prescribing alcoholic drinks as medicines and advising their patients to break the total abstinence pledge for medical reasons. Thomas Whittaker, a prominent teetotaler, remembered the agony of doubt he experienced when he resisted the doctors who told him that wine was absolutely necessary for his son during a critical illness.[67] The temperance press took the doctors severely to task when it narrated the experiences of patients who had been prescribed alcohol as medicine. One teetotaler, for example, complained that her doctors had recommended three pints of porter a day as a cure for dyspepsia. When this had failed after ten years, she had then been advised to increase the dosage to three glasses of strong brandy grog a day.[68] Mary Graham's denunciation of medicine along with drink is easy to understand in this context. All too often medicine was drink.

But what was the alternative to the mid-nineteenth-century pharmacopoeia? Was there no option for those who abjured medicines other than to bear the problems of ill health assisted only by their stoicism? The answer given by many teetotalers was summarised by Samuel Brown under the name 'Physical Puritanism', a self-help approach to preventive medicine. Writing in the *Westminster Review,* Brown described the mid-nineteenth century as 'pre-eminently the age of physiological reformers' who preached a 'new sort of puritanism' that was dedicated to 'the healing, cleansing, and restoration of the animal man'.[69] This new approach to medicine took many forms – vegetarianism, homoeopathy, mesmerism, the water cure and phrenology – but Brown saw teetotalism as 'the prime mover of the revolution'. It had taken the lead in 'the great anti-poison league of the age' which preached the need for fresh air, exercise and temperance in accordance with the organic laws that regulated human existence. These laws, not the drugs and drinks prescribed by doctors, offered the prospect of solving the proliferating health problems of mankind. [70]

Preston was one of the centres of the new health sciences; in the words of one of Livesey's early biographers, the Preston teetotalers were 'pioneer investigators of the food question'. As early as 1838, Livesey was experimenting with vegetarianism and writing in favour of 'Moderation in Food'.[71] In addition to teetotalism, *Livesey's Moral Reformer* for that year contains advice on a variety of health-related issues including tobacco, skipping and singing as exercises for women, fresh air in bedrooms, washing the body in hot weather and avoiding excess in eating.[72] In the early 1840s, Livesey took up hydropathy (the water cure), a form of self-help therapy that had recently been introduced from Austria. Having studied 'the laws of health', he used his periodicals to extol the benefits of teetotalism in conjunction with a dietary and exercise regimen consisting of hydropathy, gymnastics, vegetarianism and the avoidance of stimulants such as tobacco, mustard, pepper and spices.[73] Believing that women were more likely than men to defer to doctors, he urged them to take charge of their own well-being. They could make a start by avoiding 'the evils of tight lacing'.

Mary Graham's epitaph can be understood only when it is placed in this context. In 1868, shortly before her death, Livesey summarised his health creed in an article entitled 'Drink and Drugs Versus Nature'. In this vehement attack on what he saw as an unholy alliance of doctors, brewers and wine merchants, Livesey described contemporary medicine as an interference with the health-giving processes of nature. People were violating the dictates of natural living and contributing to their own ill-health by introducing dangerously rich foodstuffs, often in excessive amounts, into their bodies and then resorting to medicines for a remedy. What was needed was a form of preventive medicine that would strengthen the constitution and make the most of its defences against disease. This would be a holistic process that addressed the mental and moral as well as the physical needs of the human being:

> Fasting occasionally, simplicity of diet, exercise in the open air, no alcoholic disturbance, no physic, cleanliness and friction to the skin, not 'caring about many things', but a contented, resigned, cheerful state of mind, and the time well employed in rendering services to our fellow creatures – these I hold to be the true agencies of health, and a thousand times better than all the medicines and all the fiery drinks that doctors or drink sellers can supply.[74]

Characteristically, Livesey took this creed to its extremes. He had, he wrote, taken exercise, relied on water 'inside and out', and become a vegetarian. He dined daily on a diet of three buttered potatoes and a small pudding or some roasted apples. During the previous 14 years he had never resorted to doctors or medicines.[75]

Written in the same year as Mary Graham's death, Livesey's words are strikingly similar to her epitaph, a form of which first appeared in the obituary that was published in the *Preston Guardian*. Thus, for Preston teetotalers, the words on Mary Graham's tombstone would not have seemed eccentric; her decision to abandon orthodox medicine was an entirely rational one. She had died of a preventable accident at 90 years of age, and her long and active life showed what could be achieved by those who followed the natural laws of physical puritanism. She could be seen as an example of the principle that John Catterall had enunciated in 1849 when he had argued that public health could be attained by some elementary reforms: 'One disease and one only, is inherent in mankind, and that is old age. All other maladies, being accidental or contingent, may in great measure be prevented or removed.'[76] Livesey's writings portrayed the teetotal pledge as the first step to good health. It provided an introduction to cheerful forms of consociality and opportunities for public service such as those that were commemorated in the epitaphs of the people who were buried near the Monument. Teetotalism even offered a means of 'cleanliness and friction to the skin', for the free baths that the Preston teetotalers installed in their hall provided a cheap and convenient version of the water cure.[77] An exciting prospect seemed to be opening up. As the *British Temperance Advocate* explained in an article entitled 'Temperance as a Means of Physical Perfection', the possibilities were boundless for those 'of high moral feeling' who combined 'strict temperance' with 'daily ablutions of cold water':

... teetotalism is more than merely a remedy for intemperance. It is a powerful and necessary element in the means of securing the highest physical perfection of which mankind is capable – for the realization of that grand desideratum, 'a sound mind in a sound body.' The chemistry which is to change the character of the race is incomplete without it. With it (for its facts are prophetic) we may well anticipate a future peopled with beautiful forms of humanity. Our race, rising in the energy of science, literature, and religion, shall stand forth in the triple strength and grace of the highest physical, intellectual, and moral power.[78]

Thus, Mary Graham's tombstone was making its contribution to the pedagogic value of Preston's new model cemetery: illness must no longer be seen as an act of God; it was the consequence of human folly and ignorance of the ways of nature.

At the beginning of the twenty-first century, it is still possible for the visitor to experience the contemplative state of mind that the Preston General Cemetery was intended to create. The changes that have transformed the rusticity of the surrounding area into a zone of urban sprawl have not destroyed the calm and reflective atmosphere within the walls. The cemetery presents a carefully tended vista where trees and shrubs create contrasts of vivid greenery and sombre russet foliage. There are trim lawns with well-tended paths that wend their way through serried rows of tombstones that are interrupted every so often by a more ambitious artefact of monumental masonry. To stroll there on a sunny June day, interrupted only by the occasional passer-by – a young couple, a young mother with a pram, a cyclist taking a short cut – is to understand nineteenth-century references to the beauty of this setting.[79] The cemetery survives as a fitting memorial to the nineteenth-century reformers who campaigned for its establishment, and it is appropriate that John Catterall and Joseph Livesey are buried there. Like many other survivals from the nineteenth-century era of statumania, however, the teetotal monument and the *campo santo* of which it is the centrepiece have lost much of their meaning. Modern Preston does not derive its 'glory' from its teetotal history, and the men and women who lie buried around the monument are not seen as the prophets of a new society and a higher form of humankind.

Notes

1   *Preston Guardian and Lancashire Advertiser,* 22 January 1859.
2   For example Harrison, B. (1971), *Drink and the Victorians. The Temperance Question in England 1815–1872,* London: Faber; Longmate, N. (1968), *The Waterdrinkers. A History of Temperance,* London: Hamish Hamilton; Curl, J.S. (1972), *The Victorian Celebration of Death,* Newton Abbot: David & Charles; Jupp, P.C. and Gittings, C. (1999), *Death in England, An Illustrated History,* Manchester: Manchester University Press.
3   For 'statumania', see Chapter 1 above.
4   This description of the inauguration of the Teetotal Monument is based on reports in the *Preston Guardian,* 23 April 1859, and the *Preston Chronicle,* 23 April 1859.
5   *Preston Guardian,* 22 January 1859.
6   Phillips, P.T. (1982), *The Sectarian Spirit: Sectarianism, Society and Politics in Victorian Towns,* Toronto: University of Toronto Press, p. 54 writes that 'Teetotalism in Preston involved a more serious effort at developing a distinct sect than in any of the other towns.'
7   Moss, W.E. (1935), *Joseph Livesey – Friend of the People,* Sheffield: British Temperance League, p. 20 refers to one burial beneath the monument, but there is no inscription to indicate this. See also *Preston Guardian,* 10 June 1871 which refers to a burial in the Temperance Vault.
8   The implied comparison here is with the Campo Santo (Holy Field) in Rome. Associated with the early Christians, this place was venerated as a burial ground and became one of the pilgrimage sites of Rome. Thomas Lacqueur's description of the Panthéon during the French Third Republic provides another comparison: it was 'the place where Great Men were memorialised and instruction in civic virtue took place'. See Lacqueur, T. (2001), 'In and Out of the Panthéon', *London Review of Books,* 23 (18), 20 September.
9   Colley, L (1996), *Britons. Forging the Nation 1707–1837,* New Haven, CT : Yale University Press, p. 28 describes *Pilgrim's Progress* as a 'canonical text' that 'appealed particularly to the subordinate classes' and inspired generations of British radicals.
10 *Struggle,* no. 23, n.d. I am grateful to Mr Aidan Turner-Bishop of the University of Central Lancashire Library for his permission to reproduce the image of 'Storming The Castle of Monopoly' from the copy of the *Struggle* held in the Joseph Livesey Collection.
11 Their intention was similar to the one described by Ben-Amos, A. (2000), *Funerals, Politics and Memory in Modern France, 1789–1996,* Oxford: Oxford University Press, p. 92. The Paris Panthéon was intended to be 'a place of funerary pilgrimage for the members of the opposition who wished to express their protest against the regime'.
12 See Longmate, *The Waterdrinkers,* for pictorial representations of violent opposition to the early teetotalers in Preston.
13 *Preston Guardian,* 2 November 1850. See also Livesey's *Preston Temperance Advocate,* January 1837 for an exposition of teetotalism as a 'positive' reform movement with its

own temperance hotels, tea parties and processions, news rooms, reading rooms and bands of music.

14　Ibid., 22 January 1859.
15　Catterall, J. and Livesey, J. (1857), 'The Progress of Temperance in Preston', *Preston Guardian*, 18 February.
16　See, for example, Teare, J. (1847, 2nd edn), *A History of the Origin and Success of the Advocacy of the Principle of Total Abstinence from all Intoxicating Liquors*, London: Charles Gilpin, pp. 5, 18, 20, 36–7 where there are many references to Preston giving a lead to the world.
17　*Staunch Teetotaler*, September 1868.
18　Ibid., April 1868; Teare, *History ... Of The Principle Of Total Abstinence*, p. 5.
19　Hewitson, A. (1969, 1st edn 1883), *History of Preston*, Wakefield: S.R. Publishers, p. 227, uses the term 'Teetotal pilgrims'. Referring to Preston as 'the Bethlehem of teetotalism', Jabez Inwards described his personal pilgrimage to the sites of early teetotalism in 1868. See *Staunch Teetotaler*, April 1868. The reference to Preston as 'Jerusalem' is in [J. Livesey] (n.d.) *Reminiscences of Early Teetotalism*, Preston: no publisher, p. 10.
20　Swinglehurst, E. (1974), *The Romantic Journey. The Story of Thomas Cook and Victorian Travel*, London: Pica Editions, pp. 13–27.
21　For Livesey's railway trips, see *Staunch Teetotaler*, June 1868. Paid for by 'Benevolent persons and employers', these trips were for the poor, and each person was given 'a bun and milk *ad libitum*' .
22　*Preston Guardian*, 26 August 1854.
23　Alternative versions attribute the origins of the word 'teetotal' to Lancashire colloquial usage and to Turner's tendency to speak in 'an equal mixture of wit and blunders'. See *The Shorter Oxford English Dictionary* and *Preston Guardian*, 7 November 1846. Harrison, *Drink and the Victorians*, p. 126 endorses the 'stuttering' version.
24　*Preston Guardian*, 7 November 1846.
25　Inwards, J. (1879), *Memorials of Temperance Workers*, London: S.W. Partridge & Co., pp. 273–4.
26　For the evangelical ideal of death, see Jalland, P. (1996), *Death in the Victorian Family*, Oxford: Oxford University Press, Chap. 1 and her 'Victorian Death and Its Decline: 1850–1918' (1999) in Jupp and Gittings (eds), *Death in England. An Illustrated History*, pp. 232–3.
27　*Preston Guardian*, 23 April 1859.
28　Ibid.
29　Harrison, *Drink and the Victorians*, pp. 116–17. Catterall's ire was directed primarily against William Morris. Brian Harrison, *Drink and the Victorians*, p. 140, identifies a teetotaler of that name as the founder of the first teetotal society in South London.
30　For the anti-slavery 'war of the monuments', see Chap. 7 below.
31　Pearce, J. (1885), *The Life and Teachings of Joseph Livesey*, London: National Temperance League Depot, p. lxxiv. See also *Staunch Teetotaler*, May 1868.
32　Kselman, T.A. (1993), *Death and the Afterlife in Modern France*, Princeton, NJ: Princeton University Press, pp. 169–70.
33　Thompson, D.M. (1972), *Nonconformity in the Nineteenth Century*, London: Routledge & Kegan Paul, p. 91.
34　For example, Edward Miall's *Nonconformist* newspaper, 27 February and 3 April 1850, favourably reported the Board of Health's proposals for new burial grounds but expressed misgivings because they envisaged an active role for government.
35　Curl, *Victorian Celebration of Death*, pp. 46–9, 55–77. Vovelle, M. (1983), *La Mort et L'Occident de 1300 à Nos Jours*, Paris: Gallimard, p. 633, refers to eight London cemeteries in 1843 representing an investment of £400,000.
36　Curl, *Victorian Celebration of Death*, Chap. 7.
37　*Preston Chronicle*, 2 June 1849. The government inspector was G.T. Clark.

38 Catterall set out his critique of contemporary burial practises in letters to Livesey's *Preston Guardian*, 16 June and 21 July 1849. For the adoption of miasmatic theory by urban reformers, see Porter, R. (1997), *The Greatest Benefit to Mankind. A Medical History of Humanity from Antiquity to the Present*, London: Fontana Press, p. 411.

39 *Preston Guardian*, 23 June 1849; *Preston Chronicle*, 23 June 1849.

40 Kselman, *Death and the Afterlife in Modern France*, Chap. 5; Colvin, H. (1991), *Architecture and the After-Life*, New Haven, CT: Yale University Press, pp. 369–70. Hall, S.C. (n.d.), *A Book of Memories of Great Men and Women of the Age*, London: J.S. Virtue, p. 336, who was one of the early supporters of cemetery reform, refers to the condemnation they received as 'not only un-English, but un-Christian'.

41 Simo, M. L. (1988), *Loudon and the Landscape. From Country Seat to Metropolis 1783–1843*, New Haven, CT: Yale University Press, p. 6.

42 Ibid., pp. 2, 247–8, 252–3.

43 Loudon, J.C. (1981, 1st edn 1843), *On the Laying Out, Planting, And Managing Of Cemeteries And On The Improvement Of Churchyards*, Redhill: Ivelet Books Ltd, pp. 12–13.

44 Ibid., p. 1.

45 Simo, *Loudon and the Landscape*, p. 282.

46 Curl, J.S. (1981), 'Introduction' in Loudon, *On the Laying out ... of Cemeteries*, p. 22.

47 *Moral Reformer*, 24 February 1838. Livesey referred to his proposal as one that he had 'often urged'.

48 *Preston Guardian*, 8 July 1854.

49 Hewitson, *History of Preston*, p. 249.

50 *Preston Chronicle*, 15 July 1854.

51 *Preston Guardian*, 8 July 1854; *Preston Chronicle*, 15 July 1854.

52 *Preston Chronicle*, 22 July 1854.

53 Hewitson, *History of Preston*, pp. 249–50.

54 Harrison, *Drink and the Victorians*, p. 163, refers to 'Nonconformist predominance' in his sample of teetotal leaders.

55 Rugg, J. (1999), 'From Reason to Regulation: 1760–1850' in Jupp and Gittings (eds), *Death in England. An Illustrated History*, pp. 206, 226–7.

56 The preceding discussion is indebted to Binfield, C. (1977), 'Dissenting Gothic' in *So Down to Prayers. Studies in English Nonconformity 1780-1920*, London: J.M. Dent & Sons Ltd, pp. 145–9. The growing popularity of Gothic in French cemeteries at this time is mentioned by Kselman, *Death and the Afterlife in Modern France*, p. 205.

57 *Preston Guardian*, 23 April 1859.

58 Ibid., 16 July 1859. Livesey described these fountains as 'preachers of temperance day and night to all the passers by'. See *Staunch Teetotaler*, May 1868.

59 The references in this chapter to epitaphs in the Preston General Cemetery are derived from the author's personal observation in June 2001.

60 *Preston Guardian*, 14 February 1863. For obituaries of other Preston teetotalers who had supported Henry Hunt see: Ibid., 28 May 1870, 15 April 1871.

61 Porter, R. (1990), 'Preface' in Barnard, S.M., *To Prove I'm Not Forgot. Living and Dying in a Victorian City*, Manchester: Manchester University Press, p. x.

62 Catterall's obituary in Livesey's *Staunch Teetotaler*, May 1868, refers to his creation of the Teetotal Monument, his 'great interest in Cemetery reforms', his role in building the new Temperance hall, and his work for orphan schools and the Blind Institution. During the bitter Preston strike of 1853–54 he had been described as a tool of the employers for his role on the 'anti-strike committee'. See Dutton, H.I. and King, J.E. (1981), *'Ten Per Cent and No Surrender'. The Preston Strike, 1853–1854*, Cambridge: Cambridge University Press, pp. 44–5.

63 Clark, A. (1995), *The Struggle for the Breeches. Gender and the Making of the British Working Class*, London: Rivers Oram, p. 2.

64 Tyrrell, A. (1980), 'Woman's Mission and Pressure Group Politics in Britain (1825–60)', *Bulletin of the John Rylands University Library of Manchester*, 63 (1), Autumn, pp. 219–21, 229; Pearce, *The Life and Teachings of Joseph Livesey*, pp. xxxvi, xli–xlii; Weston, J. (ed.) (1884), *Joseph Livesey: The Story of his Life, 1794–1884*, London: S.W. Partridge & Co., p. 55.

65 Information about Mary Graham has been obtained from *Preston Guardian*, 1 March 1862, 5 and 8 February 1868; Moss, *Joseph Livesey*, p. 20.

66 Livesey, *Reminiscences of Early Teetotalism*, p. 38.

67 Whittaker, T. (1885, 2nd edn), *Life's Battles in Temperance Armour*, London: Hodder & Stoughton, p. 370.

68 *British Temperance Herald for the West of England and South Wales*, October 1842.

69 *Westminster and Foreign Quarterly Review*, 1 April 1842.

70 Ibid., pp. 417–18, 420.

71 Pearce, *The Life and Teachings of Joseph Livesey*, pp. cxlvii–viii.

72 *Livesey's Moral Reformer*, 6 January, 24 March, 31 March, 21 April, 28 April, 19 May 1838.

73 Pearce, *The Life and Teachings of Joseph Livesey*, pp. 55, 60.

74 *Staunch Teetotaler*, January 1868.

75 Ibid., December 1868.

76 *Preston Guardian*, 21 July 1849.

77 In a letter to the *British Temperance Advocate*, 1 November 1853, Joseph Livesey expressed the belief that few teetotalers did not also advocate the water cure.

78 Ibid., 1 March 1852.

79 This description is based on a visit by the author in June 2001.

Chapter 7

Whose History Is It? Memorialising Britain's Involvement in Slavery

Alex Tyrrell and James Walvin

On 26 September 1996, a memorial was inaugurated in Westminster Abbey to honour Thomas Clarkson, one of the best known of the British anti-slavery abolitionists. The eulogy was delivered by no less a person than the Bishop of Ely.[1] Clarkson had been celebrated in biographies and histories, but it was by no means self-evident that his memory should be perpetuated in this way and at this late date. As the guidebooks made clear, the Abbey already contained memorials to several of those who had campaigned and legislated against slavery, and Clarkson had expressed a wish that he should not be commemorated within its walls.[2] The gesture was also open to the charge that it was out of keeping with the times. The old Whig notion of history as the story of freedom and progress in which Britons of eminence and probity had given a lead to the world no longer found favour in scholarly circles. Historians had re-evaluated the lives of many 'great men' including those who had been lauded as philanthropists and humanitarians. Much had been written about 'the power of the gift', 'hegemony' and the 'social control' that was exercised by political elites. To be sure, old ideas died hard; a book that Ernest Marshall Howse wrote in the 1950s, *Saints in Politics. The 'Clapham Sect' and the Growth of Freedom*, was reissued as an Open University set book in the 1970s, but by then it looked out of date.[3] In E.P. Thompson's provocatively memorable words, William Wilberforce, the leader of the 'Saints' and the best known of the abolitionists, could now be seen as one of those who had turned the humanitarian tradition into a counter-revolutionary creed and left it 'warped beyond recognition'.[4]

The inauguration of the Clarkson memorial pointed to a disjunction between academic history and public memory that was attracting scholarly attention. 1996 was the year when a work of seminal importance by Pierre Nora and a team of scholars appeared in an English version. *Realms of Memory. Rethinking the French Past* (the original title was *Lieux de Mémoire*) was based on the proposition that academic history is a reconstruction of the past from empirical data whereas public memory belongs to the present and is attached to symbols of community. For Nora the 'analysis and critical discourse' inherent in history as an intellectual discipline make it different from public memory. History has no absolutes, unlike public memory which 'situates remembrance in a sacred context' and is 'a real part of everyday experience'.[5] Some of the historians who contributed to Nora's volumes directed attention to buildings that functioned as symbolic sites of public memory.

One of these was the Panthéon, to which, in Mona Ozouf's words, on a memorable occasion President Mitterand had summoned the French people to participate in 'a gathering of the national community around its great men'.[6] The Panthéon, however, exemplified another of the conclusions to which Nora's volumes pointed: public memory is not monolithic but pluralist and 'conflictual'.[7] Thus, as Ozouf explained, the Panthéon is associated with the Revolution, and as such it marks a 'rupture' in French history. It is only 'one of the political memories offered to the French people', and it is by no means acceptable to all of them.[8]

The parallel must not be pushed too far, but Ozouf's analysis is relevant to the study of public commemorations of Britain's involvement in slavery. Westminster Abbey is the British equivalent of the Panthéon, and the meaning that underlay the ceremony on 26 September 1996 was unmistakable. The Bishop of Ely was summoning the British people to endorse the place of honour that the abolitionists occupied among the nation's great men and to recognise that their story still forms part of a metanarrative of national identity in which Britain had shown the way to social and moral progress. The speech referred briefly to the 'brutality' of slavery, and it repudiated the 'analogous slaveries of our own day', but the sense of national guilt was transcended by a hopeful message derived from the philanthropic achievements of those who had functioned within a political system that could be brought to see the error of its ways.[9] We 'honour Clarkson's memory best', the Bishop declared, 'when we acknowledge how much our country owes to men and women of moral passion, when we ourselves engage in their vision, and commit ourselves unequivocally to discern and to do the good we have it in our power to accomplish'.

Comments at the time lingered over the juxtaposition of Clarkson's memorial and Wilberforce's statue as well as the existence in the Abbey of several other memorials to abolitionists. It was evident that Britain's involvement in slavery was being remembered in and around the persons of the eminent abolitionists as they were depicted in what was literally a sacred site – one that the British Establishment had set aside for the veneration of the great and the good in the nation's history. In addition to his birthplace and dates of birth and death, the inscription on Clarkson's memorial proclaimed only that he was 'A friend to slaves';[10] those who read it were to recall the virtues of a man who had campaigned against slavery – not slavery itself. To use a term coined by an Australian historian, this was not a 'black armband' depiction of Britain's imperial past.[11] The critical fact that Britain had been the key slave-trading nation prior to abolition had to be sought elsewhere if it was sought at all.

This was a message that had changed remarkably little since the earliest attempts to create a permanent public memory of Britain's involvement in slavery. By taking a short walk from the new Clarkson memorial, visitors could see a magnificent monument that had been erected in the Abbey early in the nineteenth century to honour Charles James Fox. It shows Fox dying in the arms of Liberty while Peace sinks with grief. The only other effigy on the monument is a negro kneeling in a gesture of gratitude to Fox who in 1806 had played a crucial role in the legislative process that ended Britain's participation in the slave trade.[12] The message was one of reassurance and harmony; good had triumphed over evil to the satisfaction of all concerned. A similar message was picked up over the coming years and repeated on memorials to abolitionists across Britain. One of the most striking of these is Wilberforce House in Hull. A whole building dedicated to Wilberforce's life and work is packed with memorabilia of the man seen to be the key British activist against slavery. The museum contains a tableau depicting a recreation of slaves suffering on a slave ship,[13] but the focus is always on Wilberforce: his face, his portrait and his imagery, from youth to angelic old age, dominate the building and its memories of slavery. (See Figure 7.1.)

Although Westminster Abbey does not conjure up a strong sense of 'rupture' in national history, it is like the Panthéon in that its depiction of the nation's past is not acceptable to all. The Abbey belongs to the established Church of England, and its memorials exude a strong sense of hierarchy together with social and political propriety. Alternative expressions of public memory have taken other forms and been directed to other commemorative sites. Britain is a country of many communities, and especially in recent years some of these have shown a strong

Fig. 7.1   A recreation of slaves suffering on a slave ship, Wilberforce House, Hull.

interest in their own history, partly from a sense that they had been overlooked in the academic and public representation of the British past. Their quest for knowledge and inclusion in expressions of national identity has been assisted by developments in academic history since the 1960s. Turning aside from the elites or placing them within a broader social context, many historians have practised a 'history from below' that focuses on those who were either ignored or patronised in the historical record: women, the poor, minorities and the subjects of colonial rule. The change accompanied and helped to promote the development of new sites of public history where dissonant versions of public memory could be set out and given emphasis. Some of these took the form of people's museums where the lives of the poor and their struggles for betterment are celebrated.[14] In the north of Scotland, for example, museums and memorials have been created around the theme of the Highland Clearances to impart what one historian has described as 'notions of trauma, dislocation and oppression as well as a sense of loss and betrayal'. The same historian also noted that this was not a dispassionate evocation of a sense of the past; visitors are presented with 'coercive' narratives. Several of the museums have even articulated a strong ideological opposition to the landowning class and by doing so have taken a stance on current issues such as land rights.[15]

Even as late as 1988 it seemed that the day would never come when public commemorations of a similar sort could be devised for the slaves, the people who all too soon had been relegated to the ranks of the unimportant and the unnoticed by the British nation that had proudly set them free. At a museums' conference in that year the former managing director of Heritage Projects Ltd dismissed the very idea of a 'Museum of Slavery': the public would never accept it, he flatly declared, and he had rejected a proposal to build one. His words brought down on him a condemnation from a Scottish journalist who pointed to some of the less savoury reasons that stood in the way of such a project:

> Now, it might be that a well-designed museum which laid bare the anatomy of the slave trade could be very useful. It could very well shed some interesting light on a vile trade which is little understood, which is still partly concealed, and in which the British, including some Scots, played a big part. Many fortunes were made from peddling black flesh. Such a museum might still embarrass some very influential families. Bristol would be its natural home.[16]

In October 1994, however, a Transatlantic Slavery Gallery was opened in the Merseyside Maritime Museum in Liverpool, another 'natural home'. The abolitionists were not omitted from the exhibits and the catalogue, but there was no doubt as to the underlying theme of the Gallery: visitors were to be brought face to face with some of the bleaker features of British history. In the words of the patron, Peter Moores, 'A visit to the exhibition is bound to disturb us – black or white'; harsh realities were exposed there 'without mincing matters'.[17] As in the case of the Highland Clearance museums, important contemporary issues were involved in this reformulation of public memory. A contributor to the catalogue went to the length of denying that in the immediate future there could be any consensus between the 'different vantage points' of those who were descended from Africans and

Europeans. One of the comparisons on which he relied showed the extent of the change that he was promoting. Ignoring the modish belief that national apologies can serve as a sufficient penitence by the present generation for the misdeeds of its ancestors, this writer went straight to a demand for compensation: Britain should follow the example of the 'Reparations ... made by the German Government to Israel for the Jewish victims of the Nazi Holocaust'.[18] This was a far cry from the message that was preached at the Clarkson memorial four years later, although the Bishop of Ely took the opportunity to deplore 'the swingeing terms upon which international debts are repaid' by the developing countries.[19] In the closing years of the twentieth century, the public memory of Britain's involvement in slavery had become undeniably pluralist and 'conflictual'.

It always had been pluralist and 'conflictual', although not in the form taken during the 1990s. From the time when the first anti-slavery monuments were erected in the early years of the nineteenth century, the public memory of slavery had been given different and competing expressions. The question at issue then was not one that set the claims of the abolitionists against those of the slaves; it was one that set the abolitionists against each other. In a way that was replicated over and over again in the reform movements of that era the question was: 'which of the abolitionists is entitled to the credit for emancipating the slaves?'[20] The answers took the form of memorials that threw into prominence some of the most bitter divisions in the society and polity of early nineteenth-century Britain.

Charles James Fox's monument in Westminster Abbey occupies an important place in the history of these early attempts to assert ownership of the public memory of anti-slavery. Its depiction of Fox dying in the arms of Liberty while a grateful slave looks on was no transient flight of fancy; almost thirty years after Fox's death a very similar image was flaunted when Earl Grey made his triumphal visit to Scotland in 1834. He was greeted at the border by a large painting that showed him 'delivering to one of a number of African slaves, a charter of their emancipation, at which the other negroes present are making demonstrations of great joy'. The painting also contained 'representations of England, Scotland, and Ireland, and a figure of Fame bearing a scroll on which was inscribed "WELCOME BRITAIN'S PATRIOT AND AFRICA'S EMANCIPATOR"'.[21] A year earlier, Grey's government had completed Fox's work by passing the Emancipation Act that terminated the status of slavery in the British Empire. These tableaux, one in sculpture and the other on canvas, created an image of the Whigs as they delighted to see themselves – the party of civil and religious liberty in Britain and its Empire. The theme had been set out more extensively on a monument that was erected in Woburn Abbey by the fifth Duke of Bedford shortly before the abolition of the slave trade. In what has been described by N.B. Penny as a temple of liberty dedicated to Fox, a frieze showed the rise of mankind from barbarism through the stages of civilization.[22] The transition was one that had been set out by Adam Smith and other Scottish Enlightenment intellectuals. In Penny's words it went

... from a primitive hunting society to a more settled life with domesticated flocks, then the beginnings of architecture, astrology and perhaps religion, followed by agriculture, technology, travel, colonization and trade. The climax of such progress is government established on equal laws, liberty, the abolition of slavery and expulsion of tyranny.

Evidently the primary function of these memorials was not to shed light on slavery or even on the campaign against it; they were commissioned to provide impressive examples of the Whigs as a civilising force in government. History, they were saying, had reached its highest point in the ideals that Fox and Grey had worked to implement. If there was a role for the slaves in this depiction of one of mankind's moments of triumph on the way to civilisation, it was summarised in the image of the deferential supplicant on Fox's monument.

What was also evident, though by omission, was the insistence of the Whigs that their leaders' claim to eminence as abolitionists was exclusive. Neither Fox's monument nor Grey's painting intimated that there was any credit to be shared with the 'Saints' or anyone else. The key dates in this history of slavery –1806 and 1833 – belonged to the Whigs. As was only to be expected, the claim to the ownership of Emancipation – one of the most potent evocations of British national rectitude throughout the nineteenth century – was not allowed to stand unchallenged. In what became something like a battle of the monuments, rival claims were given prominence in a similarly exclusive spirit. In 1816, a monument was erected in honour of Granville Sharp in Westminster Abbey where visitors could read a very different story from the one on Fox's monument. The lengthy epitaph referred to 'that Act of the British Parliament By which the abolition [of the slave trade] was decreed', but this was the only reference that could include the Whigs. The emphasis was on Granville Sharp as a man of religion and philanthropy who had set out to free Britain from the guilt of slavery. He had successfully defended the rights of 'the negro race' by obtaining a legal decision that conferred freedom on a West Indian slave who had been brought to Britain. The epitaph emphasised that this had not been a life of individual struggle; Sharp had taken 'his post among the foremost of the honourable band Associated to deliver Africa from the rapacity of Europe'. This, so an appendage on the memorial coercively informed visitors, was 'not panegyric, but history'.[23]

There was no doubt as to the identity of the 'honourable band'. The monument was 'erected by the African Institution of London', one of Wilberforce's societies, and this would not be the last attempt of the 'Saints' to stake out a claim for the ownership of the public memory of British abolitionism. In 1834, the same year that Earl Grey was hailed as 'AFRICA'S EMANCIPATOR', the foundation stone of one of the most impressive anti-slavery monuments ever to be erected was laid in Hull, Wilberforce's birthplace. Eventually a huge column, 102 feet high, surmounted by a statue dominated the skyline. The statue was of Wilberforce who had died the previous year, and around the plinth of the column appeared the words 'Wilberforce' – 'Negro Slavery Abolished 1 August MDCCCXXXIV' – 'First Stone Laid 1 August MDCCCXXXIV'.[24] This was the date on which Earl Grey's Emancipation Act took effect, and the message was unmistakably clear: the Whigs might claim that they had enacted the legislation against slavery, but emancipation was the achievement of Wilberforce. During the next few decades, this vision of slavery being overthrown by a triumphant crusade of Wilberforce and the 'Saints' was developed on memorials that were erected to honour Wilberforce, Zachary Macaulay and Thomas Fowell Buxton. Macaulay was commemorated in Westminster Abbey for his share in 'the counsels and in the labours' that had overthrown the slave trade and slavery.[25] The memorial that was erected in the Abbey to honour Buxton, Wilberforce's designated successor, enumerated a lengthy catalogue of good causes before lauding him 'above all, for the emancipation of eight hundred thousand slaves in the British dominions'. He and 'his co-adjutors' had achieved this 'final victory' on 'the memorable 1st of August 1834'.[26]

Buxton's memorial was commissioned in 1845, but by then the battle for ownership of the public memory of British anti-slavery had moved on to a new and bitter stage. This could be seen on two memorials that pointed to a date in anti-slavery history which, so it was implied, was more important than 1806, 1833 and 1834. On 1 August 1838 a Festival took place in Birmingham during which upwards of three thousand children from the local Baptist Sunday schools marched through the town to a construction site. There they witnessed Joseph Sturge, a Quaker businessman and one of the best-known abolitionists of the day, laying the foundation stone of a building that was to be known as the Negro Emancipation School Rooms. A brass plate contained the following inscription:

> The foundation stone of these School-rooms was laid on Wednesday, the 1st of August, 1838, in commemoration of the Abolition of Negro Apprenticeship in the Colonies, by the friend of the Negro, the friend of man, JOSEPH STURGE Esq., in the presence of the United Baptist Sunday Schools, and assisted by the Baptist ministers of Birmingham … .

In its report of the event the *British Emancipator* referred to 1 August 1838 as a date 'handed down to posterity as being marked by events, perhaps, more important, and more deeply interesting, than any that have yet been recorded in the pages of colonial history'.[27]

The second memorial was one that was also erected on a site belonging to the Baptist Church, this time in a mission chapel in Falmouth, Jamaica. On an interior wall a marble monument dating from 1839 gave glory to God and showed the 'Emancipated Sons of Africa' commemorating 1 August 1838 as 'The Birth-Day Of Their Freedom' and 'The Day-Spring of Universal Liberty'. Beneath the inscription, two negroes are shown burying a chain and a whip, while another rejoices in the possession of the Bible, and a woman caresses her child. Above the inscription, bas-relief profiles attribute this happy state of affairs to three men – Granville Sharp, William Wilberforce and, in the central position, Joseph Sturge. Another profile at the base of the monument showed that this version of anti-slavery history had been envisaged by the 'Rev. W. Knibb pastor of this Church', a Baptist missionary who was well known for his participation along with Sturge in anti-slavery campaigns in Jamaica and Britain.[28]

Once again the focus had shifted to bring into prominence a new and 'conflictual' form of public memory. Evidently the memorialists of the Whigs and the 'Saints' had got it wrong; the anti-slavery movement had reached its climax in 1838, and its principal activist had been Joseph Sturge. From this point of view, 1838, not 1833 or 1834, was the year when slavery had finally been terminated. The Emancipation Act had abolished the status of slavery in the British Empire but replaced it with a regime of part-time compulsory and unpaid labour that was to be phased out in two stages. This Apprenticeship, as it was called, was the work of Earl Grey's Whig Government, and it had been accepted by Buxton and other anti-slavery leaders in London. It was not acceptable to other abolitionists for whom forced labour was slavery under another name. Between 1834 and 1838, with Sturge as their leader, and against the wishes of Buxton as well as the Whig Government, these dissident abolitionists and their Baptist missionary allies in Jamaica successfully campaigned to overthrow the Apprenticeship. The monuments that were erected in Birmingham and Falmouth were attempts to commemorate their story and perpetuate their memory.[29]

The story told by these monuments had implications that went beyond a concern for recording the past. As Paul Shackel has put it: 'Those who control the past have the ability to command social and political events in the present and the future.'[30] In this case what was at stake was the leadership of the anti-slavery movement in the years to come. Beyond that lay a deeper dispute over the reshaping of the society and polity of Britain and Jamaica. The rivalry between Sturge and Buxton followed some of the most important fault lines that ran across early Victorian Britain – the divisions between Nonconformity and the Church of England, between the provinces and London and between the 'Old Society' and the new bourgeois society. From the 1780s to the 1840s, Wilberforce and Buxton infused their vision of reform with the values of the 'Old Society' of the eighteenth century where the influence of leisured gentlemen dominated public life. They knew that politicians such as William Pitt the younger, Charles James Fox and Earl Grey might need an occasional spur from the massed ranks of British Christians, but they did not doubt that the anti-slavery movement should act through gentlemen with influence. Lists of patrons of the societies that Wilberforce and Buxton set up were usually top heavy with the names of peers, bishops and men of high military rank.[31] Decades passed by while cabinet ministers were respectfully lobbied for piecemeal reforms.

Those who followed Sturge on the other hand were described as 'new people' – men and women of the provincial middle class, who were Nonconformists for the most part and increasingly intent on achieving equality in what was still in many respects an aristocratic and Anglican confessional state. They were ill-disposed to defer to Whig politicians or men of established status; they preferred to use the force of public opinion to intervene decisively in national politics. They called themselves 'Moral Radicals' who followed the politics of the Bible, and, unlike Wilberforce and Buxton who were MPs and mindful of the clash of competing interests, they saw compromise as a dalliance with sin. The words 'total and immediate' came easily to them when they were devising their demands; 'mitigation', 'amelioration' and 'moderation' – terms that were the bread and butter of everyday politics for the Whigs, Wilberforce and Buxton - had no place in their lexicon of reform.[32] William Knibb was speaking with their authentic accents when he told a sympathetic audience in Exeter Hall in 1842 that he saw the Falmouth monument as an act of triumphant assertion: 'Your missionaries are not men wedded to any system whatever; but, the advocates of the liberties of others, they will crouch to none on earth.'[33]

The 'Moral Radicals' and their Baptist missionary friends followed up the monuments in Birmingham and Falmouth by other attempts to dominate the leadership and the public memory of the anti-slavery movement. As Avner Ben Amos has pointed out with reference to France, carefully chosen place names can be a powerful means of using public spaces to create a sense of public memory with a pedagogical purpose.[34] Ben-Amos had street names in mind, but the Baptist missionaries in Jamaica had a bolder vision. In the aftermath of the Apprenticeship, encouraged by the prospects that were opened up by their rapidly growing congregations, they were intent on dominating the new, free Jamaica.[35] One indication of this was their attempt to refashion the map of the island in a way that would make it resonate with the achievements and values of the anti-slavery crusade to which they had made a major contribution. With the assistance of their British friends, including Sturge, they set up a string of free villages across the island where former slaves who had left or been expelled from the plantations could acquire small properties (with votes) and live together in Christian communities around the Baptist chapels.[36] The names of these moral power-houses were drawn from their version of anti-slavery history. Wilberforce, Buxton and Clarksonville were among the names they chose, but there were others that commemorated heroes whose names would never have appeared on a Westminster Abbey monument of this era: Sturge Town, Thompson Town, Stewart Town, Kettering and Hoby Town.[37]

The naming of the free villages was not the most combative attempt of the Moral Radicals to control the realms of memory. In 1840 they commissioned a massive painting to give future generations a vision of the anti-slavery movement as it regrouped after the campaign against the Apprenticeship system and pressed on to a new and wider role against slavery across the entire world. A letter written by 'J.P. of Islington' described the painting as 'a work of amazing interest to the friend of freedom, and will, in a future day, pourtray a pleasing epoch in the history of universal emancipation'.[38] He failed to mention that the patron was the British and Foreign Anti-Slavery Society which Sturge had recently set up in rivalry with Buxton and the old anti-slavery establishment, and that the painting mirrored the deep divisions that existed in the ranks of the abolitionists. The principal difference had been shown at the inauguration of Buxton's African Civilization Society earlier in 1840, when Buxton sought and obtained the support of leading politicians and men of established rank. Prince Albert made his first public speech on this occasion, and the society's most important venture, the ill-fated Niger expedition, was backed (with misgivings) by the Whig Government.[39] In that year, as its first major venture, Sturge's British and Foreign Anti-Slavery Society took the very different course of summoning the abolitionists of the world to a convention in London as a step towards creating an international anti-slavery pressure group, an early version of the non-governmental organisations that are so prominent in our own day. The painting to which 'J.P. of Islington' referred was commissioned as a composite portrait of the delegates and guests, the majority of whom were Nonconformists and people of the middle class. The painter was Benjamin Robert Haydon, one of the leading artists of the day.

At first glance, the outcome appears as something like a plain photographic snapshot of a moment during one of the convention's sessions, but the reality was otherwise. The painting was a 'set of heads' that was carefully constructed as a pictorial hall of fame where Haydon, guided by the secretary of the British and Foreign Anti-Slavery Society, 'ticketted all the heads according to desert'.[40] In other words, the individuals shown in the painting were chosen, positioned and scaled in size according to the Society's criteria of importance. Some of the delegates and guests were invited to participate in individual studio sittings to ensure that they would be immediately identifiable, and a special catalogue was prepared with a numbered list of names. The painting focused on Thomas Clarkson, when, appearing as the elder statesman of the movement, he was delivering his peroration to the delegates, but the symbolism with which Haydon invested this moment was unmistakable. Clarkson dominated the centre of the painting, but Sturge was given a prominent position beneath his upraised, almost benedictory, hand. At the other extreme, Buxton, who had bravely attended his rival's convention, was given 'but a second rate place' in the pictorial setting, 'because he had behaved so bad to the [British and Foreign Anti-Slavery] Society'.[41] Although Haydon seems to have enjoyed the task of promoting and demoting his sitters to the places they occupied in the painting, eventually even he was startled to find how exclusive his patrons' intentions were. In a fanciful gesture that was prompted by his recognition of a sense of pluralism in anti-slavery history, he inserted the names of Wilberforce, Granville Sharp and Toussaint L'Ouverture on the curtain in the background of the painting but was sharply reprimanded and told to delete them because they had nothing to do with the convention. He confided his incredulity to his diary: 'The Gratitude of Posterity! Without Wilberforce, Toussaint, or Sharp, no Convention would ever have been held on the subject.'[42]

By ordering Haydon to remove Wilberforce's name from a painting in which Thomas Clarkson was the central figure, Sturge and his friends in the British and Foreign Anti-Slavery Society were taking sides in the most bitter battle that the abolitionists waged against each other for the control of public memory. The battle had started in 1838 with the appearance of a biography of Wilberforce by two of his sons. The biography contained an attack on Clarkson's *History of the Rise, Progress, and Accomplishment of the Abolition of the African Slave-Trade By The British Parliament,* which, so the brothers said, belittled their father's role by implying that he had only been the parliamentary agent of the anti-slavery movement. Clarkson had even had the temerity to append something like a pictorial icon of the history of emancipation in the form of an imaginary map of a river showing the anti-slavery 'torrent' gaining its force from the confluence of many tributaries named after individual abolitionists. The image showed Clarkson's name near the upper reaches of one of the principal sources of the 'torrent' whereas Wilberforce's name appeared on a tributary much lower down-river. William Wordsworth, Robert Southey and other well-known contemporaries, the Wilberforce brothers angrily noted, had been misled into accepting the *History* as the literary monument of the campaign against the slave trade. The response in their biography was a reassessment that left Clarkson lamenting his reduction to a 'mean and degraded being'. Speaking with the voices of the 'Old Society', the Wilberforces sneeringly dismissed him as a 'nemo' (nobody) who had been paid for his services. He was not one of the 'Saints'; unlike their father who was a man of 'high political influence rarely combined with independence', he was 'half Quaker' and therefore of use mainly because he could do 'eccentric things' from which others would shrink. [43]

To insult Clarkson in this way was to insult Sturge and others who became members of the British and Foreign Anti-Slavery Society. They rallied to Clarkson's defence by publishing a new edition of his *History*. Giving him (and Sturge) pride of place in the great anti-slavery painting was part of this campaign. The gesture was more effective than it might seem. Unlike other memorials that were erected in fixed positions, this one was mobile. It was transported round the country and was even given a place of honour in the great bazaar that the Anti-Corn Law League organized in 1842. [44] It is now held in the National Portrait Gallery in London.

Nowadays Haydon's painting is often remembered as the carefully contrived memorial of another important event in British history – the denial to women of a right to participate actively as delegates at the international anti-slavery convention. Preserved for posterity as diminutive figures in the background are several American women abolitionists who had demanded the right to speak and vote. The British and Foreign Anti-Slavery Society and most of the male delegates had ruled that such a departure from established procedure was out of order. [45] Thus the obscurity to which Haydon consigned these women was deliberate, and it can be seen as a reinforcement of the inferior status of women in early Victorian Britain. A careful interpretation, however, suggests that the painting can be understood in a more favourable light. As 'J.P. of Islington' noted when he referred to the importance of the painting for future generations, several British women were given positions of prominence, [46] and they were identified in the accompanying catalogue. In other words, they occupied an honoured, if unequal, place in the anti-slavery hall of fame – one that recognised the role that women had played in the campaign for emancipation where they attended to such matters as fund-raising and petitioning. Thus the painting was bolder and more open-minded than it might seem to modern eyes. It was a brave initiative that honoured women in an active, albeit gendered, role as reformers at a time when custom frowned on their participation in the public world. This was a precedent that would be developed as the century advanced. [47]

One other recognition of the anti-slavery women deserves to be noticed. The name of Anne Knight, a Quaker abolitionist who was well known for her strenuous advocacy of advanced ideas, including women's rights, was perpetuated as Knightsville on the Baptist missionaries' map of the new Jamaica. [48] This was as far as the honouring of the female abolitionists went. In a private letter to Anne Knight, Sir George Stephen, who would later appoint himself the historian of Emancipation, described the women as 'the cement of the whole Anti-slavery building', but neither he nor anyone else pursued the image. [49] The 'statumania' of that era was not for women. [50] It remains to be seen if the present era will be different. With the exception of the way that slaves are depicted, perhaps nothing shows the limitations of the

Westminster Abbey commemorations of abolitionism more than the decision to remedy the 'wrong' done to Clarkson while the women continue to be ignored.[51]

The memorials that have been discussed so far in this chapter were assertions of empowerment. Milestones on the way to further deeds of merit, they conferred legitimacy and authority on Whigs, 'Saints' and Moral Radicals. They were pointers to a future of active leadership. The depiction of the slaves, if they were depicted at all, was very different; they were helpless victims in need of rescue. Even after they had been rescued, the role they were assigned in the icons of abolitionism showed little change – they were to be seen as figures of gratitude. The kneeling negro on Fox's monument was matched by a similar figure on the memorial that was erected in Clarkson's honour at Wisbech, his birthplace.[52] It is called 'the Supplicant'.[53] Buxton's memorial in Westminster Abbey referred to 'many thousands of the African race' sending 'grateful contributions' to assist the erection of this testimony to their benefactor. Admittedly, Henry Beckford, a Jamaican ex-slave, was assigned a prominent place in the great anti-slavery painting, but, as Haydon made clear, he was included as an easily identified symbol of the abolitionists' success. When Beckford addressed the convention it was to call on the delegates to 'look at me and work on';[54] abolitionism was their task, not his. The monument in the Falmouth Baptist chapel with its images of male and female slaves enjoying the fruits of freedom is more elaborate than most, but again it endorses a victim's role. There is even an implication that the evils of slavery have been cancelled out by the efforts of the abolitionists and the missionaries to convert the slaves to Christianity and respectable family life. The presence of Edward Barrett in the great anti-slavery painting, a former slave who, like Beckford, had been brought over by William Knibb to represent the Western Baptist Union of Jamaica, makes a similar point. Who could have said that these men would have been better off if their ancestors had been left in Africa? Some memorials in Jamaica took the form of freedom trees that were planted over coffins filled with shackles and whips, possibly as an echo of European ceremonies of empowerment, but the sites were Baptist chapels and the rituals were performed by the British missionaries. There seems to have been no recognition of any participation by the slave population in its own deliverance.[55] The deletion of Toussaint L'Ouverture's name from Haydon's anti-slavery painting was probably dictated at least in part by a reluctance to concede any agency to the slaves other the one personified by trustworthy Baptist deacons. A portrait of Joseph Sturge summed up much of the prevailing attitude. Sturge is shown against a tropical background: the documents of his participation in the emancipation campaign are on his left hand while his right hand rests protectively on the shoulder of a respectably dressed negro girl.[56]

It is this image of the slave as a helpless, child-like victim waiting to be rescued by the abolitionists that has been challenged by the Liverpool Slavery Gallery. Very much a creation of its times, this museum has directed attention to the resilience and initiative of the slaves. It has rescued their agency in history. A chapter in the catalogue entitled 'African Resistance to Enslavement' shows the visitor that whips and chains were only part of the story of slavery. There were frequent rebellions, resistance took myriad forms, and distinctive Afro-American cultural practices flourished beyond the control of the planters. In other words, slave society in the New World can now be seen as to some extent the creation of the slaves themselves.[57]

Recognising that slaves had powers of agency has been an easier task than giving them a recognisable face to put alongside the well-known features of abolitionists such as Wilberforce. Those who commemorated the abolitionists did not see this as a matter of concern; for them the slave was a symbolic figure. Apart from Knibb's Baptist deacons, the only slave to be mentioned by name on any of the memorials discussed above was James Somerset, who was set free by a legal judgment after Granville Sharp had intervened on his behalf. Public memory relies heavily on the carefully presented lives of individuals, but, as those who practice 'history from below' know well, it is often easier to rescue history's forgotten people in the mass than as individuals with distinctive life stories.[58] By the 1990s, however, it seemed that some slaves were finding their way into the public memory of slavery. Three years after the inauguration of the Liverpool Gallery an exhibition devoted to the life and work of the eighteenth-century African man of letters, Ignatius Sancho, was opened at the National Portrait Gallery in London. Centred on the Gainsborough portrait of Sancho, the exhibition incorporated his written work, music and historical significance.[59] Again like the Liverpool example, it proved enormously successful, especially for London schools, and among visitors from the Afro-Caribbean communities. Running as a motif throughout the whole exhibition was the issue of slavery. After all, Sancho had been born on a slave ship, and he had been destined for the slave island of Grenada.[60]

But of all the black figures from Britain's eighteenth-century slaving past, none has become better known than Olaudah Equiano. Virtually unknown only a generation ago, he has risen to iconic status. In 2000, an image of Equiano flickered in one section of London's ill-fated Millennium Dome, and a plaque to his memory is now located at 67 Riding House Street in London. Forty years earlier his career was almost the exclusive property of a small group of scholars: a political scientist, an Africanist and a literary scholar.[61] Today his *Narrative* is used as a text in History and Literature courses, and his name is familiar to large numbers of students in Europe, Africa and the Americas. Equiano's words are among the most quoted and anthologised of any black writer of the era of the slave trade. All this is despite lingering doubts about key sections of his text, especially those that refer to his African origins. Most curious of all, the portrait used to represent him which appears on many reprints of the Narrative, and which has been widely distributed as a poster, is almost certainly not a picture of Equiano. There is a perfectly good representational black-and-white picture (one chosen by Equiano himself) on the frontispiece of the Narrative. But modern commentators, scholars and publishers continue to choose the more striking, coloured oil painting of a handsome late eighteenth-century African. Although scholars now believe that the portrait is not Equiano, this seems to be of little consequence. The portrait has been accepted as a representation of what Equiano should have looked like. It has all the qualities we might want to see in one whose life belied the image of the African as a helpless victim; a handsome man with a no-nonsense facial expression, and a stance of defiant self-assertion. Irrespective of who he really was, it is, in effect, an idealisation of the African presence in eighteenth-century Britain. The two strands – Equiano the man, and Equiano the imaginary representative of the African presence – have become blurred in this one, symbolic portrait.

What then are we memorialising in what is almost certainly a false image of the real Equiano? The answer provides an entrée to the wider academic and public rediscovery of slavery in the late twentieth century. Equiano represents much more than the story of one man's experience in the years of the African Diaspora: the wider story of Atlantic slavery has been draped across his shoulders. His name, his words, his face (even when not his own) are implicitly accepted as a personification of Atlantic slavery at a time when attention is shifting from the abolitionists to the slaves themselves. It is an excellent example of the disjunction between the demands of public memory and the analytical procedures of academic history. This raises a more fundamental question. Why should a mythology of slavery seem better suited to memorialisation than a scholarly representation of historical reality itself? Surely the harsh realities of slavery ought to have more potency, more drama, more suffering and a deeper resonance for the modern day than anything that might be culled from the imagination? Why invent fiction when reality will suffice? Yet, time and again, the memorialisation of slavery has elevated myth above reality.

Perhaps the most notable example of the mythologising of the slave past is in Africa itself. Gorée Island off Senegal is a UNESCO World Heritage Site that has become a favourite destination for African-American tourists. They are told that many millions of Africans passed through Gorée's grim facilities. Historians of the slave trade on the other hand acknowledge that much of what is accepted about Gorée is largely mythological. It was certainly a slave fort that housed Africans before they were shipped to the Americas, but it was built late in the history of the Atlantic slave trade, and it was the location of a relatively small-scale operation in which only small numbers of Africans were passed on to the America-bound slave ships. Evidently this is less compelling than elaborate accounts of millions passing through the fort's forbidding cells, en route to bondage in the Americas. The history displaced by this process is as shocking as anything mythology could devise, but the mythology carries the day.[62]

The commercial interests involved in what is offered at Gorée are blatantly obvious – it would be a grievous blow to the local tourist industry if the opinion gained ground that much of what it claims actually took place elsewhere. But the reasons go deeper than the often remarked consequences of presenting history as a heritage attraction. Time and again, the symbolism of slavery has usurped historical reality. Until comparatively recently, slaves were marginalised in history even more than other plebeian groups, but this is no longer the case. After half a century of detailed research and publication, Atlantic slavery is now the site of some of the most interesting, innovative historical research (certainly the most voluminous) on both sides of the Atlantic. Evidently this matters not at all; myths of what happened at Gorée are the stuff of public memory.

Of the ten plus million Africans who stumbled ashore from the slave ships in the Americas, only a small proportion arrived in North America. By far the largest numbers arrived in Brazil and the West Indian islands. It was there that African slavery was to be seen at its most raw, most violent and crudest. However we analyse the data, the indices of social experience (birth, sickness, death, longevity, health) are all at their worst in Brazil and the Caribbean. It was in those regions that battalions of Africans were thrown into the enervating task of tropical field work (mainly in the sugar fields.) And it was there that their suffering was worst of all. Yet even here, where slave reality outstrips the imagination, the memorialisation of the slave past is more representational than real. The symbolic rather than the real slave is used time and again to evoke both the horrors of slavery and the resistant spirit of the slave community.

Jamaica was the prize possession among Britain's chain of eighteenth-century slave islands. Today, one of the modern state's 'national heroes' is Nanny, a female leader of a slave revolt in the 1730s. Among her many amazing qualities was an ability (so it was claimed) to catch British cannon balls in her buttocks and to fart them back at the British troops. Nanny has come to symbolise slave resistance and, of course, female spirit, despite the fact that, even in her own lifetime, she was more mythological than real. Even today we know very little about her. Nanny provides a representational juncture of varied invaluable images: African power (much of which was beyond the ken of slave owners), indomitable spirit which refused to bow before the severest of repression, and the elevation of women to equality in a world (especially a military world) dominated by men.[63] She is now remembered by a town named after her, and she has her portrait on the modern Jamaican $500 note. Significantly, the portrait is an imaginary representation.

The slave resistance personified by Nanny was of course a major theme in the story of Atlantic slavery. Indeed the history of slavery, from the first moment of enslavement in Africa, through to settlement and work on the American plantations, could be narrated via the varied forms of slave resistance. Yet the slaves only once overthrew local slavery; in St. Domingue (modern Haiti) in the 1790s. There, a confused, swirling mix of events, played out under the shadow of the French Revolution, saw the destruction of French, British and Spanish armies, an end to slavery, and the collapse of the local slavebased industries (notably sugar and coffee). This violent slave upheaval from which abolitionists as well as the pro-slavery interest recoiled with horror is represented in the Haitian capital Port au Prince by the image of a single slave: a rebellious but unknown slave. In a strikingly defiant posture, he is blowing on a conch shell, the instrument used throughout the islands to rally other slaves, and consequently feared by whites everywhere, as the clarion call of slave rebellion. One man, one instrument – to capture the greatest slave revolt since Spartacus![64]

The rebellious slave, real or mythical, has emerged as a favourite artefact in the modern memorialising of slavery. In Barbados for example, a figure of Bussa,[65] leader of the local slave rebellion in 1816, dominates one of the major approaches to Bridgetown from the airport, and it is close to the popular tourist region. It is a defiant figure, still carrying the remnants of shackles from the wrists.[66] Chains of course have a heavy symbolism for slavery, even though the armies of slaves worked in the fields free from any physical restraints. For the abolitionists and the descendants of the slaves alike, the breaking of chains has proved among the most durable of images (literary and iconographical) in capturing the slaves' struggle for freedom. Resistance to slavery, however, came in many forms, and leaders of slave resistance came in various guises, not all of them overtly violent or aggressive. In Montego Bay, Jamaica, the most famous local slave hero, Sam Sharpe, is memorialised in what seems, at first sight, to be a conventionally respectable and even pious form. Sharpe was a preacher, and his preacherly demeanour, captured in a statue in the town's main square, seems the very image of respectability.[67] The memorial, however, is at once simple and deceptive. It is not one that British abolitionists would have wished to erect. Unauthorised preaching was a subversive activity in Jamaica in the era before Emancipation, the more so if a slave attempted it. The Baptist missionaries, whose vision of a free Jamaica was one in which they would exercise dominance, were at one with the planters in attempting to define preaching as a role for recognised clergymen. They were unsuccessful. Some of the slaves, former deacons and officers in the mission chapels in several cases, set up their own independent churches. These Native Baptist churches, which worshipped according to syncretic forms of Christian and African ritual, provided one of the most important indications of the slaves' cultural resistance to white domination during the decades surrounding Emancipation. Sharpe had broken with the British missionaries and become one of the leading Native Baptists. His preaching, which unleashed a wave of slave rebellion in 1831–32, constituted an act of defiance against his missionary mentors scarcely less than against the planters.[68] There was no place for him on British abolitionist icons, be they those of the Whigs, the 'Saints' or the Moral Radicals. Sharpe represented an indigenous tradition; his statue had to await Jamaican independence.

These slave memorials are of recent vintage and they share a common factor: they speak to, and force us to reflect on, one particular feature of slavery – resistance. The daily grind of slave life, the heavy-duty field work which was the essence of slavery, has not been memorialised. It is the slave rebel, the defiant slave, the slave who spoke out against slavery, violently or subversively, who is now thought to be the best, most characteristic symbol of the slaving past. We need of course to remember that some of the societies that have chosen to memorialise slavery in this way are independent black communities, keen to strike free from the colonial past. A modern national identity has to be constructed from a history which was, in many respects, not of their own making. Public memory for these new nations is inevitably invested with a strong pedagogic component, one that can offer a radical, indigenous reinterpretation of the former colonial-inspired view. They too must have their versions of the Panthéon.

In Britain itself the memorialising of the black past took an entirely different trajectory. Until the late 1960s, very little thought or attention was paid to the history of British black people. The rise of the modern black community because of immigration after 1945 changed all that.[69] By the 1990s, there was a completely new appreciation that there had been a black population in eighteenth-century Britain – even earlier – which had simply been passed over with little more than an occasional expression of interest in the black servants that were depicted in aristocratic family portraits. Today, as modern Britain seeks to redefine its contemporary identity, there has been a concerted effort to incorporate the history of 'minorities': to describe and understand the role played by those immigrant groups (however small) in the shaping of Britain itself.

It is now seen to be important for white Britain to know that its history has been intimately linked to black life in ways that have simply gone unnoticed. For black Britain, the task has been quite different. Theirs has been a pursuit of the unknown and of the elusive. What sort of black history existed in Britain prior to the modern era? And what sense can be made of that black past (itself so intimately linked to the history of Atlantic slavery and race) for a younger generation of black Britons, often adrift in a British society which has denied them a historical role and importance? For anyone concerned about British black history, the task of memorialising has been quite different from the one found in the former slave societies. In Britain, the quest has been, initially, simply to locate fragments of a lost past. It has thus been important to preserve and reify the few major black personalities who left their historical mark. In some respects this is a disappointing development: by remembering people of attainment we return to history as the stories of great men. People who a mere generation before had been only black faces in the historical crowd have been singled out and given a centrestage role. Equiano, Sancho and others have taken on a prominence that they would have been the first to see as remarkable. Authors that they were (and therefore men who left a selfconscious historical trail), they would have been bemused to know that they have become the personification of the whole process of British black history. Equiano has the unique distinction of being variously portrayed today as an African nationalist, a pioneer of African-American writing, a spokesman for the British black community, and an Atlanticist of extraordinary range and import.[70] He even has to do duty for both sexes. As the bar-room reconstruction of the semi-mythical Nanny suggests, the present-day public memory of slavery is strangely gender-bound; Mary Prince, a slave who wrote a memoir that has been described as 'the only known autobiography of an enslaved woman from the British West Indies', has not been taken up as an icon.[71]

In their words and deeds Sancho and Equiano were unequivocally hostile to the slave system, but they were not rebels in the mould of the slave heroes of the Caribbean. They have been remembered differently, and accorded an altogether more pensive, more cerebral role, in the modern depiction of Atlantic slavery. This, in turn, is surely a revealing feature about how slavery has been memorialised in Britain itself. The image focuses on the 'respectable' ex-slave (however misleading that term might be for both these men). In the preferred image of Equiano we see the black man dressed like a propertied Briton of his day. He is a literate, devout, refined man of sensibility who at a glance could persuade white peers that here were blacks of attainment. He and Sancho were, to put it crudely, the kind of black men that white men liked to deal with. Mary Prince, on the other hand, was criticised at the time for having 'a somewhat violent and hasty temper, and a considerable share of natural pride and self-importance'. The British anti-slavery women did not accept her as a colleague; her place was as a victim.[72] Far into the nineteenth century it was the policy of the British abolitionists, as William Wells Brown put it, 'always to have in England some talented man of colour who should be a living lie to the doctrine of the inferiority of the African race.'[73] It would have been hard to imagine men such as these with a conch shell raised to their lips, or with chains dangling from their wrists, displaying the sweaty defiance of the slave rebels.

One of the most salient features of slave history in the Americas is that, despite the millions of slaves scattered across the continents, we know of very few slave burial sites or final resting places. Slaves have been as invisible in death as they were ubiquitous and vital in life. Perhaps because of their rarity, slave burial sites are now among the most prominent and obvious locations for the memorialising of the slave past.[74] The few of these that are known in Britain itself capture an image that speaks as much to slave owners as to the slaves themselves. Thus the grave of Scipio Africanus at Henbury near Bristol is a most elaborate memorial, right down to having Africans painted on the two headstones (see Figure 7:2.) It shows the affection of the slave's owner, the Earl of Suffolk, struggling against some of the prevalent images of race and colour:

> I who born a PAGAN and a SLAVE
> Now sweetly sleep a CHRISTIAN in my grave
> What tho' my hue was dark my Saviours sight
> Shall change this darkness into radiant light.

At the other social extreme is the grave of Sambo on Sunderland Point near

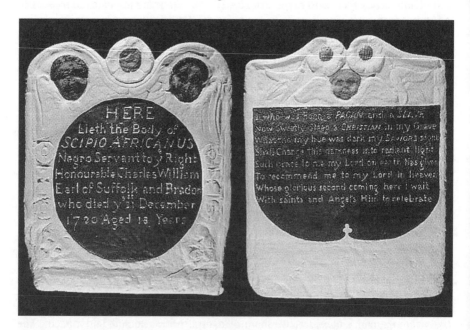

Fig. 7.2   The grave of Scipio Africanus at Henbury near Bristol.

Lancaster. Sambo was clearly a casualty of the Atlantic trade to and from Lancaster and is now remembered by the bleakest of personal details.

Here lies Poor Sambo A Faithful negro who
(attending his master from the West Indies) DIED on his arrival at Sunderland.

Repeatedly vandalised, Sambo's grave lies in an open meadow; it is currently well tended, but with an attached plea for respect. These two men, however unusual, were at least accorded a final resting place.[75] Though we know in fine detail the story of Atlantic slavery – where Africans were recruited, how they were bought and bartered on the coast, the specifics of their transportation across the Atlantic to the Americas, and the complex evolving process of slave demography in the plantation societies – we know very little about where most of them were buried.

For much of the history of slavery in the Americas, the great majority of local slaves were African; their varied cultural backgrounds, with their associated burial patterns, belonged to an African past which their owners disliked, feared and preferred not to become acquainted with. The dead were disposed of, by and large, by other slaves according to whatever rituals the slaves deemed appropriate.[76] That changed of course when the slaves were converted to Christianity, but even then the differences could be insuperable. R.R. Madden, who believed that Jamaica was 'the dearest country in the world' and made a great effort to understand the culture of the population in the 1830s, had to confess that he found this task harder than in 'countries where the obstacles to information are supposed to be infinitely greater'. When he attended a funeral and tried to pick out the words, he found that he was 'not sufficiently acquainted with nigger tongue to make out more than a few words here and there of the chaunt'. He did not believe that there were any African allusions in the service, but there was 'an abundance of scriptural paraphrases, strangely applied to their ideas of the happiness of a future state, and the deserts of the dead woman'.[77]

Madden saw more than most Europeans. Slave burial sites usually remained out of sight: physically distant from white society, and as far as possible beyond the pale of white attention and documentation. Millions of slaves went to their graves unrecorded by their former owners, save their loss as property. What makes this even more remarkable is that in life slaves were recorded in more minute detail than any contemporary free labourer. No longer items of property, in death they slipped off their owners' careful record-keeping system. Not surprisingly then, recent years have seen a remarkable upsurge of interest in slave burial sites. These can yield critical data for the archaeologist, especially about slave material culture, but the disturbing of slave burial sites, even for legitimate research, raises troubling cultural issues. Here after all are the remains of ancestors; it is not unreasonable to insist that they should be accorded similar reverence to other funerary sites.

In the Atlantic world that was once ruled by the British, we can detect a radical drift in the memorialising of slavery. What has emerged is an incomplete democratising process. From the heights of the 'Old Society' the focus descended in the nineteenth century through the ranks of aristocratic Whigs and gentlemen 'Saints' to the men and women of the middle–class Moral Radical Party. By the late twentieth century, the focus had descended further; the slave had been transformed from the humble image on Fox's monument to a person who retained considerable powers of agency and had a share in his own emancipation. Nonetheless, with the honourable exception of the Liverpool Gallery which has defined its realm of memory much more generously, in one respect the recent memorialising of the slave has been a strangely conservative development, a return to the 'great man' theory of history. The former slave colonies and the black British now have their equivalent of the men of distinction who have traditionally dominated the iconography of British national identity. The victim has become a hero but of a rather traditional kind.

Notes

1   *Address given by the Rt. Revd Stephen Sykes, Bishop of Ely at the Unveiling and Dedication of a Memorial to Thomas Clarkson at Westminster Abbey on 26 September 1996.* The Rt Revd Professor Stephen W. Sykes is now Principal of St. John's College, Durham. We are grateful for the copy of his text that he provided and for his permission to quote from it. See also *Guardian Weekly,* 22 September 1996.
2   *Westminster Abbey Official Guide,* (1969), Norwich: Dean & Chapter of Westminster.
3   Howse, E.M. (1971), *Saints in Politics. The 'Clapham Sect' and the Growth of Freedom,* London: George Allen & Unwin.
4   Thompson, E.P. (1965), *The Making of the English Working Class,* London: Gollancz, p. 57.
5   Nora, P. (1996), *Realms of Memory, Rethinking the French Past,* New York: Columbia University Press, vol. 1, pp. xii, 3.
6   Ozouf, M. (1984), 'Le Panthéon. L'École normale des morts' in Nora, P. (ed.), *Les Lieux de Memoire, La République,* Paris: Gallimard, I, p. 139. For Nora, *Realms of Memory,* p.xvii, the term *'lieu de mémoire'* is not to be restricted to buildings or topographical sites. It is 'any significant entity, whether material or non-material in nature, which by dint of human will or the work of time has become a symbolic element of the memorial heritage of any community'.
7   Kritzman, L.D. (1996), 'Foreword' in Nora, *Realms of Memory,* vol. 1, p. x.
8   Ozouf, 'Le Panthéon', p. 162. Davis, D.B. (1975) *The Problem of Slavery in the Age of Revolution 1770-1823,* Ithaca, NY: Cornell University Press, p. 146, writes that from the beginning 'the abolitionist triumph could be advertised as proof that a virtuous government would ultimately confirm, according to its own wisdom, a cause that had expanded the hearts and excited the generous sympathies of the people.'
9   *Address given by the Rt Revd Stephen Sykes.*
10 We wish to thank Miss Christine Reynolds of the Westminster Abbey Muniment Room and Library for this information.
11 The term is attributed to Professor Geoffrey Blainey by Pilger, J. (2002), *The New Rulers of the World,* London: Verso, p. 193.
12 *Westminster Abbey Official Guide,* p. 22. The monument is shown in Whinney, M. (1964), *Sculpture in Britain 1530 to 1830,* Harmondsworth: Penguin, plates 168 (B) and 169. Fox was buried in the Abbey in 1806, and in 1809 a subscription was commenced for a monument. The monument was unveiled in 1822, and the surplus was used to erect a bronze statue to Fox in Bloomsbury Square. See Reid, L. (1969), *Charles James Fox. A Man for the People,* London: Longmans, pp. 434–6.
13 Wood, M. (2000), *Blind Memory: visual representations of slavery in England and America,* New York: Routledge, pp. 295, 300, refers to the ineffectual characteristics of this sort of well-intentioned but essentially misplaced attempt to give visitors a 'total experience'.
14 See Chapter 4 above.

15   Gourievidis, L. (2000), 'Representing the Disputed Past of Northern Scotland', *History and Memory: Studies in Representation of the Past*, Fall–Winter, 3 (4), pp. 7–9. Contemporary Australia offers an interesting example of an attempt to reverse this process. Reports in the Melbourne *Age* (27–30 December 2002) have referred to 'culture wars' between the ruling Liberal Party and the curatorial staff of the National Museum of Australia in Canberra. According to these reports, the terms 'political correctness', 'predictable didactism' and 'victim episode' form part of the Liberal Party's objections to the Museum's depiction of Aboriginal history. The responses have accused the Government of intervening to impose a 'right-wing agenda, particularly in regard to indigenous issues'.

16   Rosie, G. (1992), 'Museumry and the Heritage Industry' in Donnachie, I. and Whatley, C. (eds), *The Manufacture of Scottish History*, Edinburgh: Polygon, 1992, p. 164.

17   Moores, P. (1994), 'Foreword', in Tibbles, A. (ed.), *Transatlantic Slavery Against Human Dignity*, London: HMSO, p. 9.

18   Small, S. (1994), 'The General Legacy of the Atlantic Slave Trade' in *Transatlantic Slavery Against Human Dignity*, pp. 125–6.

19   *Address given by the Rt Revd Stephen Sykes.*

20   For another example of a reform movement that was divided by disputes over pride of place in history see Chapter 6 above.

21   *Kelso Mail*, 15 September 1834.

22   Penny, N.B. (1976), 'The Whig Cult of Fox In Early Nineteenth-Century Sculpture', *Past and Present*, 70, February, pp. 96–9.

23   Lascelles, E.C.P. (1928), *Granville Sharp and the Freedom of Slaves in England*, London: Oxford University Press, pp. 145–6.

24   Information taken on site by Alex Tyrrell.

25   Booth, C. (1934), *Zachary Macaulay. His Part in the Movement for the Abolition of the Slave Trade and of Slavery*, London: Longmans, Green & Co., p. 113.

26   Again we wish to thank Miss Christine Reynolds for this information.

27   *British Emancipator*, 8 August 1838.

28   The monument is in the William Knibb Memorial Baptist Church at Falmouth, Jamaica. Information taken on site by Alex Tyrrell.

29   For the campaign against the Apprenticeship see Tyrrell, A. (1987), *Joseph Sturge and the Moral Radical Party in Early Victorian Britain*, London: Christopher Helm, Chapter 7; Tyrrell, A. (1984), 'The "Moral Radical Party" and the Anglo-Jamaican campaign for the abolition of the Negro apprenticeship system', *English Historical Review*, CCCXCII, July, pp. 481–502.

30   Shackel, P.A. (ed.) (2001), *Myth, Memory and the Making of the American Landscape*, Gainesville: University Press of Florida, p. 3.

31   See, for example, the lists of patrons for the African Institution and the African Civilization Society: *Christian Observer*, April 1807; Brett, R.L. (ed.) (1979), *Barclay Fox's Journal*, London: Bell & Hyman, pp. 197–8.

32   The emergence of the Moral Radicals as a political force in the 1820s and 1830s is described by Tyrrell, *Joseph Sturge*, Chaps 5–8.

33   Knibb, W. (1842), *Jamaica. Speech of the Rev. William Knibb, Before the Baptist Missionary Society, In Exeter Hall, April 28th, 1842*, London: no publisher, pp. 9, 29–30.

34   Ben-Amos, A. (2000), *Funerals, Politics, and Memory In Modern France, 1789–1996*, Oxford: Oxford University Press, p. 4.

35   *British Emancipator*, 20 March 1839. In an address to the Governor of the island they described themselves as ministers of religion, as the instructors of the ignorant, as friends of the oppressed and as the advocates of civil and religious liberty.

36   Hinton, J.H. (1849), *Memoir of William Knibb, Missionary in Jamaica*, London: no publisher, pp. 304–5, 308–10.

37 For the free villages see Tyrrell, *Joseph Sturge*, pp. 90–1 and Hall, C. (1993), 'White Visions, Black Lives: Free Villages of Jamaica, *History Workshop Journal*, 36, Autumn, pp. 100–32.

38 *Irish Friend*, 2 November 1840.

39 This venture is described by Temperley, H. (1991), *White Dreams Black Africa. The Antislavery Expedition to the Niger,* New Haven, CT: Yale University Press.

40 This point has been missed by Marcus Wood, *Blind Memory,* pp. 6, 61,76, who twice cursorily dismisses Haydon's painting because it is 'appallingly wooden'.

41 For a more extensive description and analysis of the painting see Tyrrell, A. (1980), '"Woman's Mission" and Pressure Group Politics in Britain (1825–60)' *Bulletin of the John Rylands University Library of Manchester,* 63 (1), Autumn, pp. 194–8.

42 Pope, W.B. (ed.), (1963), *The Diary of Benjamin Robert Haydon,* Cambridge, MA: Harvard University Press, vol. 5, p. 49.

43 The episode is discussed in a different context by Tyrrell, A. (1988), 'A House Divided against itself: The British Abolitionists Revisited', *Journal of Caribbean History,* 22 (1 and 2), pp. 43–9.

44 The *Birmingham Journal,* 5 March 1842, referred to an exhibition of the painting in Birmingham together with a selection of fetters and 'Instruments of Torture'. See also [Anti-Corn Law League] *Bazaar Gazette,* 1842, p. 16.

45 Tolles, F.B. (ed.), (1952), 'Slavery and "The Woman Question". Lucretia Mott's Diary of her Visit to Great Britain to Attend the World's Anti-Slavery Convention of 1840', *Journal of the Friends Historical Society,* 23 (supplement), pp. 22–31.

46 *Irish Friend*, 2 November 1840.

47 Pickering P.A. and Tyrrell, A. (2000), *The People's Bread. A History of the Anti-Corn Law League,* London: Leicester University Press, pp. 118, 134.

48 Knightsville was described by the *Missionary Herald,* March 1842, as near the mission station at Yallahs to the east of Kingston. See also Anne Knight's obituary entry in *Annual Monitor* (1864), p. 50.

49 Friends' House Library, Anne Knight Papers, MS Box W2, George Stephen to Anne Knight, 14 November 1834.

50 The exception that seems to prove the rule is the Sinclair Monument that was erected in Edinburgh in 1859 to honour Catherine Sinclair, a novelist and philanthropist. See Birrell, J.F. (1980), *An Edinburgh Alphabet*, Edinburgh: James Thin, The Mercat Press, p. 47.

51 Righting a 'wrong' is the term used by the *Guardian Weekly,* 22 September 1996 for the decision to commemorate Clarkson in the Abbey.

52 Darke, J. (1991), *The Monument Guide to England and Wales,* London: Macdonald Illustrated, p. 192. Boime, A. (1990), *The Art of Exclusion. Representing Blacks in the Nineteenth Century,* London: Thames & Hudson, p. 171 writes: 'Images of emancipation, like the actual emancipation rituals and ceremonies, were designed to emphasize the dependence of the emancipated slaves upon their benefactors as well as their ongoing need for the culture and the guidance of their liberators.'

53 Pevsner, N. (1970), *The Buildings of England. Cambridgeshire,* Harmondsworth: Penguin, p. 497.

54 Tolles (ed.), 'Slavery and "The Woman Question"', p. 31.

55 Henderson, G.E. (1931), *Goodness and Mercy. A Tale of a Hundred Years,* Kingston: Gleaner Co., p. 74. The freedom tree at Brown's Town lasted until 1912 when it was destroyed by a hurricane. In a hostile comment on these ceremonies, the *Jamaica Standard and Royal Gazette,* 8 November 1842 suggested that the ex-slaves may have interpreted rituals involving burials and trees within the Afro-Caribbean belief system known as Obeah and not as the Baptist missionaries intended. The writer of the article saw this as one of the explanations for the outbreak of disorder that swept across parts of the island in 1842.

56 The portrait appears on the cover of Hall, C. (1992), *White, Male and Middle Class. Explorations in Feminism and History,* Cambridge: Polity Press.

57 Small, S. and Walvin, J. (1994), 'African Resistance to Enslavement' in *Transatlantic Slavery Against Human Dignity,* pp. 42–50.

58 There have, however, been some notable achievements in this sort of rescue work, for example, Burnett, J. (ed.) (1997), *Useful Toil: autobiographies of working people from the 1820s to the 1920s,* Hammersmith: Penguin, and Burnett, J., Vincent, D. and Mayal, D. (1984), *The Autobiography of the Working Class,* Brighton: Harvester Press.

59 King, R., Sandhu, S., Walvin, J. and Girdham J. (1997), *Ignatius Sancho: An African Man of Letters,* London: National Portrait Gallery.

60 James Walvin's personal notes taken at the opening and subsequent visits, January–May 1997.

61 Walvin, J. (1998), *An African's Life: the life and times of Olaudah Equiano, 1745–1797,* London: Cassell.

62 There is a wealth of readily available material about Gorée on the Internet including the UNESCO website.

63 Craton, M. (1982), *Testing the Chains, Resistance to Slavery in the British West Indies,* Ithaca, NY: Cornell University Press, Chapter 2.

64 James Walvin's personal field-notes, Port au Prince, November 1970.

65 Craton, *Testing the Chains,* Chapter 20.

66 Ibid., Chapter 2.

67 James Walvin's notes on site, July 2001.

68 For Sharpe and the Native Baptists see Turner, M. (1982), *Slaves and Missionaries. The Disintegration of Jamaican Slave Society, 1787–1834,* Urbana: University of Illinois Press, pp. 94, 152.

69 Walvin, J. (1971), *The Black Presence: a documentary history of the Negro in England, 1555–1860,* London: Orbach & Chambers. See also Walvin, J. (1973), *Black and White: the Negro and English Society, 1555–1945,* London: Allen Lane; Walvin, J. (1984), *Passage to Britain: Immigration in British history and politics,* Harmondworth: Penguin.

70 For a discussion of these various interpretations see Walvin, *An African's life,* pp. 193–4.

71 Midgley, C. (1995), *Women against Slavery. The British Campaigns 1780–1870,* London: Routledge, pp. 87, 89. The most recent edition is Ferguson, M. (ed.) (1987), *The History of Mary Prince, a West Indian Slave, related by herself,* London: Pandora Press.

72 Midgley, *Women against Slavery,* pp. 90–1. Yellin, J.F. (1989), *Women and Sisters. The Antislavery Feminists in American Culture,* New Haven, CT, Yale University Press, 1989, pp. 8–9 refers to the weakness with which slave women were depicted in the iconography of the women's anti-slavery societies.

73 Brown, W.W. (1852), *Three Years in Europe; Or places I have seen and people I have met,* London: no publisher, p. xxi.

74 See especially the slave burial sites at Monticello, the home of Thomas Jefferson, and Mount Vernon, home of George Washington.

75 There is a picture of Scipio's grave in J. Walvin, (1983), *Slavery and the Slave Trade. An Illustrated History,* London: Macmillan, p.127. For Sambo's grave see <www.grantham.karoo.net/pauls/gaves/sambo/htm>.

76 Frey, S. and Wood, B. (1998), *Come Shouting to Zion. African Protestantism in the American South and British Caribbean to 1830,* Chapel Hill: University of North Carolina Press, pp. 22–6.

77 Madden, R.R. (1835), *A Twelvemonth's Residence in the West Indies, During the Transition from Slavery to Apprenticeship; with incidental notices of the state of society, prospects and natural resources of Jamaica and other islands,* London: no publisher, vol. 1, pp. 81, 184–5, 187.

Index